THREE MILES DOWN

James Hamilton-Paterson was educated at Oxford, where he won the Newdigate Prize. In addition to journalism for the *Sunday Times*, the *Times Literary Supplement* and the *New Statesman*, he has published poetry and two collections of short stories, *The View from Mount Dog* and his most recent work, *The Music*. The non-fiction work, *Playing with Water* was followed by his first novel, *Gerontius*, which won a Whitbread Prize in 1989, and *The Bell-Boy*. In 1992 he published *Seven Tenths: The Sea and its Thresholds*, a blend of literature and science exploring the sea. His novel *Griefwork*, published in 1993, was much acclaimed, and his most recent novel, *Ghosts of Manila*, was shortlisted for the Whitbread Fiction Prize in 1994. He lives in Italy and the Philippines.

James Hamilton-Paterson

THREE MILES DOWN

A Hunt for Sunken Treasure

V

VINTAGE

Published by Vintage 1999

2 4 6 8 10 9 7 5 3 1

Copyright © James Hamilton-Paterson 1998

The right of James Hamilton-Paterson to be identified as
the author of this work has been asserted by him in
accordance with the Copyright, Designs and Patents Act,
1988

First published in Great Britain by
Jonathan Cape in 1998

Vintage
Random House, 20 Vauxhall Bridge Road,
London SW1V 2SA

Random House Australia (Pty) Limited
20 Alfred Street, Milsons Point, Sydney
New South Wales 2061, Australia

Random House New Zealand Limited
18 Poland Road, Glenfield,
Auckland 10, New Zealand

Random House South Africa (Pty) Limited
Endulini, 5A Jubilee Road, Parktown 2193,
South Africa

Random House UK Limited Reg. No. 954009

A CIP catalogue record for this book
is available from the British Library

ISBN 0 09 958691 6

Papers used by Random House UK Ltd are natural,
recyclable products made from wood grown in sustain-
able forests. The manufacturing processes conform to the
environmental regulations of the country of origin

Printed and bound in Great Britain by
Cox & Wyman, Reading, Berkshire

ACKNOWLEDGEMENTS

My grateful thanks are not only due but cheerfully volunteered to everyone concerned with the Orca expedition: to Dr Quentin Huggett of Geotek Ltd. for proposing me in the first place; to Clive Hayley and Simon Fraser for including me; to Mike Anderson for agreeing to my inclusion. Once we had sailed, our photographer Ralph White was generous with his perspective and his gin. Thereafter, it was the greatest privilege to be at sea with the scientists and crew of the R/V *Akademik Mstislav Keldysh*, whose warm hospitality complemented their admirable and spirited professionalism. As for Dr Anatoly Sagalevitch, the inventor of the astonishing MIR submersibles, I owe him quite simply one of the definitive experiences of my life.

Andrea Cordani of Shipwreck Research Associates proved to be a sterling shipmate well before I realised her eminence in a highly specialised field. To her and her partner Nina Jenkins I owe the biggest debt of all, for without their archives, expert judgement and patient explanations it would never have been possible for me to write this book. In this connection I would also like to acknowledge Nigel Pickford's informative work *The Atlas of Shipwreck & Treasure*. In Italy my researches were greatly aided by my friend Remo Ghezzi, through whose excellent private library I became acquainted with Giulio

Raiola's definitive study of the Italian submarine fleet's Atlantic operations during the Second World War, *Timoni a Salire*. Warm thanks are also owed Elizabeth Cox for her kind permission to quote from her late father's unpublished memoirs.

I ought to add that the account which follows is an entirely personal one. If on occasion I seem critical or even downright rude about anyone to whom I have just declared myself grateful, I trust they will take it in good part and interpret it more properly as affection heavily disguised. The sea can give off a strange, lifting benevolence and I can feel it blowing through me as I write these words, months later and far ashore.

Auri sacra fames ...

ONE

It is October 1994. I am standing in a bar in Italy, trying to have a phone conversation over the noise of two nearby teenagers playing electronic games that squeal and warble incessantly. At the other end of the line in far-off Sussex Quentin Huggett is enigmatic. It sounds as though he were saying 'How do you fancy coming on a hunt for sunken treasure?' In the next lull I find he really is. 'Ah,' I say, as if quite used to hearing such propositions. 'When?'

Quentin is the marine geologist with whom I went on an oceanographic cruise in the Pacific while writing the first chapter of *Seven-Tenths*, a book about the sea. Although we are not very old friends, we struck up a rapport on that trip which was more than that of mere shipboard acquaintances. This is why I am paying him serious attention on a phone screwed to the wall of an Italian bar, my forefinger stuffed in my spare ear.

'There's the snag,' I hear him saying. 'It's pretty soon. We're hoping to sail in mid-December.'

'Mid-December sounds like being away for Christmas,' I say hopefully.

'I'm afraid so. The first stage of the cruise will probably take at least six weeks.'

'Afraid? It sounds ideal. Where are we going?'

'I can't tell you that. I'm sorry, James, I'm not allowed to. All I can say is it'll be somewhere not a million miles from the Cape Verde Islands. Sort of West Coast of Africa.'

'Christmas in the tropics?' I say. 'You're on.' Quentin, of course, is a family man. To me the idea of missing Christmas *and* a winter in Europe is pure jam. 'You might just tell me what it is we'll be looking for.'

There is a moment's silence on the line, though not in the bar. 'I don't want to sound pompous,' comes his voice. 'It's just that I'm under oath not to talk about it too much. What I've been told to tell you is it involves two Second World War vessels which were sunk while carrying quite a lot of gold. They're in hellishly deep water in the Atlantic and this salvage group has chartered a Russian research vessel with manned submersibles to do the job.'

'When you say "quite a lot of gold" . . . ?'

'Oh, you know, millions.'

'Millions, eh? That's nice. Would any of it be coming my way, do you suppose?'

'That's not up to me, I'm afraid. The point is, this is only a preliminary sounding-out. Sort of getting back in touch. I just want to be able to tell them yes or no, you're interested or you're not . . . What?'

'I said "Yes!",' I shout above the local din. 'Yes, I'm interested. What's the next step?'

'Watch this space. Keep in touch with your agent.'

'Quentin? Just . . . You know, thanks for thinking of me.'

'Don't worry. As soon as I heard about this hare-brained scheme you were the first person I thought of.'

I hang up. I have that sudden ecstatic urge to tell someone the news, something which only happens when you've been sworn to secrecy. For an instant I'm on the point of telling one of the boys, whom I know slightly, when his machine gives a cough and begins to eject coins in a series of pulses which seem to go on for about half a minute and the moment is lost. At any other time I might have interested him mildly by an airy remark about going off to look for sunken gold. But a heavy jackpot-winner is in no mood for other people's dreams.

When I go to London in early December 1994 I still know little more about the scheme than Quentin told me that morning in the bar. I know it is called Project Orca. I know that one of the wrecks we will be looking for is that of a large Japanese submarine. I know that my role will be that of the operation's chronicler. I also know I am far too late to stake even the most modest claim to any gold we might find: it has long since been divided up on paper between twenty investors and the Orca members who will be coming on the expedition. This is scarcely unfair. I am a Johnny-come-lately who has had no hand in the years of preparation. I am not even officially a member of the group, so I feel no inclination to complain. The idea of spending the year's bottom dead centre on the tropical high seas in a quest that may turn out to be more oceanography than salvage is quite good enough for me. Add to that the prospect of going to sea again with Quentin – whom I've hardly seen since we parted nearly four years earlier in Hawaii – and I couldn't care less about a share in some notional bonanza. I am going because it sounds interesting. I am going because it concerns the sea. And I am going because somebody has held out the possibility that I might – just might – get a chance to go down three miles to the seabed in a submersible.

TWO

Ships which sink do not always disappear as utterly as public amnesia might suggest. Nor is it only the survivors or the victims' families who keep them firmly in mind. Insurance and salvage companies have long memories and keep long lists, even in wartime. Casualties of war may also be actuarial losses. Valuable cargoes can remain in limbo for years – in cold storage, as it were; out of commercial circulation but by no means out of mind.

The idea of salvaging a wreck remains perennially interesting because it is understood that nobody would bother unless it involved something of great enough value to make the venture worthwhile. A wreck might be valuable for itself, of course, rather than for its cargo or the scrap value of its hull and fittings. A ship like the *Mary Rose* is of historical interest and her salvaging was more in the nature of an archaeological dig which happened not to be performed on dry land. The *Titanic*, too, is now viewed (if there's anyone left who can bear to look) in a similar light, thanks mainly to some very well orchestrated publicity which hopes to supplant the ship's poetic and melancholy status with that of a treasure-trove of artefacts. It is, indeed, becoming less of a scientifically-conducted archaeological dig than a free-for-all jumble sale. (Archaeological? *1912*? Most of the objects so far raised are the sort of inconsequential junk one threw out of one's grandmother's house after she died.)

What really grabs people's attention is the prospect of hugely valuable cargoes being found and restored to the upper air. Newspaper editors understand perfectly that treasure and treasure-hunts come very high on the list of things which induce their readers to suspend a normally serviceable disbelief. Professional salvors, meanwhile, deeply resent being called 'treasure hunters'. They prefer their activities to be described as 'cargo recovery', a highly specialised business closely connected with the world of insurance and loss adjustment. Be that as it may, as the various technologies for finding and salvaging wrecks slowly improve, so the arresting newspaper stories become less rare.

These things need to be put into some sort of perspective. At any given moment there will be perhaps thirty teams around the world seriously at work on shallow-water wrecks. These hulks might range from sunken Spanish galleons in the Philippines or the Caribbean to undistinguished little coasters in the North Sea. In many cases the wrecks lie so shallowly that the whole operation can be done by divers using scuba gear. Spanish galleons, of course, hold out the prospect (usually chimerical) of caskets of jewels and sacks of doubloons. A modest twentieth-century cargo vessel, on the other hand, may well be worth a small operation on the part of a diving club simply to salvage the ship's manganese-bronze or phosphor-bronze screw for scrap.

Although the principles of researching and locating remain common to both shallow and deep-water wrecks, the techniques are mostly quite different. Deep-water salvage is in a class of its own and world-wide there are probably only three or four companies equipped to undertake it. At the moment of writing there is a mere handful of deep-water wrecks subject to serious salvage operations. These include the *Central America* and the

John Barry. Of the two, the *Central America* is the more famous, largely because of the vast sums plucked from the air by the popular press as to the value of its cargo (up to a billion dollars). The ship sank in 1857 while *en route* from the Californian goldfields. She was known to be carrying gold in nuggets, dust, bar and coin. Newspapers have reported that around $200 millions' worth has so far been recovered, with more (endlessly more) to come. While it is true that for many reasons a company like the Columbus America Discovery Group might want to conceal or downplay the amount it actually salvages, professional salvors maintain in private that the real figure recovered to date from the *Central America* is not much more than one million pounds. On-site operations have been dragging on for years, as has some very expensive litigation about the wreck's ownership which, for the moment, has brought operations to a halt. Many feel that by the time all the sums are done the investors' profits may turn out to be comparatively modest.

The *John Barry* is a US Liberty ship sunk off the coast of Oman in 1944. She was carrying about 30 tons of silver one-rial coins destined for the Saudi Government. More than half have already been recovered. However, rumour suggests she may also have been carrying 2,000 tons of silver bars currently worth $300 million. This was allegedly being sent in secret by President Roosevelt to the USSR (then, of course, a wartime ally) in defiance of Congress. For this we have the word of the ship's purser who swore he saw bullion boxes being carried aboard. Again, this is exactly the sort of story the press likes. It not only suggests fabulous wealth but political skulduggery which, if confirmed, would be of considerable interest in itself. Many salvors doubt there is much more to be found in the *John Barry* but this is unlikely to dampen speculation, and salvage operations are continuing on the unopened cargo holds.

6

Collectively, and in one form or another, there is an inconceivable hoard of money lying scattered about the seabeds which cover more or less seven-tenths of the planet's surface. Much of it lies in international waters and is therefore pretty much free to whoever fancies nibbling at its edges. Absolutely none of it is guaranteed to prove profitable to anyone trying their hand at bringing it back to daylight. Salvage is always a gamble. The deeper the treasure, the greater the gamble because the costs of recovery go up exponentially. It is not a game for the faint-hearted, least of all for conservative types who like to invest their money so as to yield fixed returns on capital, and who keep all sorts of insurance policies handy for papering over life's unforeseeable cracks. It is, as an American salvor remarked, 'a balls-out business' designed for people who enjoy the romance of risk-taking.

In the Second World War two particular vessels were sunk in the Atlantic off the West Coast of Africa. One was a very large Japanese submarine, the *I-52*, on its way from Kobe in Japan to a rendezvous with a German U-boat. It was bombed and confirmed sunk by US naval aircraft in June 1944. The other was a liner, the SS *Aurelia* (not her real name), which the British Government had requisitioned for the duration as a troop carrier. She was on her way from Durban to Liverpool with nearly 1,900 people aboard, including 500 Italian prisoners of war. In March 1943 an Italian submarine torpedoed and sank her. There were some 1,500 survivors.

Outwardly, there is nothing to connect these two sinkings, which happened more than fifteen months apart and were separated by almost a thousand miles of ocean. Yet the vessels did have one thing in common besides being chance casualties of the same war. Each is believed to have been carrying several tons of gold.

In the early 1990s a company was founded expressly to find and raise the gold from both vessels. From the outset Project Orca was unique in several respects. The wrecks were thought to be lying in 4,500–5,000 metres of water. It would be the first time a salvage operation had ever been attempted at such a depth, especially one which might require intricate cutting techniques (the *Titanic*'s objects have mostly been scooped from where they were scattered at 3,800 metres). Both the *Central America* and the *John Barry* needed to be opened, but they lie in shallower water, at between 2,000 and 2,600 metres. It would also be the first time a deep-sea salvage operation had tackled two targets in a single expedition. Most salvors would have been daunted by either one; Project Orca seemed intent on increasing the gamble still further.

This might look like a case of greed overcoming prudence. However, in addition to the constraints of finance and opportunity one has to remember the salvage techniques currently possible as well as the peculiarities of these two wrecks. Such depths are, of course, way beyond any that could be reached by a diver. At the moment there are two main ways of salvaging cargoes from deep-water wrecks. The first is known in the trade as 'smash-and-grab'. This is done from the surface, using heavy equipment on the end of cables guided by ROVs (Remotely Operated Vehicles), which are small unmanned submersibles equipped with lights and video cameras to 'eyeball' the wreck. This is the technique being used on the *John Barry*. A team from the French oceanographic institute Ifremer adapted a deep-drilling rig with a 50-ton pair of pliers on the end of a cable. Having failed to blast a way into the ship with explosives (which are unreliable, difficult and dangerous to set at such depths), the Ifremer team resorted to the pliers and 'tore it open like a tin of sardines', in the words of the operation's chief engineer.

For all its technical wizardry (imagine trying to operate a tool dangling on the end of a cable nearly three kilometres long), 'smash-and-grab' is crude even when effective, but it does have the advantage of being safe. The other technique is the very opposite. It involves people going down to the wreck in manned submersibles which, in addition to lights and video cameras, have their own manipulator arms capable of operating precision drills and cutters. Using manned submersibles is unquestionably dangerous. Mechanical failure or a trapped vehicle could easily lead to harrowing rescue attempts, a tragic outcome and the loss of millions of pounds' worth of equipment. On the other hand, for Project Orca's purposes this was by far the cheaper alternative. To assemble 'smash-and-grab' apparatus capable of being deployed at nearly twice the depth of Ifremer's would be prohibitively expensive. The heavier ROVs, grabs, and oil drilling ship necessary for such a venture could not possibly be economically viable. Besides, it seemed likely that the Japanese submarine had broken up as a result of the aerial attack which sank it, leaving a debris field for which manned submersibles would be the only effective scavengers.

Finally, Project Orca had the opportunity to hire the very outfit responsible for filming the *Titanic* and bringing up many of the objects so far retrieved. This was the R/V *Akademik Mstislav Keldysh*, the chief research vessel of the P. P. Shirshov Institute of Oceanology (an independent branch of the Russian Academy of Sciences), with its two MIR submersibles and experienced crew. Orca could rent the *Keldysh* for five months. The brilliant engineer and chief designer of the MIRs, Anatoly Sagalevitch, would himself be aboard as head of operations. The gamble was that both wrecks could be located and salvaged in that period. Orca's backers had put up $3.6 million: they would not chip in any more as the operation progressed. It was to be all or nothing, success or failure, but arguably with the best equipment and personnel available anywhere. If Project Orca's intelligence was correct there was anything up to $83.12 million in gold to be raised for that $3.6 million outlay. As salvage in international waters and free of outstanding legal claim, all profits would go to the Project and its investors.

Yet even if it failed, there was a further way in which the expedition would be unique, one which was purely oceanographical. The area where the sunken submarine lies is known to marine geologists as 'off-axis', meaning away from the Mid-Atlantic Ridge. In fact, such regions hold little interest for the world's oceanographers. The seabed there is about 50 million years old and of a kind which geologists habitually write off as too boring to investigate – being covered with too much sediment to be interesting as hard rock yet with too little deposition to be worth examining as an example of sedimentation *per se*. This attitude is blasé, considering that marine geologists have so far seen only an infinitesimal fraction of the world's seabeds and almost nothing at all at this depth. Certainly no human eye had ever seen this particular piece of Planet Earth before. Any observers in their MIR submersibles, three miles beneath daylight and fresh air, would be the first to know exactly what it is that lies under these two patches of the Atlantic. A final irony was that they would be civilians: citizens of NATO countries using an ex-Soviet ship and its equipment to investigate an ocean which was – and to a surprising extent still is – one of the world's prime military domains. It had struck several members of the Orca group that questions of military secrecy might become interestingly involved in what was entirely a private commercial venture. This simply added a certain piquancy to a highly-researched gamble unmistakably tinged with gaiety.

THREE

10/1/95

The expedition's start is delayed. Orca members have been hanging about in London, waiting to hear that the *Keldysh* has sailed from Kaliningrad. She was expected in Falmouth on 8 December; she hasn't been able to obtain the fuel which was already paid for. The strain of waiting divides Orca into wets and hard-liners, and prompts various lines of speculation ranging from the sympathetic to the cynical. The wets begin by saying how difficult it must be for a man like Anatoly Sagalevitch to be held to ransom by the Russian *mafiosi* who nowadays seem to be running Kaliningrad port. Imagine – the eminent engineer who had designed the MIR submersibles, the Academician and operational director of the Soviet Union's most prestigious research vessel, who until the collapse of the USSR had been used to getting his orders obeyed. And here he was, having to truckle to the whims and chicaneries of gangsters who now called the shots. The only proper response from Orca's side ought surely to be one of sympathy. After all, it had taken the British more than half a century effectively to lose their imperial and superpower status, and in some respects they still hadn't adjusted to the political reality of their demotion. How much more traumatic must it be for the Russians to see their own

11

grand empire collapse in a handful of years into near-anarchy, amid the mockery and patronage of its former enemies? (And so on.)

The hard-liners are little moved by this argument. As time drags by and nerves fray, they sourly accuse the bloody Russians of being totally inscrutable, as ever. They have their own agenda. What we're seeing is nothing more sinister than their not wanting to leave before the Orthodox Christmas and New Year celebrations. Whenever they choose to leave will always have been their intended date of departure, regardless of what they promised Orca. (And so on.)

Finally, a fax arrives from Kaliningrad:

Academy of Sciences of Russia
R/V *Akademik Mstislav Keldysh*

12 January 1995
From: Anatoly Sagalevitch

OFFICIAL MESSAGE

Dear Investors,
Sorry for delay with the departure of Port Kaliningrad. We had lot of difficulties with the fuel for the ship. Last night last portion of fuel was delivered. Today we solved problems with Customs, because we have new regulations concerning 'export' of fuel and scientific equipment. Now everything is done. R/V *Akademik Mstislav Keldysh* with two 'MIR's on board departs Kaliningrad at 8 p.m. January the 12th.

We expect to be in Falmouth on January 16th p.m. Exact time we inform later.

Sorry, but we live in not so easy country now and do all our best.

See you soon.
Sincerely, Anatoly Sagalevitch, Head of the expedition.

The impression we get, sitting in London W8, is that Kaliningrad must be the direst dump imaginable. It takes an effort to recall that until 1946 it was Königsberg, capital of East Prussia, a grand Baltic city which had its own links with lost treasures. It was Königsberg craftsmen who laboured for seven years to carve the fabulous Amber Room that Frederick William I of Prussia sent to Tsar Peter the Great in 1716. This remarkable creation vanished in the Second World War after being dismantled by German troops during the Siege of Leningrad. It was last seen in the tender care of the SS, packed in twenty-two crates, since when it has been hunted by professionals and amateurs alike. Its craftsmen aside, Königsberg is famous as the city where Kant was born and spent his entire life. It was also the birthplace in 1776 of that peculiar genius E. T. A. Hoffmann: lawyer, composer, theatre director, music critic, artist and writer of some of the most haunting tales in European literature. When I was studying German at school, Hoffmann became an idol of mine. He was what I then most wanted to be: omni-competent in the arts and radically subversive. His subversiveness was very nearly his downfall. The writings and operas which made him famous brought him little hard cash and he had to resort to becoming a civil servant as a judge in Berlin. During this stint he fell foul of both the King of Prussia and his chief of police by taking the side of a prisoner accused of revolutionary nationalism. Hoffmann did so on purely legal grounds, holding it an abuse of power to prosecute someone for his views alone. He was immediately overruled. Hoffmann took his revenge in his last story, *Master Flea*, in an episode which viciously satirised the King and the police chief. This was both unwise and much to his credit; it resulted in a great thundercloud of lawsuits and injunctions massing on the horizon which he only escaped by dying of renal failure in 1822. Master Flea, I also seem to remember, had the ability to see gold where it lay hidden in the earth and so would have made a useful addition to the Orca team.

In any case, as the messages about fuel oil and petty officialdom filter through from Kaliningrad it becomes clear that a modern Hoffmann would not be short of satirical targets. Perhaps with luck that once-great city will one day revert to its original name. Kalinin? Who on earth *was* Kalinin? 'A jumped-up Kremlin peasant,' says the *émigré* writer Sergei Yuryenen bitterly, and goes on to quote an example of this intellectual's 'fantastic philosophical prowess':

> The Communist world-view is, to those who struggle for the proletarian revolution, what a giant telescope is to the astronomer or a microscope to the research biologist.

Poor Kant, poor Herder, that their birthplace should have been renamed for such a dunce. I suspect it wouldn't have surprised Hoffmann.

17/1/95

The night before Orca members go down to Falmouth to join the ship BBC television, by a curious coincidence, shows a 'Horizon' programme featuring the *Keldysh*. This was filmed only a few months previously in Norway, where the MIR submersibles were under contract to the Russian Government to take regular close looks at the *Komsomolets*, the Soviet nuclear submarine which sank after a fire in 1989, in order to measure any radioactive leakage. We study the pictures of the *Keldysh* with the interest of anyone getting a preview of their new home for the next several weeks or even months. That is the paintwork, that the furniture, those the faces we may become heartily sick of – or else come to look back on with nostalgia. That thug in the windcheater: would he be aboard? And there's the great Anatoly Sagalevitch himself, in spectacles and jumpsuit, eating a sandwich in one of his submersibles.

As for the Orca crew, they are as varied as one might wish. My five companions include the brother of the man who in 1994 famously (or infamously, if you were a Liberal Democrat) stood as a *Literal* Democrat and polled over 10,000 votes; an ex-policeman; the son of an eminent psychoanalyst; a lady who once ran a wet-suit factory and used to help run a gay helpline, and a man who taught knife-fighting to the US Marines and is a Knight of the Order of Constantine, whatever that is. Waiting in the wings is someone else who, while at Oxford in the seventies, was a member of the group which introduced Britain to bungee-jumping by leaping off the Clifton Suspension Bridge with only an engineer's back-of-an-envelope calculations about coefficients of elasticity to prove they wouldn't hurtle into the mud 280 feet below. Remarkably, this Orca man remained friends with the engineer who, before he went to the US to seek his fortune, buzzed the Houses of Parliament in a microlite while dressed as a gorilla. (Years later this same physicist was sent for by then-Prime Minister Margaret Thatcher to explain to her the technicalities of President Reagan's Star Wars Initiative).

I have no idea if this constitutes a 'normal' deep-sea salvage team. Probably it does; suggesting once again that in most human affairs of any interest notions of normality cut very little ice. When I first meet my colleagues severally (only one of whom, Quentin, I already know) there is a mutual recognition that only a project as crazy as this could have brought us together, so to some extent we must share a streak of lunacy. In rain-swept Falmouth we drink to that. It's hard to think of a more auspicious start to an adventure.

England's West Country is an appropriate place from which to set sail on a gold-hunt. There is a long historical precedent of pirates and privateers, smugglers, wreckers and salvors. Drake's Spanish gold raids were largely conducted out of Plymouth. Falmouth, though it only became established as a major port with the founding of the Packet Station in 1763, was soon perfectly familiar with gold since bullion often formed the cargo of homeward packets. Orca hopes it will be again, for the plan is to unload here in Falmouth whatever gold we raise, delivering it into the hands of the official Receiver of Wreck.

Plenty of people have left Falmouth in search of gold before us. The town's excellent small Maritime Museum has details of men like the local fisherman, Job Kelynack, who in 1854 renounced herring and pilchards for ever and sailed with his crew aboard the *Mystery* to Australia to join the gold rush. This was precisely the period of Ford Madox Brown's famous Pre-Raphaelite painting *The Last of England*, which was actually inspired by the emigration of the sculptor and poet Thomas Woolner to the same gold diggings. (Woolner created the bust of John Hunter in Leicester Square, as well as that of J. S. Mill in the Victoria Embankment Gardens. Australia can't have agreed with him. He returned to London in short order and from 1860 scarcely stirred from Welbeck Street for the next thirty-two years).

Job Kelynack and his crew made record time on the voyage, but how those tough Cornish seamen fared in so landlubberly a profession 'down under' is not stated. They would certainly have taken with them a rich variety of the sailors' taboos and superstitions which governed life, death and commercial success.

An extraordinary number of things brought ill-luck to nautical ventures. These included cats, clergymen, corpses, dead hares, haircutting, hangings, whistling, whores and – invariably – women in general. Women were famous for ruining catches. It was so unlucky for a woman to see a shoal of fish before it could be netted that in Cornish villages as late as the 1920s women were locked indoors when the fishermen put to sea. Nor did women and gold mix, at least not until the gold was safely home and had been turned into a wedding ring. At this point, of course, the old belief current from Land's End to John o' Groats came into force, that weddings brought bad weather and were best deferred until the end of the herring season. One way and another women were not a good thing, and men engaged in fishing and gold-hunts did well to avoid too much contact with them.

Naturally, oceanographers don't believe such nonsense, which is just as well since out of the hundred or so Russians aboard the *Keldysh* there are a good few women, including eight scientists. The ship lies at County Wharf across a squall-swept acreage of concrete. The two MIR submersibles crouch beneath their shelters on the starboard after-deck. A steady stream of windblown Russians goes between ship and town, clutching bags from Tesco's and Dixon's and various computer stores. A skip on the quayside is full of jettisoned boots and shoes which have presumably been replaced by more expensive but durable versions. It is hard to visualise Falmouth as consumer heaven, especially when banged about and soaked in grey January weather, but such it possibly is. It is equally hard to see the town as the gateway to a tropical adventure. Yet inland the heights of Dartmoor and Bodmin have been dusted with snow, while within a few miles of the coast the descending road is bordered with palm trees and spiky succulents; exotica testifying to the liquid radiator of the Gulf Stream, itself warmed by blazing clear days 5,000 miles away. The Cornish coast may be wet and blustery but it is not truly cold even on this winter's day.

The *Keldysh* is very well appointed for a scientific ship. Evidently no expense was spared when she was built in Finland in 1980. The corridors are wide, the stairwells carpeted. In the boardroom that we have already glimpsed on BBC television (very green the chairs look, too, in real life) are a piano and an electric organ. Elsewhere are a gymnasium, a sauna, even a small swimming pool. Quentin is much impressed. Such luxury is not characteristic of any research vessel he has ever sailed on. He and the Project's other members who settle into the ship in the days prior to sailing experience a curious stateless sensation peculiar to living aboard a foreign vessel in a home port. Much of the day is spent in an office ashore chasing up critical pieces of equipment in the succession of last-minute panics common to even the best-planned expeditions. There are also shopping trips to town: bottles of sunscreen factor 25 from Boots (hard to think of sunburn as a sharp rain drives horizontally up Falmouth's narrow main street), crates of tonic water and liquid detergent. Then dinner in a waterside pub, very English, and back to a bunk in a ship commissioned by a Soviet institution in which a loudspeaker in every cabin rasps into action at 0700 next morning with, presumably, the Russian command to rise and shine. This mixture of Butlin's and the KGB is all the odder for the view through the scuttles of the gentle grey waterfront a few hundred yards away. Nor is the reference to the KGB wholly jocular. It is soon discovered that these shipboard announcements are being made from a small room filled with radio equipment which turns out to be the communications and listening post of the secret service personnel who once accompanied every voyage. The story goes that the *Keldysh* was at sea the day in 1991 it was announced the Soviet regime had officially fallen. The captain went along to this sinister little room, opened the door without knocking, handed a large brush and a pot of white paint to the startled commissar inside and told him to get painting. His first job was to remove the hammer and sickle emblem from both sides of the ship's funnel (the outlines are visible to this day). For the rest of the voyage this man and his two colleagues laboured away like deck-hands while the newly liberated crew caroused. This room now seems to be the only one whose door remains permanently latched open. It is difficult not to see this as a slight act of superstition, symbolising *perestroika*. On this present voyage the commissar's spacious cabin is allotted to Orca's American cameraman, Ralph White. He is an old *Keldysh* hand, having filmed the *Titanic* with them for the Canadian company Imax. In fact he claims this is his ninth trip aboard, mostly in the same cabin, and the Russians sometimes refer to him more or less jocularly as 'our commissar'.

Four days to sailing. The size of the logistical problems involved in a salvage operation of such technical difficulty become apparent. The *Keldysh* and her crew are under charter for five months. Stores have to be laid in; computer systems must be tested before it is too late; mechanical and electronic spares arrive at the quayside in a constant stream. Up in Aberdeen an extensible arm is being built. This is designed to be attached to a MIR, enabling the operators to winkle gold bars out through a hole cut in the wreck's hull. It will not be ready in time and will have to be flown out for collection from Dakar in Senegal when the *Keldysh* puts in at the end of the first leg. Shore-leave for the crew at intervals of not more than five weeks is a condition of the Russians' contract. This in itself will not be easy to plan. The task of finding and salvaging two widely-separated wrecks within the allotted time means every day is precious. How to fit shore-leave, re-provisioning and spares collection in with the unpredictable exigencies of weather and what we may find on the seabed is a separate and, at this stage, largely insoluble problem. Yet firm delivery dates have to be given for Dakar. Quentin Huggett, Orca's geologist and sonar specialist, also needs an absolute promise that he will be able to fly home from Dakar on 27 February. Apart from being a family man he is running a small but growing business with a partner, Peter. Geotek's order book is full: he has to be back for crucial meetings in early March.

Clive Hayley and Simon Fraser now arrive from London. As Orca's fund-raisers and financial managers they are conscious of being responsible for the $3.6 million of investors' money sunk in the project. Clive is to join the ship for the first leg and will swap with Simon at Dakar. There is a good deal of tension and even grievance in the air. The Russians observe that it is just as well the *Keldysh* didn't arrive on schedule a month earlier in view of Orca's last-minute panics. The British reply tartly that the ship's constantly postponing its sailing date from Kaliningrad had meant it was far too risky to take delivery of expensive equipment because Orca might have been lumbered with it. A senior Russian is heard to observe that it was mad to have a woman in charge of something as critically important as stores. It would be charitable to think this was just a piece of time-honoured nautical superstition rather than simple prejudice, were it not that this distinction is itself clearly bogus, superstition being nothing but prejudice dignified as folklore.

Suddenly it becomes a little clearer why so many stories and films of treasure-hunts end in disaster. Even in a modern salvage operation like this the central factor is not the gold at all but the personalities involved. It is easy to centre one's attention on the technology: the dazzling science, precision tools, electronic wizardry. But underneath are critical chains of command, leadership issues, differences of opinion, alliances and animosities which outweigh everything else. High stakes produce high tension. In books and films, finding the gold often seems relatively simple. It is the getting it home and divvying up the profits equitably which is the tricky part, the stage when erstwhile comrades fall out. There is always someone who was the first to get wind of it, who carried his dream about with him like a map for years before realising he would need help to find it and dig it up. Invariably, it seems, he loses out to some unscrupulous late-comer. Suddenly, all becomes lost for reasons which, with the wisdom of hindsight, were not unpredictable. The clear objectives and careful planning of the Orca adventure (for such it is) ought to be proof against this sort of disaster. Yet it isn't quite enough to prevent one wondering what, to hindsight in a few months' time, might not seem glaringly obvious.

I get off to a bad start with Anatoly Sagalevitch. He calls an introduction to me as I pass an open door and I offer to shake hands with him across the threshold. 'Very bad luck,' he says smiling, but not much, and refusing to take my hand until he has stepped fully over the coaming.

FOUR

If anyone in the Orca team fills the role of the expedition's only begetter, the man who has carried his dream about with him for years, it is unquestionably Mike Anderson. Mike is the ex-policeman, and like many ex-policemen has pungent views about journalists. It was the money-men Simon and Clive who signed me up for the trip, and until we met aboard the *Keldysh* in Falmouth Mike and I had never clapped eyes on each other. At that point he thought I was a journalist; and it is a measure of his civility that he gave no indication he was unhappy at my inclusion. (It wasn't until we were well past the Bay of Biscay that the issue came into the open and was – as I believe – amicably resolved.)

Physically, Mike reminds me of the actor Dennis Waterman in *The Sweeney*, and the more I discover about his police background the more the association seems to stick. No doubt he has been told this by enough people (mostly girls, I should imagine) to have become heartily sick of it, and I'm sorry to find myself so banally making the same connection. Mike does not talk easily about himself, any more than his fictional counterpart did. He likewise gives the impression that beyond a certain point talk is a form of time-wasting, and that the only way to cut through guessing-games, hypotheses and theories of all kinds is with some good brisk action. In any case there is certainly no reason why he should talk about himself to me, a stranger and potential enemy, though I doubt if he does to anybody much. But I neither expect nor want unburdenings. I want to know about the history of this project, and his connections with it. No doubt the rest will emerge slowly over the course of the next month or two, in dribs and drabs as it generally does, only in the last days constructing a person one becomes anxious to see again but whom one probably never will. It is usually the way aboard ships.

Even before I pay a call on him for some preliminary information something has happened whose significance I can't yet judge. Mike's allotted cabin has been changed. Originally, as an old friend of Anatoly's, he was billeted in a large cabin which is something of a stateroom in the manner of 'commissar' Ralph's on the deck below. But with the arrival of the money-men from London it was decided (how?) that Clive should have this one instead, and Mike found himself moved a few doors down the corridor to a perfectly decent, but definitely down-market, smaller cabin. It was in here that he told me about his Scots father joining the police force in Birmingham, where he himself was born and brought up. Birmingham being about as far from the sea as it is possible to be in Britain, one could hardly have said that the sea was in his blood. Yet as a teenager he did want to join the Navy. Since his mother wouldn't let him, he joined the police cadets instead. 'I was determined Dad would call me "Sir" before he retired'. But soon after Mike joined the force his father was promoted to sergeant and Mike realised his ambition was unlikely to be fulfilled. While at college as a cadet he took 'A' Level Law, which interested him and which he passed well. Thereafter he rose in the ranks as a Birmingham police officer until the late seventies, when he resigned. This was not due to any particular incident, Mike assures me, but rather to an increasing feeling of restlessness and dissatisfaction. He was by no means alone: pay and working conditions were bad on the force in those days and many officers left.

Out of work, Mike took a course for artic. drivers and soon had his HGV licence. At the same time he followed up his interest in law by enrolling part-time in a course at Birmingham University. (It is not the least interesting thing about him that someone who can express such disdain for 'theory' has a real academic streak running through his career. No doubt he would dismiss this as just a means to an end, but he often betrays a slightly dogged and respectful attitude towards knowledge, as witness the effort he is making to learn Russian.) When he passed the first exam he began studying full-time, driving only at weekends and during the vacations to support himself. Part of the degree course involved writing a thesis. Since Mike had always been interested in the sea he chose Maritime Fraud as his special subject. This entailed a knowledge of insurance and loss adjusting as well as of institutions like the Salvage Association. He graduated in 1983 and began looking around for a job. Not knowing where else to start, he contacted a firm of loss adjusters. 'But,' as he puts it, 'it's a smallish world and word gets around and I was offered a job by the Salvage Association.' He joined the Salvage, Sales and Information department whose remit was to co-operate with companies wanting to do salvage work for Lloyds or for the British Government. By now Mike knew he wanted to concentrate on marine fraud investigation, which seemed a neat way of combining his experience as a policeman with an interest in the sea. Almost at once he found the department's work too bureaucratic and insisted on going out on actual salvage operations in order to learn how they were done, which was practically unheard-of. These were on shallow-water wrecks since the technology for tackling anything deeper was severely limited. The department began making money for itself and its principals, and Mike started to acquire a reputation. It was not long before he was headhunted by a large international salvage company because of his knowledge of the legal side of the business as well as for his familiarity with the politics of dealing with government departments.

So he went to work for a subsidiary of this company (which for discretion's sake we will call Salvimar S. A.). He was immediately asked to investigate the feasibility of setting up a deep-water salvage outfit to recover non-ferrous, as well as precious, metals. Salvimar already knew of about seventy or eighty wrecks that contained valuable 'industrial metals' cargoes such as manganese and copper, and were eager that Mike and his four colleagues should produce a business plan for recovering them. It wasn't long before they concluded this would be a hugely expensive undertaking, needing at least $40 million to set up (and this, of course, at mid-eighties prices). In the mean time Mike was pursuing some researches of his own. A year or two earlier he had been doing some work in the archives of the Bank of England when, quite unrelatedly and unknown to him, somebody happened to write to the Bank from Canada asking for copies of any official documents which might confirm that when she was torpedoed in 1943, the liner SS *Aurelia* had been carrying a large quantity of gold. This was Jock Walker, who had been one of the ship's officers at the time of her sinking and had overseen the loading of the gold in Durban. Now an elderly man, he was writing his autobiography and wanted to check the exact amount for the sake of historical accuracy. Could the Bank possibly help? By the time the Bank of England had delegated someone to search its relevant archives Mike was a director of Salvimar's subsidiary. When the Bank could find no record of the gold shipment it suggested to Jock Walker that he contact a professional salvage company such as Salvimar S. A. which might have access to other lines of research.

Thus it was that one day out of the blue a letter from Jock Walker landed on Mike's desk, and Mike wrote back in his company capacity. Anyone in the salvage business grows accustomed to hearing from people who know where heaps of gold can be found for the taking; it is a bit like being a tavern-keeper in Jamaica in the late seventeenth century. Although he had never heard of this man in his life, Mike was impressed by Jock Walker from the start of their correspondence. The old man showed not the least interest in making money but only in getting the facts straight for his memoirs. When business took Mike to Canada they met and liked each other. In due course Jock asked him about the salvage business and how it operated, and it was only natural they should have gone on to discuss how difficult it might be to recover the gold from the *Aurelia*. Mike said he would make some enquiries of his own to try and get independent confirmation that this shipment had ever existed, and there the matter was left.

Meanwhile, Salvimar S. A. had decided that their long-term plans for deep sea salvage would be impossibly expensive. In 1989 it cut off funds to its subsidiary, Salvimar Deep Sea Salvage, and wound it up. Suddenly, Mike was out of a job again. One of the first things he did was write to Jock Walker and tell him that unfortunately he couldn't proceed. Jock replied that by now he regarded Mike as a friend and would leave the project with him because he trusted him and anyway, he couldn't be bothered to take the whole business up from scratch again with a total stranger. Not long after this Mike was appointed Vice-President of an American salvage company, Subsal Inc. (another pseudonym), with much the same remit as Salvimar had given him: to draw up a business plan for specialist deep-water salvage operations. Mike worked for Subsal for the next two years in the course of which the company paid for him to go and interview Jock Walker. By this time the *Aurelia* was beginning to look like a genuine salvage prospect. Henceforth the ship's real name was no longer referred to and it was assigned a code name for security reasons. Since the liner had been requisitioned by the British wartime government it was likely that if any information about its cargo of gold still existed it would be in some British archive. The project was, of course, only one of several for which Mike had responsibility and he soon realised that he badly needed the services of a professional researcher on the spot in London. At the time he knew nobody suitable, but when visiting the Public Record Office one day he found a business card pinned up on a board offering the services of someone named Andrea Cordani.

In this way Mike first met Andrea, who is currently aboard the *Keldysh* as Orca's researcher. She did in fact unearth a good deal about the liner's last voyage, but still no independent evidence confirming Jock Walker's story that there had been a shipment of fifty boxes of gold aboard. She did discover that such shipments of gold to the UK were frequent during the Second World War, and not only from South Africa. One of the British Government's first acts on the declaration of war had been to disperse its gold reserves. For safety's sake it held deposits of bullion in various places scattered judiciously throughout the Empire. Whenever it needed a fresh injection of funds to finance the increasingly costly war effort, it authorised a top-secret shipment by the fastest available vessel. For preference it chose a warship, but one was not always available in the right place at the right time and a fast liner was a good substitute. The procedure for shipping gold from these outposts to England was well established by the time the liner sailed in early 1943; a complex and highly classified arrangement involving coded telegrams and often scanty documentation. The information Andrea was able to uncover, though it offered no further proof of this particular shipment, did establish that it was entirely consistent with the type of vessel used, the political conditions of the day and the loading procedures at Durban. There was one other thing that remained tantalising about Jock Walker's story. He remembered counting fifty boxes, but he couldn't say how much they weighed. Gold might have been shipped as ingots or as coins. At that time ingots came in two sizes: 400 oz. and 1000 oz., generally packed two to a box. It seems that up to 3000 ozs. of gold coin could have been fitted into a single box, so the range of weights offered by Jock's fifty boxes was large, varying in total between 40,000 ozs. and 150,000 ozs. (roughly one and four tons respectively). At today's prices this could mean anything between $15 million and $60 million.

On the basis of Andrea's research Mike concluded that even if they were to find documentary proof of the gold's existence, no investor would be likely to stump up the requisite $3 million for a salvage operation – a sum which, in view of the torpedoed liner's depth, was the probable minimum cost. However, he thought the operation might become feasible if there were another salvageable wreck to amortise costs; it ought to be possible to combine two operations for little more than the price of one. Going through the records, he found that the obvious choice was a Japanese submarine, the *I-52*. Not only was it comparatively close (three to four days' sailing), but its cargo of two – and possibly even four – tons of gold would favourably impress potential investors.

Until Jock Walker told Mike his story about the gold aboard the *Aurelia* it looked as though nobody else knew that it had ever existed. The *I-52*, by contrast, was already well known to the salvage business. The story of its gold was excellently documented and familiar enough, but it had never been seriously considered as a potential salvage target because it lay so deep. By now Salvimar S. A. had begun using remotely-operated vehicles, but ROVs have severely limited capabilities, are time-consuming to operate, and can't easily get inside an intact wreck. In the meantime Mike's boss at Subsal Inc. had heard about a Russian research vessel called the *Keldysh* and its two MIR submersibles and had wangled himself an invitation to the USSR (as it still just was) for talks. This was, in fact, a more enterprising move than it might seem today; a private American businessman going to the capital of the Evil Empire to negotiate a deal involving the Soviet Government's most prestigious scientific institution, the Russian Academy of Sciences. Much to everyone's surprise the preliminary discussions went well, and on his return the company's president was optimistic enough to tell Mike to go ahead and set up a joint *Aurelia/I-52* salvage operation. Within a year or so the much-publicised 1991 expedition to film the *Titanic* had made the *Keldysh* and its submersibles famous, and the following year Mike himself went to Moscow on behalf of Subsal in order to meet Anatoly Sagalevitch and discuss proposals for joint salvage operations.

For all Mike's legal qualifications and expertise, he must have reflected on the unpredictable – even ironic – chain of events which in the space of thirteen years had brought a Birmingham ex-copper to an oceanographical research institute in Moscow. To his surprise he found it easy to identify with the Russians' sudden political plight, and he quickly formed a close working and social relationship with Anatoly himself, as well as with several of his Russian colleagues. As a vice-president of Subsal Inc. Mike undertook to arrange the purchase in the West of some much-needed spares for the MIRs as well as equipment for the *Keldysh*, as part of a possible longer-term deal involving joint salvage operations. At the last moment, however, and to his acute embarrassment, the promised deal between the Shirshov Institute (the Academy of Science's Oceanographic branch) and Subsal fell through in circumstances about which Mike felt strongly enough to resign immediately from the company.

Back in England once more he was acutely aware of being without a job and also of seeming to have betrayed his new friends' confidence. It therefore came as a great surprise to him when a few months later Anatoly Sagalevitch called him in Cornwall and said they all realised the collapse of the spares deal had not been his fault, and could he possibly help with dry-docking the *Keldysh* in Falmouth? As it happened, he could. His relationship with the Russians thus restored, Mike and Anatoly began discussing the aborted salvage project in earnest. When Anatoly expressed real enthusiasm, Mike was put into contact with Simon and Clive in order to see how the requisite money might be raised.

Such a sketchy account does no justice to Mike Anderson the man, inevitably reducing him from a human being to a succession of career moves. Yet if nothing else, it does show how he was the originator of this *Aurelia/I-52* salvage scheme, as well as explaining how Andrea, the *Keldysh* and the Orca investors all came to be involved in it through him. I would obviously be making a mistake if I had the idea that this project was just one among many to a professional like Mike, or something which had been hanging around unresolved for so long it had become stale. 'In the course of the last six years I've been, excuse my French, shat on by Salvimar and Subsal, and I really want this to succeed so at least I can rub their noses in it a little. Of course, I also want it to succeed because it's going to make me some money. But the real pleasure I'll get if it does will come because the people who stood by me will also be rewarded, especially Anatoly and the Russians and Jean.' (This is Jean Anderson, Mike's ex-wife.)

Yet Mike is well able to be generous about the salvage industry when it is warranted since he knows it well enough to have a thorough understanding of the difficulties involved. He rates both the *Central America* and the *John Barry* projects as definite successes, regardless of how much discrepancy there may be between the amounts actually recovered and the exaggerated press reports. Both wrecks present massive technical problems. Yet even today, when deep-water salvage is still in its infancy, techniques can sometimes be formidably good. He quotes the example of a company named Oceaneering who looked for and found a single cargo door which had fallen into the sea from UAL flight 811 in 1990. Surely it ought to be possible for Orca to find a 22,000-ton liner and a 2,000-ton submarine . . . Still, the project is unique. No cargo recovery has ever been attempted at such a depth, and Orca will be the first to try using cutting tools to get into the hulls. No one in a manned submersible has ever tried to change discs on a chopsaw before.

Meanwhile the chopsaw – built recently to his own specifications – lies on his cabin floor surrounded by those polystyrene packing chips that look like cocktail nibbles. From time to time he picks it up proudly, hefts it and examines the chain drive. 'Lovely work,' he says. 'Beautiful bit of engineering.' There isn't much room on the floor with the thing laid out and I find myself still wondering about the circumstances which led to the project's originator being 'downgraded', as I can only see it, to this smaller cabin. Something else which may become clearer as the voyage proceeds.

FIVE

26/1/95
We have now been at sea nearly five days. Falmouth is a memory behind bulks of grey cloud on the northern horizon. The sea is very restless; the *Keldysh* lurches and bangs. The forepeak nose-dives and tufts of spray whip stingingly aft. Things are shaking down, gradually assuming the shapes and patterns of shipboard life which will for ever after characterise this voyage.

Back in London before the trip, the money-men had spent much time and thought on devising a code for sensitive radio messages to and from the ship. Simon and Clive hit on a cipher based on a 1965 issue of their old prep. school magazine. Today I have to record that their first attempt at coded communication has been a failure. It took Clive two hours to transcribe a few lines, and a subsequent message from Simon apparently referred to line 31 on a page which had only 28 lines and so remains a mere jumble of figures. This is some way removed from the world of 'Ultra' and 'Magic' (see p.61) which ultimately was responsible for sinking the submarine we're looking for. It was surely their mistake to have devised such a complicated method. They should have followed the example of the British tank commanders in the North African campaign as described by Keith Douglas in *Alamein to Zem-Zem*. Those ex-public

32

schoolboys relied on sporty allusion to baffle any Germans overhearing their radio transmissions, drawing largely on hunting and cricket. "'Uncle Tom, I'm *just* going over Beecher's myself, you want to hold 'em in a bit and go carefully, but after that it's good going for the whole field." "King 2 Ack," says someone who has broken a track. "I shall need the farrier, I've cast a shoe." "King 2, now that that chap has retired to the pavilion, how many short of a full team are you?"' In its way, this was the equivalent of the device used by Americans in various wars from the First World War onwards: having Native Americans talk to each other *en clair* in the certain knowledge that no German, Russian, Korean, or Vietnamese field troops would even be able to identify the language, still less understand it. I can't believe Clive and Simon couldn't have come up with a similar piece of old-school ellipsis in order to convey that the submarine had been found and the gold was being brought up. But presumably they also needed to be able to talk frankly about the Russians, and in quite un-elliptical terms.

Orca's communications system is at present a mess and hilarious to anyone who dislikes slavish technophilia. Among the five members aboard are five different computers and five different formats. Nobody can easily speak to anyone, and sending messages from the *Keldysh* to the UK (Clive to Simon, Quentin to Peter, Mike to Jean, whoever to whomever) is very far from the 'doddle' which the nerds had been predicting back in England. It's a mess of faxes and modems and Macintoshes and dedicated lines and switchboxes and Inmarsat and programs and mail-boxes and file-dumping software and Laplink and Smartcom and Winfax and Comet and WordPerfect-dumped-to-disk – as well as lugging pale grey plastic boxes and screens up to the ship's radio room to wire them up and plug them in, all of which leads to getting through at great expense to absolutely no-one. The ship's uprated GPS navigation system interferes with communication, or vice versa, while the wireless officer's own transmissions blast our fragile telephone links clean out of the ionosphere. Orca's calls to England are, in theory, bounced via Intelsat to a station in Norway where a robot voice-chip tells callers they're being relayed to the UK, where nobody picks up a receiver because the stream of digits can't make up its brainless mind whether to come out as a fax message or a voice or else some kind of celestial whisper which transcends any known system, ether calling to ether on – yes, indeed – the Ethernet.

Everyone says, 'If only the connecting cable I ordered two months ago had been made up in time it would all be so *simple* . . . ' or 'Just a gizmo about the size of a packet of cigarettes and costing £7.99 in Dixon's would have avoided all this.' I don't believe a word of it, partly because in my experience of watching people wrestle and waste time with computers this whole kerfuffle is perfectly usual, but also because there are demon electronics nerds aboard *Keldysh* who could surely sort it all out if it were at all sortable. Nik Shashkov, for example, who looks like a worried Fifth-former but is a father in real life (*sic*) back in Russia, is, according to Quentin, capable of the rare intellectual gymnastics of being able to decompile software. This is a prodigious feat of decoding, one he carried out a few years ago when trying to deal with some Finnish navigation equipment aboard *Keldysh* dating from the ship's fitting-out. The Finns had compiled its software and the source code was no longer available. Nik, working backwards, decompiled it and recon-structed the software. There's no limit to one's wonder at the ways in which people choose to spend their time. Maybe it's envy after all. Nobody is ever going to lay the laurels of an intellectual feat at my door.

Meanwhile, as the electronic fracas fizzes and chirps all

around, with people frantically labouring hour after hour trying to make their labour-saving machines save labour, it's hard not to wonder when they ever get any work done. Even today, those seafarers who really score are still the ones who can accept being cut off for months at a stretch (itself one of the great liberating perks of sea travel). May God rot Marconi. I want the days when ships *spoke* each other on the high seas, or at some scummy foreign port, and bundles of letters and messages were exchanged with a salute and a wave and each ship proceeded over the horizon to whatever destiny awaited. That was solemn and chancy. The idea of pretending in mid-Atlantic that you might just as well be calling from a phone box in a pub down the road is vile. Anyway, the thing to remember while carrying these magic boxes to and from the ship's radio room is that despite all protestations, the new communications technology is still in its infancy. The Russians still use Morse and it works every time. Modem-schmodem: we're still at the semaphore and smoke signals stage.

Meanwhile, completely unaffected by Orca's electronic chaos, our hosts are quietly getting on with real work. There are daily reminders that the *Keldysh* is a research vessel, and the scientists aboard continue working away with paper, pencils and rubbers as they always did, producing exquisite charts and diagrams which they pin to the blackboard in the 'boardroom', which I now see more as a lecture theatre. In fact, regular lectures turn out to be a feature of this trip, as they no doubt are on all *Keldysh* cruises. Serious and learned people stand up at 6 p.m. most evenings and deliver a seventy-minute lecture in Russian on a variety of topics with slides and maybe a video. Last night it was Dr Bogdanov's turn. Yuriy Bogdanov is an internationally-celebrated geologist: a large, sixty-ish man with a greying mane who sometimes faintly resembles a scholarly version of the late

George Brown MP, though more teddy bear than drunken owl. With the other Orca members I sit dutifully in the audience, lulled by the incomprehensible but mellifluous flow of Russian, drowsily reconstructing a past for him under the Soviet system, unable to imagine even the grimmest KGB lout being inclined to bully such a gentle and kindly-looking soul. He makes small, inexpressive gestures with soft mournful hands, plays with his folded spectacles, stares sadly at the table as he speaks. I catch odd words: carbonates, vulcanism, magnetic flux (possibly), dioxides. His field is black smokers and the chemistry of seabed hydrothermal vents.

Later, Quentin comes up with a hypothesis about Bogdanov's past and his geological speciality which sounds plausible. For the last eight years of the Soviet regime, to be aboard the *Keldysh* was the best posting imaginable. To be included on its prestigious scientific staff entitled one to the special perks of foreign travel, international contacts, even to a portion of one's salary being paid in cash in dollars ($5 a week). One way of safeguarding one's position aboard would have been to maintain international visibility by concentrating on 'Big Science' as fashionably recognised in the West, and black smokers had exactly the right high profile. It would have been fatal to have concentrated on some obscure and rarefied branch of magneto-metry, for example; a sure way of being dropped from this flagship of Soviet science. So my fantasies of Bogdanov as a scholar beavering away along his own lonely path, oblivious to fashionable academic shenanigans, are probably quite wrong. He wisely stuck to black smokers, a subject so popular that remarkably little real work has yet been done on them.

This may sound heretical. Yet if *Homo*'s environmental impact on the planet is ever to be assessed accurately, we shall need to know the extent of *natural* pollution. Quite apart from the numerous sources all over the world of oil seepage through the seabed, the output of chemical pollutants from hydrothermal vents has so far never been measured – not least because nobody has much idea even how many of these undersea geysers exist. The current geological 'best guess' is that each year the seabed's vents are jointly expelling more metals than all the world's mineral extraction industries produce. This, combined with a wealth of other noxious compounds (including radioactive ones), makes the seabed the planet's greatest source of chemical pollutants. The exact constituents of even a single vent are still unknown, and the same is true for its rate of flow as part of the total environmental budget. In the main, people are too dazzled by making videos of vent communities of worms, crabs and other biota to have raised much funding for the less eye-catching but more important hard-core science of measurement and analysis. (If anyone doubted the relevance of this gap in knowledge they had only to wait a few months for the famous confrontation between Greenpeace and Royal Dutch Shell, in which the oil company was obliged to abort its plan to scupper an unwanted oil rig, the 14,500 ton *Brent Spar*, even then being towed out to its proposed dump site. Despite all the popular emotion, large numbers of oceanologists and other scientists stuck gallantly to their guns by maintaining that such deep ocean dumping would actually have negligible environmental impact compared with dry land dismantling. This was not what the adherents of the Church of Greenpeace wanted to hear and no doubt it added to the further demonising of science and scientists.)

At the end of Bogdanov's lecture Quentin asked him if there was serious interest in looking for 'fossil' black smokers. The reply was that of course it was interesting, but that nobody was doing it. As a marine geologist, Quentin knew this perfectly well. He was following the old lawyer's adage that you never ask a witness a question you can't already answer. And, like counsel, he had an ulterior motive. For suddenly the *Keldysh* has begun looking like the serious scientific research vessel it actually is: more interested in intellectual matters than in some silly wild goose chase after gold. There is scepticism even from Anatoly Sagalevitch himself about the contracts with Orca he signed back in Moscow, as well as with the whole business of monetary reward. It isn't so much that he mistrusts Mike Anderson – after all, they are friends – but rather that regardless of Sagalevitch's sophistication and exposure (since the *Titanic*) to all the blandishments of the Western media, he and his colleagues seem radically unfamiliar with contracts and lawyers – maybe even with money itself. The Soviet system made for brilliant technicians, not entrepreneurs. Anatoly designed, helped build, test-piloted and has since worked his two MIR submersibles for the Academy of Sciences. In his own way he is a pioneer in the tradition of Beebe, Piccard and Cousteau, not a beady businessman at home with the idea of making the ship in his charge pay its way. Orca's charter has, in fact, put him as a scientist at that unhappy and even ruinous crossroads which Thatcherism began so ruthlessly drawing on Britain's own intellectual map fifteen years ago: how to make the serious pursuit of knowledge commercially viable. And the easiest route to take is the one leading to deep-sea expeditions, all shooting the same footage of black smokers or *Titanics* (or whatever else is the flavour of the month) for the world's television production companies, while struggling to do a little hard science on the back of it. In terms of our urgently finding out enough about the planet's ecology in time to save ourselves, it's probably a considerable mistake.

This crossroads now presents itself aboard the *Keldysh*. The point of Quentin's question is to show the Russians that at least someone on the Orca team is a scientist who recognises that other scientists aboard wish they were *en route* for a point on the mid-Atlantic ridge 300 nautical miles west of Orca's first target, *Dolphin* (as the *I–52* has been code-named). It is rumoured that another Russian research vessel has discovered a black smoker there – possibly the first ever found along this fault line. *Keldysh*'s geologists are all too aware that, thanks to the MIRs, they could actually go and see it for themselves. Some coring and sampling studies supplemented by specimens and video footage would represent a genuine scientific coup. Instead, they have to pretend to be excited by the prospect of looking for a fifty-year-old Japanese submarine which may or may not be there, and which may or may not contain gold which in turn might make them a bit richer. I'd like to think it all goes to show the prodigious inability of neo-classical economics to find simple greed at the bottom of all human endeavour. On the *Keldysh*, the scientific community's implied disdain for market forces may not reflect Keynesian sophistication so much as that purism which wants to be free to pursue knowledge for its own sake. There may be a sort of parallel here with the Internet's computing fraternity who are fighting a gallant, principled (but probably losing) battle to keep advertising from cluttering up the unsullied reaches of cyberspace with commercialism. In neither case is it laughable. On the contrary, it represents a genuine and widespread side of human beings which is uninterested in money, the side which seeks intellectual pleasure.

Individually, most of the Russian scientists will admit that the quest for gold ingots does have a certain narrative suspense, but is of no real interest compared to biology or meteorology. Or geology. For instance, in order to model what is going on at the spreading axis between two tectonic plates it is necessary to find out what happens to a black smoker when the convection system which built it moves away from the chimney through which it vented. There may be 'fossil' chimneys sticking up from the seabed, or perhaps buried deep beneath the sediment, which could tell us about mineral deposits and rates of spreading and suchlike. Unfortunately, the area in which *Dolphin* (Orca's codename for the submarine) is lying is quite ancient and probably fairly lifeless and undisturbed, geologically speaking. In short, under its Orca contract the *Keldysh* will in effect be obliged to work 50 million years away from the spreading axis. Informally, the British agree that if the submarine is found and salvaged quickly there might be time for the Russians to do their bit of science before the end of the first leg and the port call in Dakar. There is another aspect, too. In the down-time between MIR dives on the target site the Russian scientists would like to do some coring of the local sediment anyway. The problem is that it seems the only wire cable they have spooled on a winch sufficiently powerful to heave a tube of mud up 5 kilometres is the one Orca loaded at Falmouth for the sonar sled, and it is far too precious to be used in this way. It's also far too good, with its core of electronic connectors. What is needed is ordinary wire rope, given that corers and their cables are quite frequently lost. There is a kinked and frayed old wire rope, much too thin, which they might use and which would perfectly exemplify the idea of doing science on a shoe-string. In any case Orca is not about to sacrifice its cable, so the Russians are unlikely to be obliged, and certainly not so early on in the venture. This may, of course, make them still grumpier and even more refractory.

SIX

From the moment I had spoken to Quentin by phone from the bar in Italy I was impressed by Orca's desire for secrecy. At the time I naively assumed this was to prevent rival salvage operations from converging on the two wrecks and snatching the gold from under our noses. Once I had boarded the *Keldysh* and we were on the high seas I discovered this was not regarded as a serious threat. Not only did it take months to set up a deep-water salvage operation but there was only a handful of companies world-wide with the capability of mounting one. No, the real reason for Orca's secrecy centred around the sunken troop-ship, which had been code-named *Marlin*. (The submarine – *Dolphin* – was not only already known to most professional salvors, it was a foreign vessel. Nevertheless, it too had been given a code-name.) Orca was worried lest our planned attempt on the *Aurelia* should come to the ears of the British Government and they slap an injunction on us by hastily designating it a war grave. Could they do so legally? I wondered. Could Her Majesty's Government arbitrarily designate any wartime wreck as a war grave in order to freeze a diving operation? This question, addressed by both Mike Anderson and our researcher Andrea Cordani from different directions on sundry occasions, turned out to lead through some interesting legal byways before it could be answered.

Generally speaking, the British laws governing salvage are the most favourable of any maritime nation, at least from the salvor's point of view. A century ago the Merchant Shipping Act (1896) enshrined in statute the long-established procedure for delivering up a salvaged vessel or cargo to the Receiver of Wreck. (Both the trade and the law distinguish between wet and dry salvage. Wet salvage is what we're hoping to do. An example of dry salvage would be tugs from rival companies racing to get a tow on a crippled tanker.) Both wet and dry salvage might involve a Royal Navy vessel as prize; a salvor still has rights under the Act even if the wreck is Crown or Admiralty property. Until recently the UK's Receivers of Wreck were local Customs and Excise officers, a system which might have proved favourable to Orca in terms of convenience since ex-police officer Mike Anderson knew the Falmouth Customs officials personally. However, the system had recently been centralised and, from an office in Southampton, Veronica Robbins was now Receiver of Wreck for the entire UK. Her duty was to put a salvaged cargo in a secure bonded store and establish the identity of its legal owner or claimants. If there were no serious doubts, well and good and the matter could swiftly be resolved. By precedent the salvor gets the lion's share of any value, having undertaken the salvage at his own risk, while the legal owner gets a compensatory sum – typically between 5 and 10 per cent. In the case of the *I-52*, for example, if the Japanese Government provided title but renounced ownership (as it would almost certainly have to since it was not on the winning side in the Second World War), that is what would happen. If they maintained that 10 per cent of their gold's value was not enough compensation, the case would be heard in an Admiralty court which would reconsider the salvage reward. The court's decision is always final, and it would be quite possible they might reconsider downwards and the Japanese Government wind up with a share of even less than five per cent.

If the Receiver cannot trace the owner, the cargo is kept in HM custody for a year and a day, after which it is returned to the salvors minus storage expenses. The Government used to take a cut over and above their expenses but this has now been waived and a salvor can expect to keep something like 90 per cent of his cargo's value. All this is reasonably uncomplicated provided the wreck is lying in international waters. Otherwise, it can become a legal bear-garden. For instance, the Dutch Government claims rights to all sunken VOC (East India Company) ships and cargoes anywhere in the world, while the Indonesians claim absolute rights over VOC wrecks in their national waters.

Salvage law is indeed arcane and complex, relying as it does on the practice and precedents of centuries and still reflecting the oddest traditions (for proof of this contention, the curious should look into the so-called 'Doctrine of Hereditary Bottoms'). Add to this the international angle, and maritime litigation can often resemble treasure-hunting itself: a high-stakes gamble. At least Orca's two targets are indisputably in international waters. Nevertheless the larger of the two, the liner, is to some extent in the British Government's bailiwick since HMG was the legal owner of the cargo, which was presumably insured. Or was it? The War Risks Insurance Office comes under the Department of Transport. When early in the war the British Government requisitioned the *Aurelia* from the line which owned her (as it requisitioned all civilian ships), the vessel would have been insured through the WRIO for war risks but not marine (natural) ones. This insurance scheme covered both hulls and cargoes, but has led to very tricky legal arguments because in practice it is often hard to distinguish between war and natural causes as the reason for a ship's loss. Although there appears to be no official record of this particular shipment of gold, making it even more secret than usual, it is not clear whether its full value would have been covered under War Risks insurance. It seems very unlikely that the British Government would have insured its own cargo with its own insurance office. On the other hand there seems to be some possibility that this wasn't HMG's gold at all, and may never have been destined for the Bank of England. This might become clearer if we succeed in finding an ingot or two: the markings ought to explain quite a bit.

Orca's only serious worry all along has been that the British Government would get wind of the search for the liner and quickly classify her as a war grave in order to buy itself time as it beavered frantically through Admiralty and other files in the hopes of finding information about the shipment that the Bank of England itself appears not to have had. For a vessel to become a war grave it must be officially designated as such; but for practical purposes it is well accepted that any RN vessel that qualifies may automatically have this status. The *Aurelia*, as a civil liner, cannot qualify as a war grave under the usual terms even though she was engaged in war work and carried deck guns manned by RN ratings. (Given that virtually all British merchantmen in the war were civilian ships and many were exposed to the worst dangers of the most arduous convoy routes, taking terrible casualties, it seems a particularly mean kind of injustice that none of their wrecks has the status of a war grave). Nevertheless, Mike's fear is that the Government could stretch a recent Act (1986) to cover the liner if it really wanted to.

The very issue of what constitutes a war grave at sea – and

precisely what that definition does to a wreck's status – is fudged and difficult. In terms of legislation, the British Government can be seen as having approached the problem circuitously via the Protection of Wrecks Act (1973) and the Protection of Military Remains Act (1986). The first Act was brought because there was no clear legal line drawn between historical wrecks and modern ones. For the purposes of salvage there had to be a distinction in law between the *Mary Rose* and a Panamanian tanker. The Runciman Committee decided that under this Act wrecks could be scheduled and designated Protected, whether as an actual wreck or a site (as in the case of a ship entirely buried beneath the seabed, for example). Accordingly, there is a published list of such wrecks and sites which cannot be dived on or excavated without permission.

The second Act required that the Ministry of Defence supply a complete list of its wrecks, but to date the M.o.D has not done so. Until 1986 the War Graves Commission, as well as maintaining cemeteries all over the world, had the power to designate as war graves warships lost at sea. Unfortunately, there is still no precise legal definition of a war grave at sea, and the 1986 Act remains not only ineffective in its lack of a list, but badly drafted, like so much other legislation of the period. The whole subject is highly emotive and readily spills over into issues of general ponder, such as 'When is a wreck which involved loss of life *not* a tomb?' The short, cynical answer is 'When there's a valuable cargo involved.' Another, more cogent, answer might be 'When there are no longer any close surviving relatives of a victim to make a fuss or sue for distress.' Apart from anything else, different cultures have widely differing attitudes towards the bodies of their dead, some making a fetish of them while others view them indifferently as mere cast-off envelopes. Even these attitudes are pliable, especially where the bodies of a defeated enemy are concerned. And what happens when a wreck is comparatively recent, dating from the Second World War, but there are no human remains left? In neither of Orca's targets could there still be a single femur, much less an intact skeleton. The extreme pressure at that depth, combined with the salinity, ensures that even bone rapidly crumbles and disperses. Can a tomb contain neither ash nor bone yet remain a tomb? Does a mere headstone – or an Admiralty list of names – constitute a grave?

So far there are no clear-cut answers to these questions, partly because nobody can agree on them but mostly because the matter has not encouraged much serious debate. No one really wants to think about it; it is simpler to deal with case by case. A newspaper might take up a specific instance and orchestrate national outrage at the 'cynical despoliation of the last resting-place of those who made the supreme sacrifice' (or some such phrase), or else the whole thing might never come to public attention. Being a rotten cynic, I suspect that a good many people who readily and noisily invoke notions of desecration and grave-robbing are moved more by an ordinary jealousy that someone other than themselves may get his hands on a nice bit of money. Thus may dog-in-the-manger masquerade as faithful public guardian. To illustrate the rich muddle of sentimentality, greed, solemnity, moralism, expediency and the rest, one can only examine precedent.

The *Titanic*, though in no sense a war grave, neatly illustrates attitudes in the process of becoming slippery. Dr Robert Ballard, the American co-leader of the expedition that found the wreck in 1985, was scrupulous to the point of piety about not removing anything from the site, even to the extent of washing the liner's rust particles off his ROVs before hauling them in. He felt – and impressed his attitude firmly on his crew – that this mournful hulk they had found should be treated with the utmost respect. One might touch or examine things for the benefit of the camera lens but never retrieve them. In the decade since then attitudes have changed completely. Now, objects from the hull as well as personal possessions are regularly salved from the site, put on display and generally turned into the focus of a profit-making media circus. (In the summer of 1996 there was a joint US/ French attempt to raise a section of the liner itself, an attempt that failed when towing cables parted in heavy weather, leaving the *Titanic*'s remains even more dispersed and despoiled.) But why not?, the realistic demanded. Hadn't Ballard left a bronze plaque on the ship? Wasn't that enough? Back in 1986 a *National Geographic* editorial put it succinctly: 'Just as advertisers use sex to sell everything from cat food to cologne, why not use the *Titanic* to sell and develop deep-sea exploration?' And at that time, of course, there were not only relatives of the *Titanic*'s victims still alive but individual survivors as well. All that was needed was for this pragmatic approach to be given the official imprimatur of received practice. The same editorial at once did so by effectively designating the planet's entire seabed as on-limits to potential diggers: 'As one massive archaeological site, the oceans are a treasured time capsule.' 'Treasured' is the *mot juste*.

This civilian attitude can also encroach in the case of war wrecks. In reviewing the whole phenomenon one is tempted to formulate a hypothesis, which is that it is enough for a nation like Britain or the United States to have one or two celebrated and sacrosanct sunken graves to stand for all of them, and to leave the rest up for grabs. No doubt this would be strenuously denied by Pentagon and Admiralty alike, but that is how things look. That most splendid of war graves, the hulk of the battleship USS *Arizona* visibly lying beneath the clear tropic

47

waters of Pearl Harbor, is the epitome of a national monument: solemn, untouchable, the repository and shrine of far more than the 1,177 men who died in her. She, the nearby USS *Utah* and a handful of others stand collectively as a marine cenotaph, a grand equivalent of the bronze plaque Dr Ballard left on the *Titanic*. In British terms much the same applies. HMS *Prince of Wales* and HMS *Repulse* lying off Malaysia are not actually protected war graves by individual designation; yet commemorative services are still held and the White Ensign unfurled under water.

The slipperiness enters in the case of a Royal Navy vessel like HMS *Edinburgh*. She was a cruiser sunk in the Barents Sea in May 1942 *en route* from Murmansk while escorting a returning British convoy. She had a complement of 850 men and was carrying 4.5 tons of Russian gold in ninety-three boxes. As a result of repeated attacks by a U-boat and three German destroyers, the crippled *Edinburgh* was abandoned and scuttled to prevent the gold falling into enemy hands. In 1957 she was officially designated a war grave, but by the late 1970s the British Government was itself eager to see the gold salvaged. As Nigel Pickford recounts in his recent book, *The Atlas of Shipwreck & Treasure*,

Jessop Marine, a salvage company run by diver Keith Jessop, won the contract, partly because the Government felt that its methods, which used cutting machinery and divers, were more appropriate to a war grave than the more explosive 'smash and grab' techniques proposed by other contenders. Jessop Marine was asking for 45 per cent of the proceeds, and the remainder would be split one-third to the British Government and two-thirds to the Russian Government, reflecting the ratio in which the original wartime insurance of the gold had been split.

On 15 September 1981, a diver penetrated the wreck and recovered a bar of gold. By 7 October, when bad weather forced the suspension of the salvage, 431 out of 465 bars had been recovered, worth in excess of £43 million sterling.

In fact, a second expedition returned a few years later for the other thirty-four bars, an operation which has particular significance for Mike Anderson since he accompanied it. This time there was a War Graves Commission representative on board with them to monitor the entire operation. This man wielded enough authority to forbid the salvors to proceed beyond a particular bulkhead in pursuit of the last five ingots which had slipped through a hole. This was because he had reason to believe there were still some bodies in the chamber. So the last few gold bars were left in HMS *Edinburgh* with the putative bones of the men who had died protecting them.

The upshot seems to be that you can plunder a war grave with official sanction provided the rewards are high enough and provided you leave behind a tithe of the treasure to appease both public conscience and the manes of the dead: the equivalent of a bronze plaque, in other words. Mike, having watched first-hand the way the *Edinburgh*'s salvage came to public notice, has given the matter a good deal of thought. If Orca is successful in either of its targets, the matter will need careful handling. Japan, it turns out, has no such category as a war grave or else the *I-52* would surely qualify. It insists only that any human remains be returned for proper Shinto burial. In any case Orca intends to have its photographer, Ralph White, make a video record of properly reverent services being conducted aboard *Keldysh* at both sites to guard against any future accusation that we were just a bunch of grave-robbers without the slightest respect for the human tragedies which were a prerequisite for the enterprise. Arse-covering, in short.

The exact point at which grave-robbing becomes archaeology shifts with the times. In any case people in various places and various circumstances have interesting and diverse relationships with each other's mortal remains. As Kenneth V. Iserson notes in *Death to Dust*, Truk lagoon in the E. Caroline Islands (a major Japanese naval base in the Second World War) has become a renowned wreck-diving site. Until the late 1980s when the Japanese sent a team of professional divers to collect the remains of their compatriots and take them back to Japan, 'the bones of Japanese sailors were often retrieved as souvenirs by divers or used as props in underwater pictures'. Truk lagoon, of course, is shallow enough for scuba work. As said earlier, the emotive question of skeletal remains does not arise in either of Orca's two wrecks, which lie too deep. In 1993 Dr Robert Ballard was interviewed in *USA Today* about his exploration of fourteen naval craft found lying in 1000 metres of water off Guadalcanal, all victims of the fierce battles in 1943. Commenting on the ships' still-pristine condition, he observed: 'All that's missing are the bodies of the thousands of sailors.'

All in all, wet salvage is a risky business from a legal as well as a technical point of view, despite the UK's law being so slanted in the salvor's favour. Mike Anderson gave good financial reasons as to why there should be so few (probably no) companies in existence exclusively set up for deep-water cargo salvage; but potential legal entanglements and grey areas must be an additional discouragement. There is a large number of small wet salvage companies with big ideas, many of them formed around a single project. For example, a company was set up to salvage old transatlantic and other unwanted telecom cables for the huge tonnage of copper they contain. It was a good idea, but proved not practicable since the overheads were too large. Similarly, groups of potential salvors have long had an eye on the potential lying beneath the western Atlantic. During the last war German U-boats were sent to the coasts of America with orders to sink as many oil tankers bound for Britain as they could. Consequently, the entire eastern seaboard from Cape Cod to the Caribbean is littered with sunken oil tankers. Many of them probably still contain a good proportion of their original cargoes intact: hundreds of thousands, and maybe millions, of tons of oil. The only trouble is the overheads . . . But the techniques for getting at these cargoes do exist, and the proof is on board the *Keldysh*. The Rockwater cutting tool which Orca has brought along was very recently used with great success to drill holes in the hull of the German warship *Blücher*, lying in Oslo Fjord, to drain the ship's leaking fuel tanks before oil could contaminate Norway's beaches.

The wet salvage industry can be subdivided into modern (basically twentieth-century, steel-hulled wrecks), historical (shallow-water Spanish galleons, for example, whose salvors are often referred to as 'treasure hunters') and archaeological (such as the *Mary Rose*, Roman galleys etc.). Mike Anderson asserts that Orca members are most certainly not treasure hunters but simply deep-water modern cargo salvors. As he has pointed out, very few salvors have ever set up business to concentrate just on cargo salvage, whether in deep or shallow water. The only British company of any note to have done so since the last war was one named Risdon Beazley. This was formed around a nucleus of ex-Royal Navy divers who, once they were demobbed, pooled their experience and the knowledge they had acquired and decided there was a living to be made. From 1945 until about 1980 they were so successful in recovering cargoes world-wide for both the British and French governments that they achieved a kind of semi-official status, and this despite only ever having a depth capability of some 400 metres. (Their chief researcher, T. H. Pickford, did much of the original spade-work in uncovering details of the *I-52* in the late 1940s and 50s. It is his son Nigel who wrote the authoritative *The Atlas of Shipwreck & Treasure* from which I quoted above.) Mike Anderson's view of Risdon Beazley's demise is that they simply failed to keep up with technological advances. They were bought by the Dutch salvage giant Smit who had all sorts of grandiose plans for developing their new subsidiary; but it turned out that not even Smit had the resources to go into full-time deep-water cargo recovery, and so far nobody else has either. The dreams, the plans, the brilliant fantasies abound. The ocean floors are thick with golden opportunities. But the business of recovery is as specialised in its way as that of space exploration; much more dangerous, and very nearly as expensive.

SEVEN

As to meals, there are four of us at our table: the engineer Viktor Brovko, Anatoly Suslyaev or 'Goldenhands' as he is respectfully known in both Russian and English, our researcher Andrea Cordani and myself. Mostly there is tea for breakfast. A stainless steel kettle at the end of the table holds espresso tea, as one might call it, incredibly strong and bitter, while a larger kettle contains hot water for diluting it. A dish of lemon slices. Cold sausage and cheese. At lunch and dinner the kettle is filled with *kompot*, a sort of watery prune juice. Nothing wrong with any of this at present, but if it goes on for six weeks it could become monotonous. I'm glad to see Viktor can't bear *kompot*, any more than 'Goldenhands' can stomach onions. When the Russians are picky about their own food it will make it easier for Andrea and me to balk at anything which turns out to be really inedible. Further-sighted Orca members have brought along a selection of un-Russian things like marmalade, lime pickle, Marmite and tabasco sauce, all of which nice Viktor has tried but which mostly caused him nearly-concealed distress. Still, it hardly behoves the British to be sniffy about other folks' cuisine. Only a nation of hard-core gastronomic philistines could possibly think 'Slam in the Lamb' was any way to treat food, still less be a selling slogan.

This morning we have to touch briefly at Funchal in Madeira, an unscheduled visit made necessary by a loading mistake at Falmouth in which drums of red hydraulic oil were put aboard instead of petrol for the *Zodiac*'s outboard motor. We're to stand off while a launch delivers it. No shore leave, no delay. Sensibly, Clive is trying on the ship-to-shore phone for a case of Madeira to accompany the drums of fuel.

This is a scientific vessel, all right. Apparently the early wake-up announcement this morning gave our ETA off Funchal as well as the water temperature, wind speed and barometric pressure. I actually heard it up on deck, where I'd long been. The prospect of land always makes one eager. The dawn breeze is warm. Somewhere over the horizon is Africa; we have left Europe and its winter behind. Even after a lifetime it never fails, a landfall at break of day. The sky is pink and turquoise and the other colours of being young. Out of last night's blank ocean a volcanic bulk of land has swum up, lines of lights twinkling up its slopes, unknown citizens invisibly getting up and seeing the distant white toy of the *Keldysh* through their bedroom windows and maybe wondering who we are, where we have come from, but more likely not paying such a familiar sight any heed at all.

Pink basalt cliffs deeply ravined and holding up tilted green slopes strewn with white houses. Quentin, who has put in here on more than one occasion while on field trips in HMS *Discovery*, speaks highly of the place and observes, 'If the sea were warmer this would be Hawaii: same latitude, same sort of vulcanism, similar cliffs.' He believes the world's highest cliffs are to be found here, as measured top to true base deep undersea. I can't but be fascinated by the broad prospect since this very landfall is the one I needed to imagine when writing my novel *Gerontius*, having never clapped eyes on the place where Elgar's ship touched on its way from Liverpool to the Amazon in 1923. It's a bit lower than I envisaged. '*Vulkan*', says a Russian standing nearby. He is one of a dozen shapes in track suits and T-shirts scattered about the decks, each doing morning stretches and bends in a private patch of space. (I like this reminder of the Far East, where total privacy can be had inside paper walls, within invisible boundaries drawn in air.) '*Vulkan*,' I agree. Madeira is indeed so obviously volcanic, and my somewhat geological way of looking at landscapes now so accustomed, that I no longer see it as I probably would have done as an undergraduate, in a literary way, as 'floating' on the sea among the early mists. Rather, it is a chunk of the earth's crust pushed up from below, the continuous crust above which we have been sailing and which was last visible to us as the dinghy-strewn foreshore at Falmouth: a different kind of poetry.

To be frank, this island we're approaching really doesn't look much like the place I envisaged when writing my novel after glancing through a contemporary illustrated guide. Not that it matters. But it does seem a silly pastime all the same, writing novels, as if that sacred totem 'the imagination' were somehow superior to or 'realer' than whatever leaps to the gaze when we're not writing or dreaming but leaning on a ship's rail and watching a new land approach in the sardine-smelling light of early morning. Being here now is better than remembering having been here will be, and very much better than pretending to have been here disguised as a man of sixty-six.

Once at anchor the *Keldysh* is met by a busy little cutter called *Mosquito* from which three dapper-uniformed Portuguese officials, an elderly agent, a fat man and a floozy climb up a rope ladder. They leave 400 litres of petrol, a precious case of John

Blandy's best five-year-old Bual and an outrageous invoice for $2,600 made up of $454 for the petrol and $68 for the Madeira, the remainder being padding such as 'Launch hire', 'Boat attendance', 'Fiscal stamps' and a whacking $903 'Agency fee' to the Brothers Blandy. Such are the hidden on-costs of treasure hunting – as well as the hidden roots of the Blandy dynasty's hegemony on (and in) Madeira.

Within the hour we're under way again. The sun climbs; land falls astern and the wheeling seabirds thin to a couple of mournful die-hards following our wake. Barring the unpredictable we shan't see land again for at least a month. We're off to give a wrecked submarine our undivided attention.

EIGHT

What was a Japanese submarine doing off the West Coast of Africa in 1944? Why was it carrying two tons of gold? And how did it appear to run straight into the waiting arms of the US Navy?

There was in fact a surprising amount of submarine traffic to and from Europe and the Far East. Very occasionally, German U-boats joined forces with Japanese submarines to attack Allied cargo ships in the Far East, the only joint military operations by Germany and Japan of the entire war. Mainly, though, these lengthy voyages were for ferrying much-needed supplies. In the spring of 1943 the Germans converted seven large Italian submarines to carry cargo. These, together with three Japanese and a number of German operational submarines, ran the Allied blockade of Europe. The commodities shipped out to Japan included alloy steel for aero engines, bottled mercury, optical glass, industrial diamonds, ball bearings and electronic gear. Coming in the reverse direction were tin, rubber, quinine, opium, molybdenum and gold bullion. There was also human cargo: diplomatic officials, engineers, spies, assorted technical experts and occasionally politicians. In early 1943, for instance, one such Japanese submarine took the Indian nationalist leader Subhas Chandra Bose to Singapore after a secret meeting with

Hitler to discuss how the nationalist movement might harry and destabilise the British Raj. (From there Bose, who was describing himself as the 'President of the Provisional Indian Government', was flown to Tokyo to hear Prime Minister Tojo pledge his support for Bose's Indian National Army.)

The need for the Japanese to ship gold to Europe was a belated development. From the outbreak of war Japan had needed supplies of a neutral currency to cover her diplomatic, commercial and espionage expenses in Europe. Until early 1943 the Germans kept the Japanese supplied with as many Swiss francs as they needed. Then, suddenly strapped for cash themselves, they began demanding payment in gold not just for the currency but also for commercial services such as providing patents. The Germans were assuming that the Japanese were getting at least 80 tons of gold a year out of their mines in the occupied Philippines alone, but this was a serious over-estimation. In fact, by that time the Japanese Government had begun buying up or requisitioning any private gold still in its own citizens' hands. In order to continue financing their war effort in Europe, to say nothing of paying the rents for their various embassies, the Japanese had to resort to all sorts of dodges to raise the estimated 40 million Swiss francs they needed annually. (At 1943 exchange rates this was the net value of roughly eight tons of gold.) They sold quantities of pearls, as well as supplying their Lisbon embassy with forged US dollars to be exchanged on the black market for escudos.

In mid-July 1944 the German Foreign Ministry instructed the head of their economic delegation in Tokyo to use all diplomatic means to induce the Japanese to send fifty tons of gold to Germany as quickly as possible. By now both countries were becoming desperate for funds. Since the Germans were expecting the Japanese to ship the gold to Europe entirely at their own risk, and since the Allied blockade was growing more effective by the month, Tokyo was increasingly reluctant to pour further precious money down the bottomless Nazi well. Even as Dr Wohltat was pleading his Führer's case, Tokyo would have been getting the first coded messages from their Naval Attaché in Berlin about the presumed loss of the *I-52* together with two more tons of much-needed gold.

By Second World War standards the *I-52* was a very large submarine indeed. She had been completed at Kure Naval Yard on 18 December 1943 and this was her maiden operational voyage. She displaced 2,000 tons, was over 108 metres long and carried a complement of ninety-four men and officers. Her range was astonishing: 27,000 nautical miles at twelve knots (surfaced), or clear around the globe and to spare. She could also manage 105 nautical miles submerged, travelling at three knots on electric motors. Her maximum operating depth was 100 metres. After fitting out and trials she reported in March 1944 to Osaka Minor Naval Station and took on a high-value mixed cargo: a total of 228 tons of tin, molybdenum and tungsten; 2.88 tons of raw opium; 3 tons of quinine and 54 tons of raw rubber. On 10 March she also took aboard 2 tons of gold from the Bank of Japan. Her orders were to rendezvous with a German submarine, the *U-530*, in the Atlantic off West Africa and take on three German radio technicians and some electronic equipment before proceeding cautiously through the Bay of Biscay to the French port of Lorient 70 miles south-east of Brest. As soon as he had the gold safely stowed and these orders in his pocket, Commander Uno Kameo left Osaka and took the *I-52* 160 miles west to Kure where she touched briefly before leaving for Singapore around the middle of March. She finally departed

Singapore on 23 March on her three-month voyage around the Cape.

The only remarkable thing about these rather ordinary details is that they were all known to the United States Navy before the *I-52* ever left Japan. Not long after she had sailed, the Americans learned some further small facts about the most precious item of her cargo:

From: Tokyo

Action: Berlin

To Financial Commissioner Yumoto from the Head of the Foreign Affairs Dept. of the Ministry of Finance:

1. The gold being sent by the 'MOMI' [*I-52*] on her present voyage is for the replenishing of the gold fund special account, and details are as follows:

 a) Number of gold bars: 146 (49 boxes)
 b) Total weight of bullion: 2,000,229 grammes 0
 c) Purity of bullion: 2,000,003 grammes 5
 d) Fineness: over 995 fine
 e) Inherent value: 7,700,128 yen 64 (if one gramme be taken as 4 yen 80 sen, 9,600,016 yen 80).

2. Please arrange to handle the matter as on previous occasions.

The interpretation, decoding and translation of this top secret cable represented an intelligence coup which meant that the US Navy had months to prepare a plan of attack. It is a sad irony that even as Cdr. Kameo watched Singapore dwindle astern in a haze of diesel fumes and prepared for the long haul westwards, the Americans knew practically as much about his 'top secret' mission, his cargo and his brand-new vessel as he did himself. To that extent the *I-52* was doomed from the start, together with all those young ratings unwittingly sunning themselves on deck as the submarine ploughed on through Japanese Empire-controlled waters with a life expectancy of three months.

In point of fact this intelligence coup was merely a single instance in what was undoubtedly the best-kept secret of the entire Second World War: that the Allies had broken the Axis powers' operational codes. British cryptographers had been successful slightly earlier than their American counterparts and had usually, though not invariably, passed on what they learned. (Sometimes the British cipher-breaking operation is loosely referred to as 'Ultra' and that of the Americans as 'Magic'. Actually, 'Ultra' was the British classification of broken ciphers described variously as 'Ultra intelligence' or 'Z-decrypts', while 'Magic' was the name the Americans gave to those decrypted messages which were mainly diplomatic traffic and formed the 'Magic diplomatic summaries' prepared daily for the Pentagon.) By 1944 the Americans had long since caught up with British decrypting skills, especially in the Pacific theatre. That the Allies could read their enemies' traffic was itself a great achievement; contriving to keep this fact secret was truly astonishing. They did so by pretending to a world-wide network of spies and agents so highly-placed and extensive that by sheer weight of numbers they could keep one step ahead. By means of this prodigious fiction they managed to account for successes which would otherwise have looked suspiciously like miracles.

In this way the *I-52*'s mission to Europe was known about even before she sailed, as were the names of her officers and the precise co-ordinates of her planned rendezvous with the *U-530*. The US Navy's problem, therefore, was to arrange for her interception without it looking as though she were expected. How does one casually plan a battlefield in advance without giving the game away? The Pentagon dared not even let its own

Naval commanders into the full secret. The most it could do was what it did: order its pioneer anti-submarine hunter/killer group into the general area of the planned rendezvous. The nucleus of this group was the aircraft carrier USS *Bogue*, which by the end of the war was to become the highest-scoring Allied escort carrier, receiving a Presidential Unit Citation and three battle stars. The *Bogue* and her support ships thereupon began a series of routine sweeps which would bring them plausibly within striking distance of the meeting place.

There was something else special about this operation which ensured it would be most carefully observed and recorded. It was to be the first battle trial of a new and secret anti-submarine weapon the Americans had been developing. This was the Mk. 24 mine: a Second World War 'smart bomb' with a propeller which, when dropped from low altitude, would home in under water on a submarine's acoustic pattern no matter how much the submarine altered course. On board the *Bogue* was a civilian technician, Price Fish, who had helped develop the Mk. 24. Fish was from Columbia University and had been seconded to the US Navy's Underwater Sound Laboratory in New London, Connecticut. He came along as an expert observer and had even been briefed to fly on 'live' missions and monitor on the hydrophones his pet weapon's underwater performance. There was therefore a good deal of high-level interest in how this new aerial torpedo would perform; and while nobody could have foretold that its first major test would be against the *I-52* (for the *Bogue*'s group might have engaged any enemy submarine it happened to meet) it was doubly hard luck on the Japanese – now nearing the end of their long voyage – that they should have had such a powerful adversary ready and waiting for them with a new weapon.

The story of what happened when the *I-52* met up with the *U-530* as arranged and was shortly afterwards engaged by the

US Navy is a model of what a modern salvage operation often has to contend with when trying to plot a wreck's exact position. From start to finish the action was documented from several points of view so that in broad outline there seems little doubt what happened. And yet on closer examination the evidence is frequently contradictory and leaves curious gaps which have to be filled with conjecture, informed guesswork and hypothesis. For a start, there are two sides to the account, as represented by the American and the German versions (for the *U-530* got away and survived to surrender in Argentina a year later, complete with her log book). On the American side alone there are as many separate narratives as there were ships and pilots taking part.

There is no question that the rendezvous went off as planned. The *U-530*'s log book records that the *I-52* was sighted at 2315 on the night of 23 June 1944, bearing 280°. The two submarines were alongside each other within fifteen minutes, and between 2330 and 0145 on the morning of the 24th some radio or radar equipment was transferred to the *I-52* together with three Germans described as 'Kapitänleutnant Schäfer and two radio-men'. These are thought to be connected with difficulties the Japanese expected to encounter in negotiating the Bay of Biscay and making a landfall at Lorient. Conditions on the French coast were changing from day to day as a result of the Allied landings of Operation Overlord, and French waters were becoming steadily more dangerous for Axis craft. In any case, once the transhipment had been made the two submarines parted, the *U-530* noting her own course as due south.

It is not clear whether the two submarines heard the *Bogue* and her escort ships on their hydrophones, nor whether the *Bogue* heard the submarines. But at 2203, according to the carrier's battle-log, Lt. Cdr. Jesse D. Taylor of the USNR 'took off to search to 75 miles on a routine anti-submarine mission'. Taylor, who was still very much alive in 1995, aged 79, was flying a Grumman TBM-3 Avenger, a chunky three-seater aircraft designed specifically for anti-submarine warfare. (The 'TB' stood for 'torpedo bomber'; 'M' designated General Motors, who built it. The Avenger was the aircraft the future US President, George Bush, was flying in another theatre that very year.) It was a fine night with a light wind and no moon. As he stared ahead through the whirling airscrew of the bulky radial engine, did Taylor genuinely think this was a routine sweep or did he suspect there might be a particular target in the minds of his superior officers? In any case, within thirty-six minutes of taking off he reported a contact. He dropped a flare and saw a large surfaced submarine outlined starkly on the dark sea below him. Coming around for another pass, Taylor followed the flare with some conventional Mk. 54 depth charges. By now the submarine must have been crash-diving for its life even as Taylor was working up to testing the new weapon, or 'FIDO' as it was known. In order to monitor the submarine's movements once she had disappeared, as well as that of the new missile as it homed in on its target, Taylor first dropped a pattern of sonobuoys. The principle of these transponders was simple enough. They listened for, and relayed, the noise of propeller cavitations. Each buoy was colour-coded and broadcast the underwater sounds it picked up on its own radio frequency. Since the buoys' positions were known exactly, it was possible to determine the direction of moving underwater sounds, according to whether they became louder or softer relative to each sonobuoy. Taylor, like the other pilots, had been carefully coached. The new missile had to be launched from level flight at an altitude of between 150 and 300 feet and at a speed of 125-150 knots. He carefully lined his aircraft up, made his low approach run and dropped the FIDO, noting the time on the cockpit wire recorder as 2347.30.

The Mk. 24 had been designed for use against submarines that had already dived before an attacking aircraft could depth-charge them. It was essentially a torpedo, 7 feet long with a warhead of 100 lbs of TNT fused to explode on contact. It had a rated endurance of fifteen minutes underwater as it homed in on its target at 12 knots, faster than most submerged submarines of the day could manage. As Taylor circled he, his radioman and the gunner could all hear on their headphones the orange sonobuoy somewhere in the darkness below them as it transmitted the propeller sounds of a submarine in a crash dive. Exactly three minutes after Taylor dropped the Mk. 24 'a loud explosion was heard on the orange sonobuoy which continued for about a minute and was followed by a noise which the pilot later described as "the sound of a tin can being crushed". The radioman thought it sounded like "the breaking of twigs or crumpling of paper but heavier and deeper in tone" while the gunner compared it to "the sounds of a pile of small brittle twigs being stepped on" or "like paper being crumpled into a ball." All propeller indications ceased after the explosion . . . ' An original wire recording has recently come to light in the US National Archives and on it Taylor's voice is clearly audible shouting 'We got that sonofabitch!'

Meanwhile, other aircraft had taken off from the *Bogue* to join in the hunt, all tuning their radios to listen to the sonobuoys. The same explosion was heard by several of the approaching planes who also were to report that it lasted between fifty seconds and a minute. (In fact, this is not exceptional for an underwater explosion. Irrespective of whether the sound of the FIDO exploding had been followed by secondary explosions as the submarine's own ordnance detonated or it began imploding once it had sunk below its dive limit, the sonobuoys would have gone on picking up the echoes for a long time as they bounced continuously back and forth between the seabed and the surface.) At 0022 a pilot named Hirsbrunner reported hearing faint submarine noises on the orange and yellow sonobuoys. Lt. Gordon took off at 0028 with the expert civilian, Price Fish, in the gunner's seat trying to listen to the buoys above the roar of the engine and the chatter on the intercom. At 0055 he and Gordon both heard the sounds of a propeller from the yellow and orange buoys. By 0125 the sounds had become louder, and Gordon and Hirsbrunner independently estimated the submarine's course as due North. At 0154 Gordon dropped his own Mk. 24 mine, which he heard explode at 0212. Immediately afterwards, all submarine noises were reported as having ceased on all the sonobuoys.

So what did happen? All the crackling and crunching which followed the explosion of the first FIDO sounded to expert ears unmistakably like a submarine breaking up. How was it, then, that more than two hours later propeller noises were still audible to Hirsbrunner and Gordon until they dropped the second mine? Had they picked up the sounds of the *U-530* as the Germans desperately fled the battle zone? But this seems impossible, not only because that submarine survived, but also because her log had given her course as due south whereas the propeller sounds were heading due north. (The *I-52*, on the other hand, would indeed have been heading north if Commander Kameo was obeying orders, since he had already received a signal from the Japanese Naval Attaché in Berlin which read: 'Rendezvous point is 15.00N 40.00W. Route after rendezvous: You will proceed North along longitude 40W'.) When laid out schematically, using the times given by the various pilots and ship's logs, it is difficult to match up all the recorded events. The *U-530*'s log seems broadly to confirm the engagement, for at 0251 it notes the sound of aerial bombs and one mine coming from between 10 and 20 miles to the north. This was almost certainly Taylor's opening attack, which the Americans variously recorded as being between 2345 on 23 June and 0015 on 24 June. The complicating factor is that the submarine's log book shows the Germans were operating on a different time system to that of the US Navy. It looks as though they were on GMT, whereas the Americans were altering their clocks according to the time zone they were in.

Over half a century later, all this may sound like a nit-picking confusion, which in a sense it is. Yet to a salvage operation it represents data which, if properly evaluated, ought to yield the co-ordinates – or at least a limited area of probability – where the Japanese submarine went to the bottom. If the details of that night's engagement back in 1944 seem not completely clear, dawn did nothing to improve matters for potential salvors. In fact, daylight on 24 June made things distinctly worse.

At 0800 the next morning the USS *Haverfield* was at 15.16N 40.11W looking for debris at the presumed scene of contact. Neither she nor the *Bogue*'s aircraft circling the area could find anything. The *Haverfield*'s commanding officer, Lt. Cdr. Jerry A. Matthews, had a hunch that the *Bogue* had made a navigational error during the previous night's engagement, giving her position wrongly at the time. It would probably not have been politic to point this out in so many words. Instead, Matthews radioed the carrier to request permission to head eastwards. Having done so, the *Haverfield* came upon the entire pattern of sonobuoys floating 8 nautical miles away. The box search of the area was expanded still more and an aircraft from the *Bogue* finally reported a large oil slick a further 8 miles to the east of the *Haverfield*. By noon the *Haverfield* was on station there. 'We discovered a heavy brown slick,' wrote Matthews in his ship's war diary, 'circular in shape and about 1,500 yards in diameter, with air and oil bubbles rising intermittently.' He launched some boats to search for debris and found some floating bales of crude rubber, a plank, a rubber sandal with Japanese markings and 'some flesh tentatively identified as oriental'. The ships in the area, including the USS *Janssen* and the *Haverfield* itself, went on searching the slick until dusk, but nothing else was found and at nightfall the search was called off. The specimen of flesh was ferried over to the *Bogue* preserved in alcohol and formalin. The MO examined it and identified it as tissue from the upper arm, with a vaccination scar. He found it to be full of small splinters of wood. Another specimen was of many strands of 'straight, black, course [*sic*] hair', some 6 inches long, which had been removed from a block of rubber. These embeddings being consistent with a powerful explosion, Cdr. Matthews wrote: 'My conclusion ... was that Japanese sub., loaded with cargo of crude rubber was damaged by initial aircraft attack, and finally sunk by second aircraft attack.'

This evidence, taken with the size and quality of the oil slick, looked to all the Americans involved like convincing proof that they had indeed sunk a Japanese submarine. The MO's identification of the flesh as Japanese seemed conclusive (though it is an interesting irony that had a piece of one of the three Germans aboard the submarine been found instead, it might well have suggested that the vessel had been the *U-530*). In any case, from that day on the *I-52* was officially regarded as sunk. There has only been one moment of serious doubt, which was when the war diary of the German Navy's U-boat High Command (BdU – *Befehlshaber der U-boote*) came to light after the war. Several entries suggest that signals had been received from the *I-52* in the

Bay of Biscay on 30 and 31 July. This has always been assumed to be a mistake. Beyond having caused a mild flutter among potential salvors, it has never induced anyone to change their minds. Certainly the Royal Navy has always shared the American view, which is that the *I-52* was definitely sunk on the night of 23/24 June. A Rear-Admiral, writing to a colleague in the historical section of the Admiralty in 1956, was in no doubt: 'Oriental markings and characters on some of the debris made it quite obvious that the victim was "a Nip".'

It is equally clear that by the end of July the Japanese themselves feared the worst, even though the BdU no doubt told them they thought they had picked up signals from the submarine in the Bay of Biscay. Two intercepted messages from their Berlin Naval Attaché to the *I-52*'s Commander Kameo survive from this period. The first reads:

Although the German escort vessels waited for you on Aug. 1st, 2nd and 4th at the rendezvous point outside LORIENT harbour as per instructions ... they did not meet you. They are now waiting at LORIENT. Was there not some error? Please inform us again of your expected date of arrival at the rendezvous point.

The second, on 8 August, has the sad air of a message the sender knows is being transmitted to a ghost:

Though we have had no communication from you, we pray for your safety. As it has become dangerous in view of the rapidly developing war situation to enter LORIENT or other ports along the French coast, proceed to either TRONDHEIM or BERGEN in NORWAY. If convenient, inform us as soon as possible of your condition ...

Months later, on 20 November, the Attaché sent a telegram to

Tokyo which made it clear that he accepted the *I-52* had been sunk, and identified the three luckless Germans who had been taken aboard so shortly before. The first name does not quite tally with.that given in the *U-530*'s log, but no doubt the spelling was the result of foreign names being transliterated into Japanese, encoded, and finally decrypted by Americans.

> Lt. Alfer Schiefen: liaison officer ['Schäfer' in the *U-530*'s own log]
> Chief Radio Petty Officer Schultze: signalman
> Chief Petty Officer Roik Behrendt: pilot
> Because the co-operation of this liaison officer, pilot and signalman was deemed to be indispensable for Japanese submarines to sail into the Bay of Biscay, the above-mentioned three persons should be invested with appropriate decorations as victims of Japanese-German combined operations.

One wonders if this suggestion was ever acted on in Tokyo. Given the outstanding loss to the Japanese of ninety-four young men, a brand-new submarine and an extremely valuable cargo, it was a decent thought to have had in the circumstances.

NINE

The Russians have now been given all Orca's file material on the sinking of the *I-52*. This is in line with Orca's insistence that this be a joint venture, not just a matter of the ship's charterers giving orders. It is hard not to suspect a degree of condescension behind this, a feeling that it would be judicious to include them as much as possible in order to keep their interest on the boil if (incredibly) they don't seem sufficiently motivated by the thought of financial reward. Actually, it's becoming plain that the ship is full of extremely brilliant and competent people, and Orca would anyway be well advised to take advantage of their combined talents.

Whatever their thinking Orca, over many days and after interminable and often obsessive meetings, have already reached their conclusions about the most likely place to start looking for *Dolphin*. They have done so via all sorts of hypotheses concerning the German U-boat commander's psychology (aided by nearly illegible xeroxes of his log entries) and that of the Japanese (hindered by the obvious lack of any log book). Also taken into consideration were the American pilots' debriefing accounts, the logs of the USS *Bogue* from which they flew and the USS *Haverfield* which found the oil slick, floating bundles of rubber and the rest of the debris. Quentin has given his views on the significance of the sonar reports, as on the speed differential between upwelling oil driven by the current and a surface slick pushed by the wind.

These various and often conflicting accounts have been neatly correlated and redrawn on a vast sheet of graph paper by Ralph White, our American photographer. Nothing is made any clearer by the fact that the German and US navies were using different times, while the German Navy employed a complex grid system of coded squares within squares within squares to define co-ordinates instead of the conventional longitude and latitude. And finally thrown into this reconstruction of a small event in a war more than half a century ago is the submarine's position as recently sold to Orca for $1,500 by a Mysterious American with seeming access to a 'mole' in the US Navy. This man not only claims to know the exact co-ordinates, but actually to have seen a photograph of the wrecked submarine. This is not reassuring. Presumably the US Navy, not being interested in conventional salvage operations, would have found the *I-52* by chance, if at all, while surveying the seabed in that area of the Atlantic for its SOSUS anti-submarine listening devices. SOSUS, or Sound Surveillance System, was begun in the 1950s and spans the globe with a network of microphones grouped in arrays and linked to shore stations by 30,000 miles of undersea cable. It can track a moving sound source over thousands of miles. As part of budgetary cut-backs the US Navy is currently preparing to shut down up to 80 per cent of the SOSUS network. It is an interesting irony, as well as a sign of the times, that the very scientists and environmentalists who would most have opposed the network's hugely expensive construction for militaristic purposes are now appealing for its conservation as a powerful tool for monitoring such things as seaquakes, whale migrations and vessels suspected of illegal fishing. Indeed, SOSUS has lately been used for all these purposes. Next generation's civilian technology will probably be represented by GOOS or the Global Ocean Observing System, an idea that grew directly out of the 1992 Earth Summit in Rio de Janeiro. This will involve more than a hundred nations in a joint oceanographic enterprise spanning the globe, as the system's name suggests, and using networks of transponders and satellites to measure an extensive range of marine variables.

If, as the Mysterious American implies, the submarine is intact rather than the debris field Orca is hoping for, might not this information have already been passed on in secret, maybe years ago, and the gold long since salvaged by a commercial outfit? Orca's judgement is that this is virtually impossible. The world of deep-sea salvage is so small that there are no more than two or three companies in existence who would be even slightly tempted, and they lack the equipment to do the work. In any case there's nothing for it but to press on. Here we are, somewhere off the coast of North Africa and heading south-west, and this Mysterious American's co-ordinates do indeed fall with uncanny precision right into the search zone as the Orca team has just computed it. So all this information has been turned over to the Russians for them to draw their own conclusions. This morning both parties agreed where to start the search and the area of maximum probability which will have to be covered by the sonar survey.

As it turns out, the German Naval system of mapping by means of a grid of nested squares has its uses. Quentin suggests everyone should choose a tiny square and the winning square-holder be given a prize. ('The lens from the top of the periscope,' he proposes. 'A gold bar,' says Sagalevitch with a certain firmness.) The analogy, of course, is with a treasure-hunt at a fête where a tray is divided into small numbered squares, one of which contains a coin, and is then covered with sand. People buy a ticket with the number they think has the buried treasure ... This turning it into a competitive game implies that the *Keldysh*'s crew, despite (or because of) their extreme competence in their own fields, may not quite believe in this project and need jollying along. A professional salvage team in the company's vessel would presumably not require these little carrots. It's anyone's guess whether a project like this works better with greedy plodders or with the brilliant but uncommitted. There's not much doubt who one would rather sail with: it's wackier and more interesting. Probably the choice isn't quite as simplistic as this makes it sound.

A Russian celebratory party out on deck in late afternoon in recognition of the *Keldysh*'s fourteenth year since her commissioning. There are still six members of the original crew on board, including the First Engineer. Anatoly gives a speech which one knows will lead to the first of many vodka toasts – he is holding a tumbler entirely full of something which resembles water – pointing out how world-famous this ship now is as an oceanographic and scientific vessel. He contrives not to mention Orca by name – speaks only of 'our welcome guests' and wishes the cruise 'success'. The word 'gold' passes nobody's lips but a good deal of vodka does. Tables are set out on deck spread with plates of salad, roast chicken and cartons of fruit juice. The entire ship's company circulates with increasing abandon and the Orca team, distinguished by its brand-new Orca T-shirts (which are later going to be handed out to everyone on board) begins tentative ice-breaking conversations with the Russians. Ralph White cranes about, camcorder on his shoulder like a grizzled pirate with a black parrot. It's the first real social occasion.

Several women nobody can recall seeing before have emerged in their finery, and various crew members have likewise come up from unsuspected regions wearing stiff jeans with shiny rivets on them.

The MIR pilots are clearly the social élite: highly skilled, nerves of ice, tending to wear tailored ex-Soviet military fatigues. In a film they would be played by Tom Cruise. They are the ones whose pulse-rate doesn't alter when, 5,000 metres down, they hear *psss!* and a needle-jet of sea-water springs from a connector hole. They know it takes three hours to get back to the surface and they know the leak will inexorably increase the submersible's air pressure to the point where eardrums rupture, and will go on increasing far beyond the moment when the screaming stops and you are dead. But they also know they will be found still sitting at the controls without any expression on their blood-streaked faces, having perfectly performed every possible trick and manoeuvre to stave off the inevitable. They have all put in hundreds of hours on the world's seabeds, peering at black smokers and sediment and tube worms and wrecked nuclear submarines. They eat sparingly off paper plates and gaze out across the sea which today, because of the overcast, looks metallic and faintly menacing.

By far the best represented social type aboard, however, is the common nerd. I am introduced to Roman Pavlov and am instantly disarmed by his warmth and geniality. I remember having been told he is even more of a genius than Nik Shashkov. When we were still in Falmouth a printer was loaded aboard for use with the side-scan sonar. One of its distinguishing capabilities is that it can print sixty-four different shades of grey. Roman soon decided it could be vastly improved for the particular use he wished to make of it and, without even bothering to use an interface card, completely reprogrammed it in a single morning. 'I am artist,' he says impishly. 'I want to meet you because they say you are also artist. We are artists.' He rests an oily hunk of gnawed chicken on the still-wet edge of the newly-painted swimming tank. 'Machines are stupid. I create new mind for them. Creating is artist work, OK?'

The more I work with scientists, the more feeble I find the customary 'arts' claims to a monopoly of creativity and imagination. I have been captivated recently by some research currently being done at Scripps Institution of Oceanography at La Jolla. Three physicists there are trying to find a way to 'see' under water without using either ordinary light (which water quickly absorbs) or sending out sonar pulses (which betray one's position and may disturb nearby creatures). The imaginative leap came when they had the idea of using ambient noise, of which there is always some under water, to 'illuminate' objects in exactly the same way that objects on dry land are illuminated by ambient daylight. It is thus entirely passive. Called 'acoustic daylight ocean noise imaging system', or ADONIS, it strikes me as an elegant and creative *idea* that puts the average novel plot or slim volume of verse to utter shame. We writers have much to be humble about.

In the mean time, somewhere down in one of the labs is the American company's brainchild that Roman has been creatively 'improving', presumably now able to print in 128 shades of puce and double as a coffee percolator. Roman is clearly right. He *is* an artist: a mischievous genius who can't look at a computer system without wanting (and being able) to reconfigure it. Actually, he is God because he has The Language: the unwritable, unspeakable Language which transcends everybody else's paltry dialects (Basic, Fortran, C, Pascal etc). The Word of Roman goes to the heart of every machine he touches and lo! the machine outperforms its design specifications. What is this if not

76

a sure sign of divinity, as defined by generations of school chaplains?

Everywhere, everyone is talking science. An intense lady is discussing bathymetry and another, who looks like a flirtatious version of Iris Murdoch, explains one of her toys on the bridge deck: a huge green fibreglass flowerpot which pings every four seconds. She says it would be dangerous to hold your hand over it. A laser beam shoots upwards for a nanosecond and bounces off the cloudbase, enabling her to assess the amount of atmospheric pollution by measuring the scattering effect of particles along the beam's path. And if this didn't punch a tiny hole right through you, the radar housed in the big white golf ball on a tee right next to it would already have fried your gonads. Science is so much more *interesting* than literature it's really quite shocking. A small, twinkling fellow with a bushy beard, a beret and a horizontally-striped T-shirt lurks on the fringes of this conversation. He looks a dead ringer for the part of an anarchist in a film of *The Secret Agent*. All he needs is a round black bomb with a sizzling worm of fuse. I wonder who he is. He radiates something attractive: competence and self-possession, maybe. He's certainly not a nerd.

The subject of bombs and explosives comes up only a few minutes later. I'm talking to one of the engineers attached to the MIR group. In a sober sort of way he's drinking fruit juice and gazing out to sea, but wants to practise his English on a passing writer. He has also been reading Orca's file on *Dolphin* and reminds me that when some Avengers had ditched while trying to take off from the USS *Bogue*, their bombs had exploded as they sank even though they weren't armed. The pilots, who had been rescued, had reported that the concussions had been extremely unpleasant, even though their having survived at all must have meant the bombs didn't go off until they were very deep. The engineer explains that explosives become quite unpredictable at depth and nobody fully understands why. It turns out that he has particular knowledge of the subject since explosives can be used to cut holes in wrecks and it was one of the possible ways of salvaging the gold discussed (and rejected) back in Moscow. He explains that as a general rule, the deeper you use explosives the more carefully they need to be shaped and placed. An explosive works by suddenly generating a huge volume of gas. This has to go somewhere, and sets up a shockwave. At great depth, however, under the enormous pressure of the surrounding water, the volume of gas created is nothing like as large, so explosives tend to be ineffective. The way around this is to contain the charge in a pressure case tailored to the shape of the metal surface it needs to make a hole in. This case also contains a significant amount of air space into which the gases can expand. A typical charge, if perfectly set, will punch a neat four-inch hole in the sheet steel of a ship's hull. The problem with this type of hole cutting is that it's extremely expensive. The site has first to be precisely measured using an ROV or manned submersible so that a case can be machined to configure exactly to the surface. (Obviously, each case is an expendable one-off.) Placing such a charge with the required accuracy at, say, 5,000 metres, would be a long and tricky job, even allowing for the six hours' travel to and from the surface. And because of the unpredictable nature of explosives under water it is a dangerous procedure ... The engineer smiles and quaffs his fruit juice. 'Nyet problem' he says; Orca is going to use only mechanical cutters to open the target wrecks. We're carrying no explosives aboard. Just as well, he says. Ifremer's attempts to use explosives to break open the John Barry failed completely.

Somebody – presumably a member of the Orca team – has

hung a large Jolly Roger from the rail above the deck where the party is being held. This seems like a gaffe. These are serious people, unlikely to be charmed by being reminded that their research vessel's course is being largely dictated by a bunch of British buccaneers. Commerce may be one thing but treasure-hunting is surely infra dig for such highly-qualified and eminent men and women, the majority of whom are over thirty and some – like Yuriy Bogdanov – very senior indeed. Never mind; the First Mate has devised a dart-board based on the now-agreed search zone for the Japanese submarine. Ovals of different sizes drawn in ink and slightly resembling the schematic outline of a teddy bear represent the areas in their degrees of probability. Everyone throws a dart at the board. The one whose dart turns out to be closest to wherever the submarine is found will get a reward. Perhaps because the teddy bear has been drawn by the First Mate and the game is explained entirely in Russian, darts are thrown with alcoholic good humour. A nerd misses the board entirely (it measures about three feet by two) and holes the bench against which it is propped. This is considered hilarious. Now and again I catch Sagalevitch's eye and try to figure out the various barrels over which he is bent. It is open to speculation as to whether the Russian Academy of Sciences actually knows the true pretext for this, the thirty-fifth cruise of the R/V *Keldysh*, the flower of their fleet. Would so august a body really have sanctioned the use of their prestigious ship in a private enterprise treasure-hunt by foreigners, complete with party games? It seems more likely that the cruise was represented as a scientific expedition on which it would also be possible for some foreigners to conduct a weird salvage project of their own, but the Academicians could rest assured that fun and games would never be allowed to get in the way of serious science ...

It's a cause for wondering, though, and no more so than when the issue of the side-scan sonar's towing cable comes up in conversation. This is the cable which was spooled on in Falmouth. The Russians' own sonar cable was unreliably the worse for wear, so Quentin arranged to buy one cheap for Orca through the Institute of Oceanographic Sciences at Godalming (now the Southampton Oceanography Centre). This cable is second-hand, but warranted in good condition. Orca affected to be scandalised by its price (£15,000, of which only £5,000 has yet been paid pending its good performance), even though it would have cost over £80,000 new. It is 4 miles long and weighs 11 tons. In a day or two we shall be in waters calm and deep enough for it to be deployed to its full length. This is partly so it can be tested electrically, to make sure the sonar data will travel from one end to the other, but also so its own weight will put it under equal tension throughout its length when wound back in again for the sonar sled to be attached. This is most important. If the innermost windings of the cable on the drum are left untensioned, the tensioned upper layers will bite down between them and jam everything up. A four-mile-long steel cable under tension is a dangerous thing. When it is fully wound, the pressure on the drum can sometimes cause the winch to explode.

A story now circulates that Sagalevitch, not wanting to lose time by slowing the ship, plans to deploy the cable at 8 knots. Quentin says this could be fatal since at that speed – even if the *Keldysh* could maintain it with so much drag in the water behind her – the cable would wind itself up, owing to the screwlike twist of the wire strands. If the ship then lost way or a sudden wave caused some slack in the tow, the cable could instantly form a loop which would pull out into a kink and snap at that point. He says that in the course of some thirty oceanographical cruises he has seen several cables lost. If we lose this one Orca will be sunk before we've begun. However, Quentin is electing to say nothing. The Russians, too, are highly experienced. Sagalevitch has himself towed sonars hundreds of times; he knows perfectly well it has to be done at $1\frac{1}{2}$ knots. But what (I wonder) if he *intended* the cable to snap? Wouldn't that free him to head west to the black smokers he and his scientists are yearning to visit? This is a cynical notion and I keep it to myself: a grim but comic hypothesis which – since I don't yet know him well enough – might hardly amuse Clive as the investors' representative aboard. Anyway, this whole 8-knot rumour could well be a deliberate tease floated by Sagalevitch as a way of winding up not so much the cable as these frightful interlopers aboard his ship. The mere fact that this sort of speculation is going on already suggests the mild paranoia of a closed community.

Tomorrow we cross into the Tropic of Cancer. No shades of Henry Miller. Appalling decorum on all visible sides, but who knows what goes on down in the ship's hotter regions? There is a rumour that the Soviet Navy's old tradition of providing a daily glass of wine for each crew-member in the tropics will also hold good aboard the *Keldysh*. It's supposed to be medicinal. Our days are not precisely drink-free as it is.

Another odd thing. Down in Ralph White's 'commissar's' cabin is a portable telephone-sized GPS unit which he has brought with him. Nowadays, anybody from yachtsmen to weekend walkers can buy themselves a Global Positioning System receiver which will tell them where they are to within a hundred metres, thanks to a network of satellites in geostationary orbit. However, the US military – which owns the satellites – is a jealous god and tries to preserve the system's extremest accuracy (10 metres) for itself by degrading the signals which everyone else receives. It does this by building in a 'wobble' or fluctuation in the data which reduces it to 100-metre accuracy.

In Falmouth a couple of experts from Oceonics came aboard to install some expensive and complex equipment designed to restore the 10-metre accuracy to the ship's GPS system. This apparatus is known as DGPS, or Differential GPS, and it works by comparing 'civilian' GPS data to a fixed point whose position is known to an accuracy of centimetres – in this case a station in Lagos. It is one way around the US military's meanness. The whole thing would be unnecessary if we had access to their so-called 'P' code which makes GPS accurate to 10 metres. Ralph's little box of tricks turns out to have the 'P' code, giving him the most accurate positioning system on the ship and neatly trumping all that Oceonics stuff. Who *is* this guy?

TEN

Who is Ralph White? For immediate purposes he is an American cameraman – the only non-British member of the Orca party – whose job is to film the expedition. To say he is well qualified is an understatement. He, if anyone aboard this ship, has been there, seen it, done it and lived to tell the tale, which he not infrequently does. Ralph Bradshaw White is on life's 'A' team. A couple of paragraphs from one of his printed CVs give the flavour:

> White's first professional filming assignment was as the sky diving cameraman for the Ivan Tors series 'Ripcord'. He served as a Marine Corps Force Reconnaissance team leader, and was a member of the US Marine Corps Competition Parachute Team and the 1964 & '65 United States Parachute Team. He retired after 18 years as a Captain from the Los Angeles County Sheriff's Reserve Forces as one of their most honored officers.
>
> He is a Knight of The Order of Constantine, and The Military and Hospitaller Order of Saint Lazarus. A Fellow and Past Vice Chapter Chairman of the Explorers Club, and a Past President of the Adventurers' Club. The Underwater Society of America awarded him the prestigious 'NOGI' for his lifetime achievement in underwater photography. He is a highly sought-after speaker on the

Titanic and his many other exciting adventures.

The *LA Times* Magazine (27 October 1985) quotes Ralph as lamenting 'I always wanted a nickname like Rock or something,' Bradshaw being 'too effeminate'.

Most people don't give too much away initially, and one slowly builds up a description of them which hopefully may fit as acquaintance deepens. Ralph comes from the opposite direction, loud and clear, as a fully-fledged character. The friendly stranger's task is to demolish the self-description in order to glimpse the interesting person Ralph actually is. Ralph the public figure is so much larger than life that life itself gives a nervous cough and retires a pace or two. If you welded Hemingway and Superman together and squeezed the result into a black one-piece jumpsuit stuck all over with *Titanic* badges (which would be the envy of any red-blooded eleven-year-old) you would have the version of Ralph White he has elected to present to the world. 'I'm an ardent former Marine ... And if you haven't done your time in the Marine Corps, you still haven't fulfilled your military obligation.' The rest of the world, therefore, starts out at a considerable disadvantage.

This being said, the second thing one notices about him is that he's affable, courteous, generous with his time and his Beefeater gin, and genuinely knowledgeable about almost anything involving the derring-do branches of science and technology. He is also an excellent photographer. The trouble is that we both belong to such radically different cultures: something which wouldn't occur to me were he Nigerian or Chinese. He strikes me as contaminated by having had to earn his living for so long in the up-front, balls-out world of La-la Land. It does something dishonest to the contract one has with mortality. He has made his career hanging out his hide: in a parachute harness three miles up, in a submersible three miles down, in pressurised cockpits at 2,000 m.p.h. and so on, his eye glued to a viewfinder as with a knife clutched in a spare hand he fends off a great white shark. This peculiar way of life takes a toll on certain aspects of the imagination. The apprehensive, wounded and disillusioned creature we most of us are has in Ralph's case seemingly vanished inside a tough nugget of actuarial data which only tells him laconically that he can't survive indefinitely ('It was getting kinda hairy up there and I guess I was thinking, well, you old SOB, it's only a matter of time').

Another thing I've been noticing about Ralph is that he keeps his own counsel. Smoking away in his spacious 'commissar's' cabin (which still has the KGB safe and firearms cupboard in it), he works hard on his charts and analyses of the *I-52* data, his natty little GPS gadget propped in front of him, the BBC World Service coming softly from a speaker behind him. He attends all the meetings but wastes little time on fraternising. This is, in fact, the beginning of the picture I have of him as 'Old Hand Ralph': someone who has been aboard this ship many times, who has known Anatoly since 1988 (longer even than Mike Anderson), someone who can be his own person. When I described him as looking piratical at the party with the video camera perched on his shoulder I wanted to convey something of the pirate's self-possessed aloofness; that confidence which is partly professional and partly the result of having lived long enough not to give too many damns (he and I are the same age to within a couple of months). He has that kind of reserve which allows him to be a shameless extrovert, just as I would imagine a pirate to be. I'm delighted to discover the Jolly Roger that flew above the party the other day belongs to him. I was wrong, then: it wasn't a gaffe by an ebullient Brit but a Ralphism, far too intentional and gung-ho to be anything as feeble as a diplomatic lapse. My immediate problem, meanwhile, is to find a way past his water-tight self-description, so I begin circuitously by asking him about Anatoly. He gets off to an indifferent start. 'What you've got to realise is that Anatoly's a Renaissance man.'

I wonder if there is any hope of declaring a moratorium on this particular cliché? Anatoly is obviously a brilliant engineer who has the ability to lead from the front. That he also plays the guitar, sings his own songs and loves jazz suggests to another European nothing more than that the man is ordinarily civilised. I try again and this time Ralph does better.

'Anatoly feels like a prostitute. You've got to understand that science – specifically, engineering – is his love and passion. He hasn't managed to resign himself to the change, that all over the world the money for pure science is drying up. Even an oceanographic institute as famous as Woods Hole is short of funds. If Anatoly's bitter it's because he knows that if he's to survive he, too, has to sell himself. Somehow he's got to find an honourable route to mix science with commercialism.

'He also sees himself as the victim of a plot. In 1990 he was told – by let's say certain Canadian and US parties – that if he ever did commercial work he would discredit the Keldysh's reputation for science. In fact, these parties were pretty anxious to discourage him because they were scared he'd be competition. I mean, they had their own schemes. You bet they did. Anyhow, Anatoly was chartered by the Mexican Government to look for a Spanish galleon [the Nuestra Señora del Juncal, wrecked off Veracruz in 1631 with a cargo of gold and silver]. The Mexicans gave him a completely wrong search area, spent $1,400,000 and found nothing. OK, from Anatoly's point of view it was a job, but it didn't really help him any. Sure, he'd like to see Orca successful, but he's apprehensive about what all this treasure-hunting's doing to the ship's reputation, to say nothing of his own. He doesn't want to become known as the leader of a salvage vessel, no matter how much money it makes for him. His last pure science trip was back in 1990. Since then he's had some short foreign science charters e.g. the Cambridge University/ NERC trip in 1994 to the Transatlantic Geotraverse (TAG) site, but the main jobs have been the *Titanic* in 1991, *Komsomolets* – the only Russian job – the Mexican Government one and now Orca.'

This may or may not be an accurate account of how things stand for Anatoly. It certainly tallies uncontroversially with the received wisdom going around Orca's part of the ship. It gives little enough away about Ralph's own relationship with him, which must surely be interesting seeing that he tells me this is his ninth trip in *Keldysh* and that he manages the ship's banking services in the US. I switch to a more congenial topic by asking him to put the MIR submersibles into some sort of international context by giving an overview of the current state of the art of diving. He perks up and promptly runs through a schematic list, ticking the points off on his fingers. This is stuff after his own heart. Mine, too; and I pass it on as he gave it to me:

1. *Surface to 200 ft.*: conventional divers and scuba divers using ordinary air.

   200 ft. to 700 ft.: divers using a mixture of oxygen, helium and some nitrogen.

   1000 ft. to 1500 ft.: divers using mixtures of 'exotic' gases, including hydrogen. The proportions of these gases have to be absolutely precise. Any slight variation can be lethal.

   With the latest technology it is now possible for *unprotected* divers (i.e. not wearing pressure suits) to work down to 1300 ft., if they are physically exceptional and well trained. Unprotected dives below that depth are entirely experimental and restricted to a tiny handful of unusual people able to resist a pressure of sixty atmospheres. The suits they wear are not pressurised but have hot water injection. They also wear a fibreglass helmet known as a 'rat hat' (named after the helmet Bob Ratcliffe invented for Oceaneering International). An umbilical supplies the hot water and a 'tri-mix' of helium, hydrogen and oxygen. Obviously, these need to be supplied at a pressure high enough to keep the heating tubes and the diver's lungs from collapsing, but the body itself is under enormous load from every direction. (By way of comparison, the present world record for free diving – i.e. with a lungful of breath at atmospheric pressure – is Tanya Strecter's 370 ft., which is approaching the point beyond which the human lung collapses beneath the ambient pressure of ten atmospheres.) The umbilical is connected to a nearby PTC or Personnel Transfer Capsule, a sort of glorified diving bell into which the diver retreats at the end of the dive and is winched aboard the mother ship and straight into a fortnight's imprisonment in a decompression chamber. (This part of the operation sounds like the final, clinching argument against saturation diving: two weeks of nothing to do but make squeaky phone calls in your helium voice, leaf through a tattered collection of porno mags and watch TV while 'ascending' gradually as the pressure inside is reduced to match the atmospheric pressure outside.)

Two thousand feet effectively represents the unprotected human body's absolute limit, and then only for one person in a million. The pressurised exotic gases upset the central nervous system and radically change the chemistry of cerebro-spinal fluid. Splitting headaches from pressure in the finely-divided skull bones (sinuses, antrums etc.) are habitual. During decompression the crown of one diver's tooth exploded due to the infiltration of helium under pressure. In addition, most professional divers lose much of the top end of their hearing range, so the phone conversations in the decompression chamber must be odd affairs, with incoming voices hard to hear and the outgoing voice sounding like Minnie Mouse. (The question arises: why do it? If you can go deeper more safely in a pressurised diving suit and accomplish work into the bargain, why go the exploding fillings route? One *could* go firefighting in the nude, too).

2. One-atmosphere pressurised diving suits will operate down to 2,500 ft. These are 'spam in a can', astronaut-style heated suits made of special fabrics, complete with heavy boots.

3. Submersibles. These divide as follows:

   a) Conshelf boats: to 3,000 ft. These will reach the world's continental shelves.

   b) Mid-range boats: to roughly 12,000 ft. The group includes craft like the Canadian *Pisces* (such as Ralph and Anatoly dived with in Lake Baikal and which the Shirshov Institute still has mothballed for lack of operational funds), the ageing *Alvin* (as used by Dr Robert Ballard in discovering the *Titanic*), *Turtle* (the US Navy's relative of *Alvin*), and *Cyana* (run by Ifremer and nearly decommissioned in 1994 because there weren't enough projects for it and the maintenance costs were being passed straight on to the scientists).

   c) Six thousand metre boats: to 20,000 ft. There are really only five in the world: the US Navy's *Sea Cliff*, France's *Nautile* (also run by Ifremer), Japan's *Shinkei* 6500 (operated by JAMSTEC – the Japan Marine Science and Technology Centre) and the two Russian MIRs.

   d) Max ocean boats: to 36,000 ft. or the very deepest parts of the ocean. There are just two of these at present: the

Archimède and *Trieste 2*. Both employ the usual steel or titanium sphere which is the basic capsule common to all submersibles, but slung beneath a huge lightweight tank containing 60,000 gallons of petrol. Since petrol is lighter than water this acts as a float. In order to descend, the craft has to be loaded with ballast heavy enough to counteract the positive buoyancy. This is simply dumped when the crew want to come up again. (Apart from the danger of fire on the surface with such a quantity of inflammable liquid flimsily contained, the system seems by modern engineering standards oddly primitive. It remains essentially an underwater balloon exactly like Auguste Piccard's original bathyscaphe, FNRS 2, dating from 1948.)

This run-down of Ralph's reminds me that one of the recurring topics of his conversations – both text and subtext – is *pressure*. His anecdotes are strewn with men in space capsules facing deadly vacuums or else in submersibles risking horrendous implosion. The reason for this interest may become clearer as time goes on.

Ralph has no formal training as a scientist, and it seems to me that possibly his most impressive feat of all has been to have turned himself into a person who is nevertheless scientifically valuable. He explains this by saying that as a cameraman he became painfully aware of being a JUFO ('Just a Fucking Observer') who was taking up a valuable seat. So he qualified as a co-pilot on the MIR and *Nautile* submersibles. Normally a MIR pilot needs a university background in engineering, electronics or hydraulics. 'You can leap this level, but very rarely,' he says. Again, this must say something about his relationship with Anatoly, who has absolute discretion as to who even gets into one of his MIRs, let alone is allowed to handle the controls.

A second aspect of this feat of Ralph's is more intellectual. On many purely scientific submersible trips – especiality in the US – he noticed that a lot of data were being wasted because, for instance, 'rock-hounds' weren't recording the zoology and biologists wouldn't remember to turn on radiation meters as well as temperature sensors. (This tallies with my own observations in similar circumstances: some scientists' refusal to see anything beyond their own narrow speciality can suggest old-fashioned union/labour demarcations of the pettiest kind.) Ralph worked out that by being both a cameraman and a co-pilot he was able to record an 'overview' of many different kinds of data. 'Finally, even scientists came to realise that sending me and Emory [Kristof, a *National Geographic* staff photographer] down produced good science as well as good coverage in *National Geographic*, which frankly did them no harm either.' Ralph describes his and Emory's working partnership as 'underwater photography's SWAT team'.

He next takes up a point that Anatoly makes about how *Keldysh*'s 1991 IMAX expedition to film *Titanic* yielded some serious science into the bargain. According to Ralph, biologists were able to identify twenty-eight species of animal never before seen together in a deep-ocean artificial habitat. What was more, geologists and metallurgists had a closer look at two new phenomena first seen in the hulk of *Titanic*: the so-called 'rivers of rust' and 'rustsicles'. The 'rustsicles' take the form of icicles or stalactites, long reddish-brown growths hanging from steel surfaces, whereas the 'rivers' are more like streams of mud or lava flowing down a metal surface and following gravity across the seabed. In the late 1980s a Woods Hole expedition had failed to bring up usable samples of these phenomena. The difficulty of bringing samples of nearly anything (and especially delicate biota) from such a depth is a constant problem in all deep ocean scientific work. There is a great risk of contamination from different components of the water column or changes in state on the way up. It was Russian scientists from *Keldysh* who first successfully took samples of these newly-discovered rust formations and brought them intact to the surface for analysis. The upshot was the identification of a bacterium which eats ferrous metal and excretes iron oxide and mucus. The mucus acts as the bonding agent in the 'rustsicles' and as lubrication for the 'rivers'.

Meanwhile, back in 1979, Ralph had been on the expedition that first discovered black smokers. This was on the East Pacific Rise, and represented 'the first time any life form had been found whose metabolism depended on chemosynthesis rather than photosynthesis'. The basic chemical presence in these hot water vents was sulphur in the form of hydrogen sulphide together with a good admixture of iron, and many of the bacteria had metabolic systems which depended on sulphur instead of oxygen. At the time, this was unheard-of; prevailing wisdom would have said unequivocally that such high-temperature water chemistry was far too poisonous to support life. Among the many discoveries was a bacterium dependent on iron which formed the bottom of the food chain, feeding clams and shrimp. These in their turn were eaten by crabs, and a sinister whitish-grey hooded octopus about five feet long lived on the crabs. Many of these highly-adapted creatures were albino-looking externally, but the clams' meat was bright red as well as radioactive from the radium it contained. Though they had eyes, the shrimp were blind and relied on an infra-red sensor in a stripe on their backs to prevent themselves from being inadvertently boiled alive by swimming into the columns of 750°F vent water.

This great discovery led to the finding of other hydrothermal vents along the 28,000 miles of the 'Ring of Fire' which marks the edges of the Earth's tectonic plates. There is a good site at roughly 25°N and 42°W, halfway between Florida and Africa, the Transatlantic Geotraverse or TAG site. (The site on the Mid-Atlantic Ridge which the Russian scientists would prefer to visit instead of looking for a submarine is one Yuriy Bogdanov himself discovered about 600 miles south of TAG.) A large volcanic structure has been found at TAG about the same size and shape as Houston's Astrodome and containing all three of the main hydrothermal vent types: 'black smokers', 'white smokers' and 'sparklers' (clear water plumes, bubbling and shimmering with convection currents). This dome is believed to be either a blister on the Earth's crust caused by magma pushing up from below, or to consist of the collapsed chimneys of vents and smokers. The iron-eating bacteria at such sites are thought to be the same as those discovered at the *Titanic* site, but this hypothesis is not yet proven. Confirming it is one more thing the Russians yearn to do on the back of the Orca expedition.

Certain things in Ralph's delivery of all this information warn me off trying to get him to clarify points of scientific detail. I don't want to hear him flounder, and he is not a person who easily says 'I just don't know'. Now and again I think I catch the voice of the 'highly sought-after speaker' with marvellous tales to tell (and they *are* marvellous). If I recognise this voice it is because I, too, am like him in that no matter how competent we may become at our respective skills, we remain to some extent professional bystanders – he with his camera, I with a series of tatty notebooks. He is more dazzlingly brave than I could ever be; but now and again I wonder how scrupulous he is about his facts, which requires a different kind of bravery. Men's men who worry about their mere names being thought effeminate often lack a neutral intellectual terrain where factual matters can be queried and discussed without an implied doubting of their entire persona. I suspect that if I start saying, 'Here, wait a bit, Ralph, animals don't depend on photosynthesis; nor were sulphur bacteria first discovered at hydrothermal vent sites: they exist in all sorts of marine habitats both shallow and deep and had long been known about', it may sound like a challenge.

Yet it usually turns out (and it may take months to discover this) that Ralph's science stories are neither inventions nor much embroidered. Their occasional apparent implausibility is due more to the pressure of his own enthusiasm, which can lead him to omit vital footnotes in the telling. Thus the story of the diver's exploding tooth (it happened to the late Danny Hoi) depends crucially on knowing that under pressure helium, being extremely light, has the ability to penetrate places that air and water cannot reach. In decompression chambers the watch crystals of these record-breaking saturation divers may also explode and cause injury because helium has seeped into the otherwise watertight cases. Unless one already knows of this property of helium's, such tales can sound fanciful and even dubious. In the long run it is better to hold one's hasty scepticism in check, to keep silent and take notes and admire this genuinely strange and complex fellow who never saw his father until he was nearly five because the man had had the misfortune to go on a business trip to Hawaii a week or two before Pearl Harbor and was neatly swept up by war.

There is no doubt Ralph has already classified the Orca group as a bunch of amateurs, which I can't hold against him. If appearances are a measure of professionalism, no one could look less professional than Quentin or myself when glimpsed staggering up to the radio room most evenings with plastic carrier bags of modems and electronic clutter, laughing helplessly and trailing wires. Here in Ralph's spacious cabin the charts and equipment, the gadgetry and instruments in neat leather cases, the badged and logo-ed jump-suit hanging in the closet, all speak of the professional. And that natty little GPS device with the military's 'P' code?

'Oh, that? I'm just field-testing it for the manufacturers. It's called Magellan.'

But then, he wouldn't have admitted working for the CIA or the Pentagon even if he were. Never mind SWAT teams; I've got ex-Marine Ralph down as the Oliver North of underwater photography.

ELEVEN

31/1/95

Early this morning we crossed into the Tropic of Cancer. Where is our free wine?

The sonar cable has been tensioned and stowed, the efficiency of both winch and technicians so impressing Quentin that he has made a note to find out where the winch was made. He is wearing his business hat today and thinking cannily as a supplier of oceanographic hardware. Geotek Ltd., his company, designs and makes geophysical instruments and sensors.

We are supposed to reach the *Dolphin* search zone by the evening of 2 February. Orca's communications foul-up continues. Endless and increasingly tetchy discussions abound in cabins and corridors about a 'stuffing programme' which doesn't delete once its message has been sent and so goes on incrementally adding each message to the last, day after day. Orca is going to wind up with a phone bill like those which European parents trace in horror to their bored teenage children caught calling up transatlantic porno hotlines in New York and San Francisco. In Orca's case they haven't yet managed to receive anything half as exciting for their money, although Simon's messages have begun to take on a certain dominatrix flavour the more Clive fails to decode his end of their school magazine cipher.

The sauna is going strong and the nearby swimming pool full. In the context of the sauna this is now revealed as more of a plunge bath. It's a tank about 5 metres long and 2½ wide so anything like serious swimming is impossible. There's an elasticated rig which can be worn in order to 'swim on the spot' like a tethered frog. After lunch at 11.30 a.m. the crew and scientists take time off and reappear in ones and twos in bathing costumes. The ship's complement is comparatively elderly and we are sombrely reminded of our poor human envelopes – some of us less than others, however, and usually those with most reason for self-consciousness. Among the younger swimmers are the MIR pilots who discreetly wait for middle aged lady biologists to climb out, blowing, the water briefly quacking and pluppling against their nyloned nether regions hoist above the surface. Then these lean young men – who, though brimful of the Right Stuff and as Top Gun as any American fighter jock, are far less self-aware and do not hold themselves as if for the gaze of lenses – drop silently to the bottom and remain there motionless for five minutes. One has a winged tattoo on his upper arm. This maybe represents a pledge of desperate comradeship as a crack parachutist in Afghanistan or some-where; it looks like a regimental insignia. There is a short fellow with a mouth containing more gold than *Dolphin* probably does and who is an ex-*Spetsnats* operative. This is 'Little Lev', as he is known. He pilots the *Koresh*, the tender which services the submersibles during launch and recovery. His is a critical and sometimes dangerous task, and for a while the lives of the exhausted aquanauts wallowing in their MIR at the end of a long dive are in his hands. He is rumoured to be able to kill a man with his little finger, should this prove a useful thing to do. Ralph's wisdom is that he must be given a wide berth. One finds oneself giving him a wide smile instead and hoping it's not misinterpreted, though he seems amiable enough, just not very fluent in English. Why should he be?

Most of the other bathers look nerdy, further evidence that the condition is genetic and exists independently of the plumage they shed. This is an important anthropological observation. It is nice to copy the Russians' example and be able to do some hard science of one's own on the back of a treasure-hunt (which I really must remember to call a salvage operation). *Homo nerdus* is a separate species. It might be worth faxing Richard Leakey with the news, if one could fax anything at present – which one can't unless one's a nerd oneself.

Still no flying fish. Obviously the water isn't warm enough yet. All sorts of equipment is being deployed from stem to stern of the *Keldysh*. Various pingers and transponders are laid out in readiness on deck, derricks are swung out and greased. Scientists haul up the antennae and probes of their various experiments. A marine biologist prepares a large plankton net. The meteorologist tends her beehive above the bridge, a white cupboard with louvred doors. It's a contented sort of bustle, familiar on any working research vessel. Long filmy hammocks strung vertically from either side of the foremast winnow particles from the atmosphere. More than a few particles are meanwhile thrown over the side, including brightly-coloured fruit juice cartons from the party. They tumble in the wind and bob away astern. There is an instruction sheet in every cabin, one of whose injunctions reads 'YOU MUST NOT throw any matches, cigarette ends or rubbish over the side of the ship.' It was the same aboard the *Farnella* in 1990. (Incidentally, Quentin tells me that the poor *Farnella* has since been lengthened by being literally sawn in half and having a prefabricated 20-metre section inserted in her middle before she was welded back together again. She has been renamed and is for charter, mainly to the offshore hydrocarbon industry.) On the *Keldysh*'s deck the Russians play volleyball beneath a huge net suspended from a jib.

Why do Russians sunbathe standing up? I think I also noticed this on an old picture postcard of a Black Sea beach. Is this a leftover from some piece of fifties' Soviet medical wisdom whose practice has stuck?

At sunset the Anarchist appears on the bridge deck. He is wearing a plain T-shirt and very short shorts. He has a rounded, muscular bum whose cheeks bunch and dimple with the roll of the ship. He stares straight ahead into the sun's molten path, eyes intense between beard and beret. His expression is sad and intriguing.

1/2/95

The buffeting glooms of the Bay of Biscay are a dim memory. The wind is still strong but the water here appears to weigh less or to be lighter-hearted, with drools of foam spiffling merrily up from the crests as they race past. The ocean is that rich luminous blue one never sees in northern latitudes. In the space of five minutes we sight a sperm whale blowing six times and then sounding with a distant crash of flukes, and the first flying fish curvetting off between the rollers. The sun pours down and a summery, laid-back mood infiltrates the ship. 'Relax. Enjoy yourselves,' calls Anatoly with a stricken smile, doing a honeypot jump into the plunge bath, drenching us.

Suddenly the weather feels like a gift, a reprieve, bearing in mind the dead of winter we've left behind. The sun is lavish and democratic. We are no longer British or American or Russian, just animals emerging from hibernation and basking, 'half-crazed for larger light' (as Tennyson once described his own youthful longing for sunnier climes than Lincolnshire). Some days humanity seems quite indivisible, homogeneous throughout, barring small local variations in skin colour and culture. On others utterly dissevered, forever fragmented by profound gulfs of attitude which divide all knowledge and experience into unrecognisable categories. Neither version is correct, neither is wrong. It's all part of the usual Undecidable, often thrown into sharp relief by nothing weightier than brilliant weather.

These 6 p.m. lecture/seminar sessions are quite serious. Tonight's is a pre-operation effort to make sure we all understand the technical procedure when we reach the *Dolphin* search zone tomorrow: what happens, and in what order.

Although it's practically all in Russian, and taking place in the ideal hour for sitting above the bridge with a G&T to watch the sun set, this lecture makes it hard not to be fond even of the nerds as they take it in turns to stand up and face their colleagues as well as these unaccountable foreigners in their midst. Obviously underpaid, absolutely earnest, the whole room attentive, they talk above the murmur of the geochemist acting as our interpreter. They have carefully prepared large felt-tip charts and diagrams which are taped to the board behind them. Now and then they wave a hand at them: scatty hair, frayed trousers, socks the colour of blackberry fool visible behind the panels of their GUM store sandals.

Quentin observes that by going to sea one becomes like a clock getting progressively out of step with a central time source. One returns to land all at odds, in a different time zone, at a tangent to everyone else. How will one ever catch up? We know from the BBC World Service that floods are presently drowning Holland and threatening much of the rest of Northern Europe, but we don't really care. This ship is all the world there is. The formalities and customs of a working shipboard life constitute a country of their own. I can hardly remember the names of people and places ashore and we've barely been at sea ten days.

It's a remarkable phenomenon, one known throughout history (Patrick O'Brian's naval characters often refer to it). Wives and husbands, children and lovers: they are rinsed from seafarers' brains as though by the pouring past of so much water. Seen from the top deck the horizon is about fifteen nautical miles away. Since leaving Falmouth we have fallen over 200 horizons.

It now turns out that Clive's impatience with Simon's alleged cock-up of their school magazine cipher has been misplaced. In fact, the columns of digits he found on his screen day after day and ploddingly tried to translate into plain English were the computer's own hexadecimal coding of perfectly ordinary messages complaining about the extravagance of our case of Madeira, etc. In other words Clive was attempting to read DOS or something. When I learned this, over a large glass of the said Madeira, I had to lean weakly against a scuttle as the setting sun shook itself all over the horizon. There is an immense pit of self-inflicted electronic obscurity into which great numbers of people wilfully leap with cries of abandon, a sort of inverted Tower of Babel. Up in the light of ordinary day the casual passer-by glances down into this hubbub from which a sacred word emerges, repeated over and over again: 'Communication!' The passer-by (if he's not fool enough to be writing a book), is tempted to philosophical reductionism, to speculate that communication is in fact not only unnecessary but undesirable. Kurt Vonnegut's harmoniums, contented life-forms living plastered to the wall deep in the caves of Mercury, had reduced all communication to two possible messages, each being the automatic response to the other: 'Here I am, here I am, here I am' and 'So glad you are, so glad you are, so glad you are'. That's really about all that's needed. I would cheerfully settle for 'Good morning', 'Good evening' and 'Goodbye'. Quentin, who has not yet read *The Sirens of Titan* but who is much smitten by the notion of the benign, placid harmoniums now reminds me that Mike Somers, a physicist at Southampton Oceanography Centre and recently an OBE, has coined the phrase 'communaholics' to describe the phone-toting, keyboard-rattling, modem-interfacing, e-mailing inhabitants of the new Democratic Republic of Nerdia. I remember Mike Somers coming aboard the *Farnella* in Hawaii to do a leg of the USGS survey as head of the sonar team. He carried no computer and wrote all his work in longhand. 'He dislikes communications as a form of intrusion into the solitary experience of going to sea,' says Quentin fondly. And enviously.

But Clive ... Clive Hayley's persona is as intriguing as his position aboard *Keldysh* appears compromised. I had never met him until we were introduced in Simon Fraser's house in London while waiting for the Kaliningrad mafia to release the ship's fuel, but in an odd way I felt I had. His late father was a much-loved analytical supervisor to two of my closest friends, and I had heard a good few Tom Hayley stories over the years, told with affection and hilarity. Tom had evidently been one of those brilliant eccentrics the British used to be so good at producing: a Colonial Office administrator in India – a District Commissioner – whose anti-Congress propaganda to promote the war effort so impressed the Congress leaders that they invited him back to assist in the rural development of Assam. He must presumably have organised Indian opposition to nationalists like Subhas Chandra Bose. After the war he took up psychoanalysis and was friends with Freud's English translator, James Strachey. His widow is still a practising anthropologist.

This about exhausted my knowledge of Clive's background before I met him, yet knowing even that little made him seem less a total stranger. We were still tied up in Falmouth harbour when Quentin reported having just gone on a local shopping trip with him and Jean Anderson. Jean had asked Clive whether he'd rather buy his provisions at Tesco or Sainsbury's. 'Don't mind,' Clive said amiably. 'I don't think I've ever been in either of them.' In anyone else this would have sounded an outrageous affectation. In Clive's case it was probably true, it being not long since he had moved out of the very West End family home where he was born and had lived for over thirty years in circumstances which presumably did not require him to do much in the way of catering. It is unusual nowadays to meet someone whose London office is in the house of his birth, and still more so if he has never had occasion in his entire lifetime to visit either Sainsbury's or Tesco's. Quentin recounted their shopping trip with an air of amused wonder, Clive's evident unfamiliarity with the most ordinary household products being quite genuine. Jean Anderson said it was like going shopping with a tribal African.

Even with our present slight but growing acquaintance, I do know it would be a fatal mistake for anyone to assume from such an unworldly image that Clive is either a dreamy intellectual or a Woosterish bon viveur. He is, as a matter of fact, endowed with a beady intelligence and a taste for good things. He also has an excellent and cynical sense of humour which extends generously to himself. (Nobody who took himself too seriously would drive an ageing Aston Martin about town – that fashionable James Bond barouche of quite thirty years ago.) The thing to remember about Clive is that he is a successful lawyer. That alone ought to dispel any lingering notions about his supposed unworldliness. Even so, it doesn't seem to be the right corrective to the impression he makes on certain people, the legal profession being one of those – like politics and journalism –

which are held in almost zero esteem even as their potential clout is contemptuously feared. Sagalevitch, for one, is luxuriously suspicious of him, though suspicion seems to come as naturally to Anatoly as nest-making does to a bird. Both Mike and Andrea have their own reasons for resentment, too. This maybe has less to do with Clive the person than with the position he occupies as the investors' representative aboard. They are the grizzled prospectors with the map and the dream who only grudgingly concede that one needs money to look for money. Mike, though, has an additional and more immediate reason for resentment. I now believe it was Clive and Simon who summarily moved him by *force majeure* out of his original stateroom and into his present poky cabin. No doubt they argued that the stateroom was more commensurate with holding critical meetings, taking weighty decisions and generally acting as one of the expedition's command posts. If true – and if we *don't* find the gold – I expect this single act will acquire considerable symbolic weight as the trip wears on.

None of this means a row of beans to me, though. I like Clive because he is, in a quite different way, a fellow bohemian. I like his amused and unsentimental view of everybody's inherent criminality (including his own), his recognition of the anarchy of people's true desires and of the world's sub-plot that bears so very little resemblance to life as purveyed in the media's semi-official version.

His friend Simon, on the other hand, presented a very different character when I spent several nights beneath his hospitable roof in Holland Park. For all his City connections he looks plausibly like the ex-RN officer he briefly was: brisk and chiselled, and capable of a chill, headmasterly eye. If Clive disconcerts some people by being socially unreadable, Simon – at first sight – would be more reassuringly a 'type'. I suppose the contrast between them might simply reflect very diverse upbringing. The distinction is not one of class, but of milieu. Clive's background is intellectual and eccentric while Simon's immediate personality suggests a solid grounding in the conventional, even if his intelligence pays it scant regard. It turns out I have a faint connection with him, too, in that his father's medical partner was the Queen's gynaecologist, with whom my mother had occasionally worked as anaesthetist. In the league of oddball tearaways, Queen's gynaecologists rank appreciably lower than psychoanalysts.

If it would be a bad mistake to think of Clive as unworldly, it would be an equal misreading to assume Simon was stuffy. He, too, has a wildness tamped down there somewhere as though his student recklessness (alpine hang-gliding) has lived on, acceptably transmuted into enthusiasm for risky and offbeat business enterprises. He has a sharp eye for money-making schemes that involve the sort of pressure Ralph likes: racing cars, deep-sea salvage, stuff like that. At that level he and Clive unexpectedly share a distinct taste for having fun, seeing no reason why earning a living shouldn't also be entertaining. When together, Simon and Clive can appear to play a kind of good/bad cop duo in that Clive is ebullient and laughs a lot whereas Simon gives a more reserved and unsmiling impression. In fact, it's a brilliant act. Underneath they both pick up on, and remember, everything, while Simon's sense of humour is quite as active as Clive's, with a good line in deadpan asides.

No doubt all of this explains why they're both perceived so differently, and perhaps why Anatoly is managing to suggest that when he comes aboard at Dakar, Simon will have to be punished for being Simon – a punishment which he hints with much beaming innuendo will take place at the 'Crossing The Line' ceremony. Poor Simon. In his absence he has become the focus for all Sagalevitch's dislike of Orca, the repository for all his loathing of what he sees as City slickers, Western capitalists, cheats in suits, the purse-holders and string-pullers of the new world in which he finds himself trapped. That this is grotesquely unfair to Simon, who is none of these things, is no deterrent. Somehow it is implied that Anatoly disliked him from the start, and Anatoly's allies such as Old Hand Ralph take much pleasure in sketching out exactly what will happen to Simon when he is haled before the 'Court' in which Sagalevitch plays King Neptune. Ralph dwells lovingly on the violence of this ceremony he has so often witnessed aboard *Keldysh*: of people being thrown overboard (from the bridge deck this means a fall of 60 feet to the sea, which is not inconsiderable); of one fellow being hurled so inaccurately into the swimming tank that his head struck the edge with an impact loud enough to be heard on somebody's video recording; of a squad of ex-*Spetsnats* men scouring the ship from top to bottom in search of malingerers; of a terrified Russian being dragged from under his bunk to attend King Neptune's pleasure. (All of which seems a good enough reason to be leaving the ship in Dakar.)

Clive, meanwhile, who presumably started this trip tarred by Anatoly with much the same brush as Simon, is starting to win Sagalevitch's grudging respect, possibly because he is not in the least fazed by the Russian's belligerent tactics at public meetings. But then, head-to-heads are Clive's speciality. Quentin recently remarked that at heart Clive was really a barrow-boy. This was admiring rather than snobbish. It simply acknowledged that Clive is someone who functions superbly well as a salesman, an advocate. He likes to get among people and manipulate them – not maliciously, necessarily, but at least partly for the private mischief of seeing the outrageous things he can get away with. Both watchful and amused, he expects any other intelligent person to behave similarly. In short, he's a lawyer and not a banker. It is not obvious to me that Simon, who spent time in Wall Street, takes anything like the same pleasure in observing human weaknesses, including his own. It is this, together with his understated sense of humour, which gives Simon his apparent vulnerability. (All this is, of course, only what I think I've observed, and on very slender acquaintance. Like many writers – most, probably – I'm a poor judge of character.) On occasion Mike is openly sceptical about Simon, as when he said that Simon might well have been in the Royal Navy for a while but he still asked Mike how many gallons of fuel the *Keldysh* needed when she was delayed in Kaliningrad. 'Gallons!' exclaimed Mike scornfully. 'That really inspires confidence in the man's nautical knowledge. And he's supposed to be coming aboard in Dakar to run things for Orca.' It is beginning to be possible to have some ideas about Mike's own emotional state. I would not put it past Simon to have set him up for that one.

TWELVE

3/2/95

We are now on-site. Bathymetry has started and finished. Overnight and using echo-sounders the sonar team have drawn a seabed profile of the *Dolphin*'s search zone so that when the side-scan sonar sled is deployed they won't inadvertently fly it into the side of a seamount and ruin it. The area turns out to be nearly ideal: just enough features to use as navigational reference points in case we find the submarine but nothing high enough to threaten the sonar seriously, being roughly 10 per cent rocky outcrop and 90 per cent sediment. There is therefore a 10 per cent chance that the submarine will be lying on a seafloor of naked basalt and won't show up on the sonar. According to the agreed listing of search areas in terms of their priority we are in a '68 per cent confidence zone'. Luckily at this depth and position both currents and deposition rates are so slow there is little chance that the submarine would be buried in sediment after a mere fifty years.

The principle of using sonar to obtain a detailed image of the seabed is simple enough if it is viewed as a sort of underwater radar, bouncing sound instead of radio waves off objects. The actual technology is complex. The ZVUK sled we are using is very much home-grown in that it was developed by the Shirshov

Institute, which also runs *Keldysh*. It is a rectangular stainless steel frame about two metres long by one wide towed slowly behind the ship (at between one and two knots) on the end of enough cable to allow it to drift just above the seabed. In water as deep as it is hereabouts this can mean 7 kilometres of cable, so the ZVUK is a very long way beneath and behind the ship. On each side of the sled, facing out and angled slightly downwards, is a bank of 'pingers' which send out a fan-shaped beam of sound once every second. This fan has little thickness but extends up to three-quarters of a kilometre on either side of the sled. Each second the same banks of transducers receive the acoustic echoes and send them as electronic impulses up the cable and on to the sonar lab's computer screens, where line by line they build up an image. As far as interpreting the picture goes, it is quite similar to aerial photography in that objects cast shadows. Reading the images is not in itself a difficult technique to learn, but experience turns out to count for everything. This will become obvious as soon as the long strips of print-out are laid side by side. Geological features which clearly run off beyond the edges can't always be matched up conveniently with their continuations on the neighbouring strip.

This neatly exposes the biggest difficulty of all side-scan sonar surveying: that of knowing where you are. Since orientation is inextricably linked to navigation it means a host of variables must be taken into account. Theoretically, the ship should tow the sonar sled at a constant speed in dead straight lines, building up slightly overlapping strips in a technique graphically known as 'mowing the lawn'. In practice, of course, this doesn't happen. It is very hard for a ship with so little way on her to maintain a straight course: there is always a slight wind or cross-current or waves nudging her bows to this side or that. At any given moment the ship has to 'know' precisely where it is in relation to an imaginary point on the earth's crust immediately beneath it – hence the need for GPS and other navigation equipment. This electronic knowledge is fed into the sonar's computer so that it can automatically correct for things such as drift and variations in speed.

However, the sonar picture at that same instant is of an entirely different piece of seabed several kilometres behind and – if there's a current running – off to one side. This in itself is bad enough. But when the ship turns round at the end of its leg to make an exactly parallel strip from the opposite direction all the variables have to be reversed, by which time, of course, the wind may have changed. It is for this reason that a net of transponders is put down before the sonar scanning can begin. Tethered just above the bottom, these provide a grid of fixed reference points, each transmitting at its own frequency exactly like the colour-coded buoys the American pilots dropped before the *I-52* was sunk. All of which goes to show the gulf between a quite simple theory and actual practice. The entire operation can easily degenerate into a nightmare of difficult towing conditions and conflicting electronic data resulting from trying to square the ship's and the sonar sled's 'pictures'. A sonar image may not be visibly skewed, but it can stubbornly refuse to match its neighbour when the print-outs are laid side by side. Errors of distance which look tiny on a print-out can later translate into a submersible, blind inside its little pool of light, entirely missing a significant-looking feature mere yards away. This is why deep-sea salvage is such a nail-biting affair. All too often there is that feeling, which every treasure-hunter knows, of 'if only'. If only the spade had gone in just 18 inches to the left . . . ! If only the submarine hadn't chanced to settle behind a low cliff of basalt which so exactly masked it . . . !

It is an overcast, sombre morning and the *Keldysh* has slowed to under two knots as she heads across the target area towing the fully-deployed ZVUK sled for the first time. A few months short of fifty-one years ago this area would have been full of grey-painted warships and carrier-borne aircraft patrolling the battle zone: the *Bogue*, the *Haverfield* and the rest. Oil and flesh would have been floating on the surface, and chunks of raw rubber. Now, three miles below us and somewhere among the low hills and gullies must lie the *I-52* without its ninety-four Japanese and three Germans. It is easy to feel a diffuse melancholy on their behalf, hard to find the place itself memorable. The battlefield no longer exists, after all. The featureless water is not the same featureless water which saw that single small action in a war long ago. Nothing is the same except this moving restlessly about the sea's surface with a smell of diesel in the air and surrounded by gently trembling warm metal surfaces. Nothing is left; the sea takes no prisoners. There will be no skeletons, not after half a century at that depth and hydrostatic pressure. Not even the opium could have survived. Resin would long since have dissolved. Nearly 3 tons of raw opium is not as good as 2 tons of gold but it could certainly have brought some cheer.

Suddenly everything about this enterprise, this chain of events which had its roots so long ago, afloat on this ocean, seems trivial. The boundless waste of human intelligence in war, the waste of lives and loves and time; the futility of power; the sense that gold itself is no more than compressed emptiness, a locus of dreams. All this contributes to a melancholy which is never far away on this voyage, hanging like dark smoke just over the horizon.

We are now roughly two hours away from the co-ordinates recently supplied by the Mysterious American. Tension is mounting, if that's what tension does. Russian technicians wearing blue boiler suits are huddled together in the sonar room, including the one Clive has nicknamed 'Brains' after the character in the old TV puppet series, 'Thunderbirds'. They are watching the trace on the monitor or else examining the print-out. This may not be evidence of mounting tension, however, just of professional oceanographers happy at last to have their precious instrument down there with hard data coming up. Now and again one of them looks at the trace on the right-hand part of the screen which shows the sonar sled's height above the seabed, and gives an order on a radio. Out on deck the winch operators spool off some more cable, allowing the sled to be towed a little lower, a fraction closer to the unknown landscape below. It is presently flying at its optimum height of about 100 metres above the bottom of the sea.

At teatime (3.30 p.m.) we find a mug of ice-cream beside each place and a litre carton of Spanish red wine. Presumably this vital dietary supplement has been ordered by the ship's doctor. This gentleman, vastly fat, beringed and bearded, looks like Holbein's Henry VIII and is clearly someone who takes quantities of his own medicine. The wine is only 10 per cent alcohol, making it more than small beer and less than grog. It's a reminder that never a day goes by aboard the *Keldysh* without its pleasurable *bizarrerie*. One day at tea they served large platefuls of unadorned cottage cheese; the next, porridge.

One can eat well aboard the *Keldysh*, but largely between meals. If one asks the cook for a plate of things to go with drinks he will come up with excellent morsels: cheese, spiced sausage, olives and so on. I shouldn't like this cook – an obliging and often sober fellow – to take umbrage at my remarks. You can only build with the bricks you have. I imagine the penurious

Institute back in Moscow has rigid ideas about riotous living aboard its research vessels, and caters accordingly. And it wouldn't at all surprise me if there were also dietary rules laid down for the Proper Nourishment of State Scientists which specify minimum daily allowances of vitamins, protein, calories and stuff like that and entirely leave out more vital quotients such as inventiveness, pleasure and satisfaction. Anyway, one should remember that American research vessels are strictly dry.

Meanwhile, our researcher Andrea has discovered the fat doctor's secret. He is living with a tomcat named Kisulkin (which apparently means 'small cat') in a cabin she describes as 'a tip'. One can't imagine having a medical condition so extreme it would induce one to submit to the ministrations of this gross sawbones. The cat is only one year old, but to judge from the smell which pervades Level 5 of the ship its little glands are in fine working order. Andrea reports the reek in the cabin as startling. The animal is a native of London. Its expectations as to a suitable lifestyle may once have been quite different. On the other hand so may the doctor's. More and more he seems like an anomaly aboard the *Keldysh*. The ship's complement is as remarkable a collection of characters as one ever did see, but they mostly appear serious and fit and do exercises on deck at dawn. The doctor, for all that he may be an amiable fellow, is unquestionably a slob. One wonders how he wangled himself aboard. There'll be some dark reason; there always is at sea.

Since there has not so far been a single meal which hasn't contained many handfuls of parsley (I bet it figured prominently in the doctor's medical school textbooks as a rich source of vitamins), Andrea hazarded the guess that they were growing it hydroponically in huge trays down in the hold. Viktor Brovko, the estimable engineer whose table we share at meal times, didn't know about that but he did tell us that the Russian for parsley is *petroushka*. It would make a charming name for a ballet.

It is hard to believe we are now actively in search of the submarine, methodically pinging the black kilometres of ocean directly beneath us. There is nothing to do now but wait, so after tea Mike, Clive, Quentin and I go to the gym to play ping-pong as we do most afternoons. Around the walls of this room is ranged a selection of contemporary torture instruments: rowing machines, dumb-bells, weights, racks and a comprehensive thing of sinister black padded upholstery, pulleys and chrome handles. It looks like a cross between a dentist's chair and an ejector seat. We play doubles, or one against three, or just about anything, depending on who happens along. Odd men out feel obliged to do a little exercising with decreasing self-consciousness while the ping-pong ball skitters around their spreadeagled legs. It is quite impossible to overrate the boredom factor involved in pumping iron. It is undignified, hurts, and now and then smells. By general consent ping-pong is deemed far better exercise and altogether more fun, solitary pursuits on wall bars promoting no friendships and few laughs.

Quite often a mountainous Russian with an affable round face comes in while we're playing and whirls some cannonballs with handles casually about his head. He resembles the 'Mr Clean' of American kitchen floor-cleaner fame. He also reminds me of a character in a long-ago naval novel: one of those war stories by Alistair Maclean or Nicholas Monserrat one read aged eleven. A hatch cover on a stricken British warship is jammed; nobody aboard can free it save one man, a Swede who – as in all books of the period with Swedes in them – is a giant named Larsen. They call for Larsen, who arrives holding in one hand a bunch of immense crowbars as if they were *grissini*. That's our Mr Clean. In fact, he turns out to be more generally known as 'Captain

Zodiac' since he is in charge of the Zodiac inflatable dinghy used in launching and recovering the MIRs. He is reputed to be the strongest man on the ship. Now and again as he whirls his cannonballs, he breaks off to field someone's stray shot, stares at this tiny thing cupped in his palm like a wren's egg lodged in the dish of Jodrell Bank radio telescope and says 'Rrrussyan ball *nyet* good!' Alternatively, he's a born minor character in an early James Bond movie. Sports note: it is quite difficult to play table-tennis on a moving ship.

Afterwards we go up to the deck above the bridge to drink our cartons of wine. We are surrounded by antennae, RDF loops and revolving radar scanners which are probably sterilising us as we sit. Clive tells us about a British press baron whose female employees know him contemptuously as 'Blow job or No job', while Quentin regales us with tales of employment he once took as a penniless student, operating a porn shop in Soho. He and a friend have devised an ingenious scam – so far not put into practice – which involves placing discreet advertisements in personal columns for the services of a company called Penis Extension Ltd. One of their courses will cost a mere £15 and comes with a 'No results – No pay' guarantee. The idea is that as soon as the money is received, P.E. Ltd. will send back an instant refund but drawn on a cheque of such obscene design nobody would have the courage to present it to one of the dainty tellers in his high street bank. As well as the picture in the cheque's background there would be a rubric in large print: 'Reimbursement for Failed Penis Extension'. There is, Quentin asserts, not a cat in hell's chance that anyone would ever claim their refund, thereby exonerating P.E. Ltd. from liability under the Sale of Goods Act. Nor is anybody likely to make a fuss about a paltry £15. In the thin glow induced by our medicinal Spanish wine this seems quite a likely money-spinner and ingenious enough to be worthy of the brother of Britain's first (but not only) Literal Democrat. At any rate it makes us consider the devastating effect on Quentin's mind of many years' study of abyssal sedimentation rates.

One of his observations does seem germane to the ship's present idiosyncratic progress on a course which, it now seems, will take us relentlessly a mile too far north of the Mysterious American's magic co-ordinates. From long experience he knows how a ship which has to steer a highly accurate course while covering a grid for a sonar survey can show distinct anomalies in the read-outs for twenty minutes every four hours. This, he says, is because each time a new watch comes on to the bridge he has his own way of running things and it always takes twenty minutes to settle down. It apparently happens regardless of the ship. This is interesting since it might well explain some otherwise quite inexplicable anomalies in the logs of the American warships as they recorded the engagement which sank the I-52. There would be a temptation for the new man on watch to try to make sense of previous entries by rationalising them with respect to current readings of course, speed etc., thereby creating his own narrative variant.

This takes Quentin into further reflections about certain practices aboard the *Keldysh* which at first horrified his British-trained scientific expectations but which he now thinks are highly original and effective. In many respects Russia and 'the West' evolved quite separately over the last thirty years. Russia was solving exactly the same scientific problems, but in entirely different ways. And they work. 'It's all quality stuff,' as Quentin says. Their ZVUK side-scan sonar sled has a skirt of rubber sheeting fixed all around the edge of its banks of transponders. Five years ago, according to Quentin, the Pentagon and NATO naval intelligence generally would have killed for a sight of this single piece of equipment, which until this morning was lying about the after-deck for anyone to sit on and take notes. 'Even *they* don't understand precisely how it works. But it does, and it knocks spots off a lot of our best stuff.' Quentin sometimes lectures the Royal Navy's nuclear submariners, so one presumes he knows.

At supper later we all have to acknowledge the genius of Russian science on the grounds that the soup contains proof of a chicken genetically engineered to consist entirely of neck and feet. As we eat, Sasha the radio officer makes a noisy announcement over the intercom to the effect that from now on, all phone calls from the ship to Moscow will cost $1 per minute. When this is translated the Orca people look at each other in wild surmise. A dollar a minute! We have been spending £10 for three minutes on calls which seldom get through but which are charged all the same. No one dares add up how much Orca members have so far spent on failed communications, for all their zingy little boxes and wires. And here's this heavy-duty 1948-style Russian radio system which bulldozes its way through the ionosphere and allows Oleg to chat to Ljudmila across 4,000 miles. Why don't they go into competition with Inmarsat and use sheer, old-fashioned reliability to cream off the business?

THIRTEEN

4/2/95

According to gossip they missed the *Titanic* four times, even with the correct co-ordinates, and she was vastly bigger than the *I-52* as well as being 1,200 metres shallower ... The *Titanic* is beginning to haunt this trip. Not merely the wreck itself but the *finding* of it has evident mythic weight in the salvage trade. The re-losing and re-finding are endlessly quoted as a sort of salvors' mantra: if the *Titanic* could be found, then so can some *pissant* submarine; if the *Titanic* can be lost again you're excused for not finding a thing. Certainly dawn brings with it the very opposite of a feeling of progress, whatever that might be. The *Keldysh* is crawling along over a calm, blackish sea as various stains appear in the eastern sky behind lumps of cloud. Beneath the cloud, hundreds of miles away, lies Africa. On the other side of the ship, even further off, lies America. Since leaving Madeira we haven't seen a single ship; we're obviously well away from all normal routes. The *Keldysh* barely moves, black symbols hoist up her foremast: ball, diamond, ball; the international code warning others that we cannot make manoeuvres. The tedium of treasure-hunting.

At the regular 9 a.m. meeting it is revealed that during the night the towing cable was damaged at 7,000 metres. The spooling gear on the winch seems to be not quite as brilliant as Quentin thought. It apparently lays the turns of the cable so tightly they chafe. A strand has broken. If two more break at the same point they may have to wind in the sled and abandon the entire operation. There is no technology aboard capable of butt-welding the strands of cable when it's under several tons of tension, and in any case the heat of the welding is always likely to damage the electronic connectors in the core. On the other hand, the team did find a target overnight which was about the right size for the *I-52*. So if the sonar is rendered *hors de combat* at least the MIRs will have something to investigate. Anatoly says sceptically, 'Maybe someone has been dumping a load of old refrigerators.' He and his Russians are so hardened to it all that drama is hard to detect.

This 'target' is most likely to be no more than a rocky ridge poking up above the surrounding sediment. Nobody even mentioned it at the meeting: I learned about it casually from Quentin two hours later. Or I thought I did. Actually, he now reminds me that he did show me a pencilled note of some co-ordinates at breakfast with the words 'There you are, me 'andsome. 'Ere be gold, loike.' Not unreasonably, I had taken it for another prank. Clive, who has to face the investors when he gets home, is prepared to be pretty serious about this first real prospect of finding the submarine. Mike, who hopes to buy a farm on the proceeds of this venture, is pretty serious about it. Andrea, who lives the penurious life of a self-employed scholar and also stands to benefit, is pretty serious about it. The rest of us, including ninety-odd Russians, think it's a bit of a lark or a load of old refrigerators. Down below in the MIR group lab is a computer showing the ship's position as a white blob on a black sea crossed by thin grid-lines. Some wag has programmed the word GOLD in gold letters to flash up randomly in a variety of positions across the screen, many of them miles outside the target area. Quentin detects Nik Shashkov's hand in this, evidence of an unsuspected sense of humour, and he and I warm still further to these Russians.

Still, Quentin's acting all casual about what is to Orca fairly momentous and heartening news is suggestive. It looks like evidence of that old egoic professionalism, the instinctive tendency of all priesthoods to vouchsafe small nuggets of information to non-initiates at calculated moments with just the right air of 'I'm sorry – didn't you know?' or 'Oh, *that* submarine. We found that *hours* ago.'

Something else I didn't know at the time was that there was a white-knuckle moment earlier this morning when the sonar team flew the ZVUK into the seabed. When this happens there are really only two things to do. One is to pay out as much cable as possible, stop the ship and back up. Even at $1\frac{1}{2}$ knots it takes time to stop, especially if she's going with wind and current. The other recourse is to plough on and hope the sled tears loose, which is what happened on this occasion. Luckily it seems to be undamaged since it's still sending back signals. It's not unlike fishing: having to judge how hard to pull when you've hooked a tree stump or some underwater object. But in this case the cast is worth half a million pounds sterling.

Meanwhile, as it is Saturday, Quentin and Clive are suspending interest in sonar screen-gazing after lunch in order to listen to the England–France rugby match on the World Service. The scene on the deck above the bridge at 2.00 p.m.: cans of cold McEwan's, two plates of cheese and salami slices with olives, a short-wave radio, sudden outbursts of 'Swing low, sweet chariot'. In the middle of the Atlantic ocean it is a hearty Twickers singalong with Clive and Quentin. Numinous names

R/V Akademik Mstislav Keldysh

Search zone meeting: (*from left to right*) Andrey Lvov (*back to camera*), Nik Shashkov (*extreme left*), Quentin Huggett, Andrea Cordani, Anatoly Sagalevitch, Yuri Bogdanov, Evgeniy Chernjacv, Mike Anderson (*extreme right foreground*).

Analysing the sonar scan print-outs.

The SVUK sonar sled, until recently a top secret piece of Soviet equipment.
Behind it is the escape capsule (out of order for lack of spare parts) intended.
as a safety backup for the MIRs.

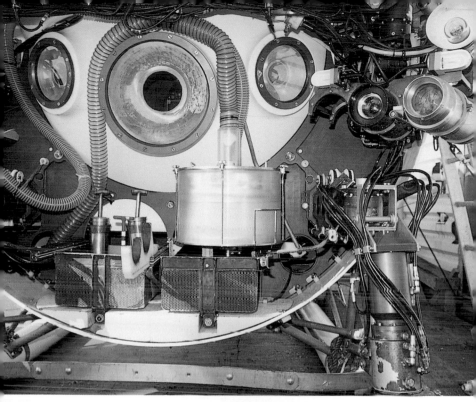

Above: Front of a MIR showing Viktor Brovko's vacuum collector for live organisms.

Left: The MIR's designer, Anatoly Sagalevitch.

Before a launch: (*from left to right*) Nik Shashkov, Mike Anderson and Viktor Brovko.

Andrea Cordani climbing into *MIR 2* before a launch.

MIR 1 being hoisted from the *Keldysh* and lowered.
The bows of the tender *Koresh* are visible behind it.

MIR 1 almost ready to be towed to a safe distance to submerge. Lonya releasing the
hoist, Zodiac dinghy with 'Captain Zodiac' alongside and *Koresh* with the tow rope.

Above: Money-man takes a bath. Simon Fraser enjoying Russian hospitality on the expedition's second leg.

Left: Photographer Ralph White in his Captain Marvel outfit; Andrea Cordani in hers.

Below: Christmas in the tropics: (*from left to right*) Mike Anderson, Clive Hayley, author, Quentin Huggett.

Left: Sergei Smolitskiy ('The Anarchist') atop *MIR 1*, in charge of the critical task of closing the hatch before a dive.

Crossing the Line. Mike Anderson kneels before King Neptune,
possibly in atonement for the entire expedition.

whizz about in the sun, transmitted from an overcast playing field over 2,000 miles away: Jeremy Guscott, Rory Underwood, Rob Andrew ... It turns out to be a crushing victory for England, heading for their third Grand Slam in five years. The Frogs are routed. 'I vow to Thee, my Country ... '

The smell of belch and sun lotion, blown away over the bluest sea outside a child's painting. It's curious to see the true origin of a convention: the average British primary schoolchild has probably never seen a really blue sea, yet their paintings faithfully portray a tropical rendition. In the Far East I once saw a sunrise in which rays shot like spokes from the sun exactly as in a child's painting – again, it's unlikely most British children would have seen this effect which is, of course, faithfully stylised in the Japanese naval flag.

We learn that in eight minutes the ship will be passing directly over the Mysterious American's co-ordinates for the *I-52*. However, it will take another two or three hours for us to know whether or not the sub's there, since at this speed that is how far behind the sonar sled is trailing. At the appropriate time the Orca team troops downstairs to the sonar room but is rebuffed by the Russians who are too intent on not flying their precious machine into the ocean floor again to welcome distraction. They have scant patience with these eager, apprehensive foreigners. Mike goes and stands at the port rail, his face stricken. It seems there actually is a shadow on the print-out which might just indicate a debris field: something else for the MIRs to investigate in three days' time when the sonar survey is complete. But later, at the magic co-ordinates, there is nothing whatever – just featureless sediment. It begins to look as though Orca may escape having to pay the American his $6,000 bonus.

Unconcerned, the unoccupied crew play volleyball with Sagalevitch on the upper deck, a pneumatic lady romps in the plunge bath and the man we know as Vaseline – who looks more like a pirate than any extra in a Douglas Fairbanks film – runs round and round the funnel wearing fluorescent orange oilskins. So much sweat pours off him his track is marked by a trail of blotches on the deck planking. The sense of holiday is palpable. Who wouldn't rather be adventuring on a tropic ocean than sitting in an office in February-shrouded Britain, or Russia? The unexpressed conviction is: This is the life.

Later that evening down in the sonar lab Quentin looks more closely at the two long rolls of the ZVUK's print-out. Each consists of a central blank strip flanked by two views of roughly a kilometre and a half's terrain on either side. Roman's re-programmed printer has faithfully reproduced each scanning line in sixty-four different shades of grey. The impression is that of long, narrow pictures of an unknown asteroid's surface taken from a passing spacecraft. They give a broad impression of lumps and craters, but Quentin looks at them with the attention that sees a good deal more. Sometimes he half squats and gazes at the scene from a low angle, reading the geology and the geography so that for a moment he, too, is on the seabed, looking out across a clear view of escarpments and ridges. It is for this task of interpretation that Orca hired him; he is acknowledged as one of the best. It looks like an anachronistic skill since it so closely resembles the reading of aerial reconnaissance photographs in the Second World War. What the onlooker misses Quentin stares at obliquely in silence for minutes at a stretch. It may be that he *is* looking at a fragment of the Second World War.

Quentin: 'See this? That could easily be a debris field and it's slap bang on this American's co-ordinates. We were wrong earlier . . . These black dots? They're shadows cast by individual objects, chunks of rock, whatever they are. No, look, the sonar scan's coming from the left of the picture here, so the shadows are all on the right. The Russians are claiming the ZVUK can get a definition of one metre, but I'd guess the smallest objects visible here are about five. This is definitely a target for investigation. They'll mark it with a grid of transponder beacons, then fly the ZVUK as low as possible for a close-up look of the area. Then the MIRs will have some co-ordinates to navigate by when they go down to see what's what ... '

Another possible target is found: a whitish lump in which it is only too easy to imagine a submarine's outline. It would be about 80 metres long, too, which is roughly right. That will also need investigating.

The new coincidence of Quentin's debris field with the magic co-ordinates gives the Orca team a real fillip. It would be wonderful enough to find the submarine intact, a minute metal cylinder lying on the bed of this vast Atlantic ocean; but to find it conveniently in pieces is almost too much to hope for, despite the implications of the huge explosion reported by the American pilots. The most ironic possibility has long haunted Mike, in particular: we find both the sub and the liner but there is no way of getting access to the gold. Now there is the faintest of faint chances that this debris field might turn out to be the remains of a Japanese submarine rather than just a jumble of rocks, the boxes of gold scattered handily about the seabed among the rest of its cargo simply waiting to be scooped up.

Quentin ends the session with a sincere tribute to Roman Pavlov and the rest of the tired Russians sitting around their elderly electronic equipment. This clearly pleases them greatly, just as they are evidently happy to be working with someone as experienced and knowledgeable in their own line of business. Later, he remarks how extraordinary it is that they can get such beautiful imaging with back-up electronics which, by 'Western' standards such as those of the British TOBI system, appear antediluvian. The truth is that not only are these scientists and technicians as good as – or better than – the best of 'ours', they really love their work and have years of experience at doing science on a comparative shoestring. Theirs is a world in which equipment isn't instantly replaced or uprated. What may look like a tangle of wires and army-surplus oscilloscopes *works*, is understood, and can be modified almost endlessly. If you can't rely on funds for the latest toy you are obliged to become ingenious and improvise. As someone asks later, How would you prefer to be stranded by a breakdown in the Sahara: in an old Land Rover with a box of hammers and spanners, or in some snazzy Japanese off-road vehicle full of computer chips and electronic fuel injection? Of course, this piece of rhetoric is really just a way of giving ourselves confidence in all the rest of the Russians' equipment. For the moment is now approaching when some of us will be going down in their MIRs. Everyone knows the Shirshov Institute is chronically strapped for cash, and the MIRs themselves are now getting on for ten years old. According to Sagalevitch they were both completely overhauled last year in Finland, down to the spheres being unbolted into their two halves and checked for cracks. Even so ... Down at 5,000 metres, at a pressure of 500 atmospheres and among 50 million-year-old rocks and rifts never before seen by human eye, there are no such things as slight defects, only fatal flaws. It wouldn't take much more than a single hair lodged in one of the many holes drilled in the pressure hull to cause a tiny leak with large consequences.

This, of course, is the unstated background to each of the daily Sub Group meetings at 8 a.m. Orca members rarely go to them, with the exception of Mike and Andrea. In some ways it looks as though these meetings might form the centre of Anatoly Sagalevitch's day. He is freed, for once, from having to sit in his cabin with Natalya, his partner, and haggle over banking arrangements and contracts and budgets as though he were a businessman rather than a scientist. Down there he's back in his spiritual home with his beloved MIRs which are just outside the door on deck, reefed down tight under their individual garages of white-painted steel.

6/2/95

Now men and machines are being readied for the first dives. The sonar scans have yielded several possible targets that need to be looked at directly. This morning the lab is crowded with the ship's aristocracy: the pilots and technicians who know every last screw on the two submersibles. To a non-Russian speaker the atmosphere seems completely democratic. Men chip in with remarks and comments – worker participation, maybe, but tinged with whatever it was that transcended even the comrade-ship which pilots in the old Royal Flying Corps once shared with their riggers and fitters. For the room is full of people who regularly put their lives in each other's hands. If there's an élite aboard it is unquestionably the MIR Group, not the money-men and the foreigners, nor even the pure scientists. These are the engineers whose skill makes it possible to visit the planet's most forbidding environment. Even an internationally-known geologist like Yuriy Bogdanov is a mere passenger when he is down there among the canyons and the black smokers. And after all, it is the two MIRs that have made the *Keldysh* famous.

The sonar survey is over for now. They have hauled the ZVUK up. It leaves puddles on deck the colour of milky tea. It ought to look changed after its three days' passage through an unknown world three miles down but it doesn't, apart from a bent towing bracket caused when the sled hit the bottom. The tea is draining out of the tubing of its runners, which are full of pinkish foraminiferous ooze. Calcareous, Quentin tells me. Much of the colour itself comes from the Sahara whose dust has been settling right across the Atlantic for millennia. After three days at 4°C and in pitch darkness, the thick steel starts to warm in the sun on deck. I notice that all its structural tubing has small holes drilled in it. This is so that water can fill every part of the frame and equalise the pressure. Any tube without a hole and hermetically welded at both ends would be crushed with sufficient violence to risk the destruction of the entire sled.

As on any day before a dive the time is spent in laying a pattern of transponders at carefully calculated positions. These large orange buoys are thrown overboard with sinkers that take them down so they hang like barrage balloons a hundred or so metres above the seabed. They will act as beacons for the submersibles to navigate by, down in that trackless darkness. Each MIR pilot will have a bathymetric map of the particular area he needs to cover, marked with the targets which need investigating and the positions of the transponders, each of which operates at a different acoustic frequency. These will be recovered as soon as the MIRs are back. At an acoustic signal from the ship, each buoy jettisons its weight and floats back up to the surface where a flashing light is activated so it can be seen at night. Because they incorporate a pressure case strong enough to protect the instrument package and communications gear they are extremely expensive. That, together with the syntactic foam which forms the body and gives it the necessary buoyancy, brings the price of each to at least £10,000, so the possibility of losing one is not taken lightly on a ship whose motto is 'make do and mend'.

Ralph shoots the buoys being thrown over the side as part of the documentary film Orca have engaged him to make. 'Seen it, done it,' he says in self-mockery. I wonder how many miles of videotape he has shot of identical scenes over the years. At least a writer in similar circumstances might be able to say, 'Seen it, but never noticed *that*.' So although I have indeed watched transponders being dropped before, I have never paid attention to the care with which they are 'armed': the long sealed tube of the strobe light being screwed into the top, the automatic release shackle on the base being tested. For much of the day the *Keldysh* sails a slow and minutely-accurate course while gangs of men wait with a buoy poised on the rail until a radio signal reaches them from the bridge and they push it over. As it bobs astern they pay out the 100 metres of tether line and throw the lump of iron (never again to see the light of day) after it. The weight disappears with a *galoof!* A minute or two elapses while it sinks until it is vertically beneath the distant buoy, which itself then vanishes.

'Oceanographers, of course, do not believe such things,' I wrote a little over two weeks ago when considering the superstitions of Cornish fishermen and others. Tonight:

Mike: I hear you've been asked to stop whistling.
Me: No. (Quite truthfully.) No one's said anything.
Mike: Perhaps it's someone else. You mustn't whistle aboard a ship, you know. It's bad luck. Whistle up the wind ...
Clive: Sounds fairly typical, I must say.

Tomorrow the MIRs are deployed for the first time. At our 6 p.m. briefing Anatoly, Genya and the Burt Reynolds look-alike are all wearing boiler suits with 'мир' patches. There's now a real sense of excitement. Although the two JUFOs will be geologists, Yuriy 'Black Smoker' Bogdanov and 'Misha' Mikhail, the Orca group knows it's theoretically possible that by this time tomorrow night the wreck of the *I-52* will have been found and *even* (just) one of the boxes of gold brought up . . . Orca decides this calls for a drink – a decision it has always taken with more fluency than any other – and Ralph's Beefeater is broken out of bond unbeknownst to him. The fact is that Clive and Mike very unwisely parted with eight bottles of our Gordon's as a donation to the Russians for their deck party. They must have thought this judicious: a decent gesture at a time when we needed all the favour we could curry. This was before it became clear that the Russians will drink anything. In Falmouth we did put aboard a case of Chivas Regal 'for the natives', as Clive remarked, but alas only one. It was still a terrible mistake to have sacrificed our Gordon's for the party. We can only assume that Mike, who rarely drinks anything stronger than an occasional can of warm McEwan's, didn't realise the gravity of his actions. In any case Ralph's Beefeater goes down well and the rest of the evening lacks focus, except for an hour spent in the wireless room while Quentin's computer received a message from the UK which must have cost him hundreds of pounds.

At 2 a.m. I'm woken by aero engines passing really low. I guess from their sound it's a visit from the US Coastguard – a P3 Orion like that which buzzed *Farnella* off Hawaii. I get up and go out on deck. There is no moon so it's impossible to identify the aircraft which keeps circling. Even when it flies over at a couple of hundred feet it's still only a group of winking navigation lights. I go up to the bridge, which is in darkness. The First Officer is trying to talk to the pilot, who is definitely American. I do some interpretation in between messages since the First Officer's English is none too good. It seems the Americans are claiming to have picked up emergency signals from a beacon aboard the *Keldysh* which has mistakenly been switched on. This is not implausible. More than 90 per cent of automated mayday calls from ships are false alarms, according to the UK's Marine Safety Agency. But in the small hours of morning on the darkened bridge of a Russian ship, the First Officer says 'Huh. CIA,' and it doesn't seem unlikely there could be a link with some sort of military intelligence. The US Navy's underwater SOSUS network will have been picking up signals from the transponders we dropped and the Navy will have asked Woods Hole Oceanographic Institution what a Russian research vessel could possibly be doing here. Woods Hole will have replied that there's no geology of any interest in these parts, far away from the Mid-Atlantic ridge as we are. Baffled, they've decided to give us the once-over. Whatever his mission, the pilot finally flies away, saying he has 'no more questions at this time' and is heading off to Barbados – about 1,800 miles.

FOURTEEN

7/2/95

When I tell Orca members about last night's visitor they go into a huddle about codes and things. When the MIRs go down today the US Navy will be able to eavesdrop on their acoustic signals as they talk to the *Keldysh* and each other. Suppose the dreaded word 'gold' is mentioned? We always suspected we'd be on navy screens, and now that we've been so elegantly told we are, Orca's worst suspicions are confirmed. And so the authentic atmosphere – slightly paranoid, conspiratorial, excitable – has finally been established. You can't hunt for lost gold without it.

The launching of MIR 1 is dramatic and moving. Conditions are not ideal. A brilliant tropic sun with clots of cloud but a lurching sea. Suddenly, all the familiar faces (the Anarchist, Mr Clean, the Cowboy, Goldenhands, Burt Reynolds and quiet Viktor Brovko), become part of a skilled and dangerous ballet which they've performed together many times. The Anarchist turns out to be the man who closes the hatch and hooks the MIR to the crane. He is still in beard and beret but now looks less conspiratorial than motherly as he squats on the roof of the bulbous orange submersible. (How stupid it is that when one doesn't speak a language one is reduced to caricature in order to individuate people.) Anatoly climbs up the ladder on to the

MIR's back and gives the assembled cameras a jaunty wave as he kicks off his slippers before vanishing down the hatch in his socks and blue boiler suit. Bogdanov, who is no stripling, has rather more trouble easing his teddy bear form down the narrow hole. Closing the hatch, which is chamfered and has a sort of piston ring embedded in its steel cheeks, proves difficult and there's a slight delay. Inside, Sagalevitch, Mikhail and Bogdanov must be sweating. Not only is the sphere generally hot and stuffy at the beginning of a dive in the tropics but it can't be reassuring to know the hatch isn't seating easily. Now it finally closes, the crane lifts the MIR and swings it outboard. From the rail above it resembles a fat orange-and-white helicopter fuselage without a cabin: the pressure sphere with its three tiny viewing ports is hidden beneath the smooth upper bulk of syntactic foam. Tossing and wallowing in the lively sea (there's a stiff breeze today), Mike's pride, the *Koresh*, is waiting with Little Lev at the helm. According to Mike the MIRs' tender was built to very strict specifications in Falmouth, having been designed largely via fax in a long series of exchanges between Moscow and Cornwall. It has a big Volvo Penta engine and an oversized propeller. It can't do more than six knots but has the power of a small tug. It is used for towing the MIRs a safe distance from the *Keldysh* while they do their final pre-dive check, and later for towing them back to the ship's side when they've surfaced. (*Koresh* is apparently a Russian colloquialism for 'friend', but for me it connotes the leader of the Branch Davidian sect which came to such a spectacular end in Waco, Texas, a couple of years ago. In that Biblical context the name is actually the Hebrew version of Cyrus, which itself derives from the Persian word for 'throne'.)

Near the *Koresh* lurks muscular Captain Zodiac in the rubber dinghy with the Suzuki outboard. His companion today is

Lonya, the Cossack, naked except for swimming trunks. Once the MIR is in the water beside the ship the Zodiac comes surging up and Lonya leaps from it on to the back of the submersible. He goes into a crouch and with a terrific downward yank uncouples the MIR from the crane. Then he hitches a tow rope from *Koresh* to the submersible's nose, dives clear and is picked up by the Zodiac. He is a lithe youngster and needs to be. The entire operation takes only a matter of seconds, but in a sea as rough as this it all depends on timing, catching the MIR on an upward lurch when there's enough slack in the crane coupling to allow it to be disconnected. For a moment as he crouched on its back he was completely submerged and we could see his blurred shape turn green as he wrestled with the release gear. Now the *Koresh* takes up the slack in its towrope and the wallowing orange back with its aircraft-style tail fin slides away from the ship.

The atmosphere among the crew and observers left anxiously staring behind is that of a family seeing a child off to school on the day of a crucial examination. Nearly everyone aboard watches the launch, which is the first in many months. This explains the tension. It will remain until both MIRs have safely returned (*MIR 2* is scheduled to be launched later). No one is whistling. Most must have seen it dozens of times, yet it is still an astonishing thing to watch three men being sealed into a pressure case that will not be opened for maybe eighteen hours, in which time they will have reached one of the least accessible places on Earth, pressed in upon by utter dark and caught in a huge cramp of salt water. What happens if there's a pinhole leak? Ralph, leaning on the rail, assures us that at such pressure the needle of water would 'cut through a body like a laser'. And if a seal goes and there's an implosion? 'You might just hear a click. Then the shockwave would turn you into a liquid about as thick as consommé, while the atmosphere would be compressed to a volume about the size and temperature of a white hot pea. After the other MIR had retrieved yours, they'd pour you out of the hatch. They might just find some buttons or a zipper.' This explains why Orca members watch with an attentiveness which has nothing of ghoulishness about it: sooner or later (they hope and dread) they will be doing the same thing.

Even at this moment of writing, an hour after the orange whale turned green and vanished, Anatoly and his two companions are still only a third of the way down, about a mile and a quarter deep, sinking steadily at 30 metres per minute. It's impossible not to visualise them huddled in that chilling, armoured golf ball down there and remember the great pioneers: Beebe, Piccard, Cousteau. There is something immensely grand, even solemn, about the whole enterprise, and it rubs off on everyone aboard, especially Orca. What has been a project for so long is at last putting men's lives on the line. If ever it had seemed to some little more than an expensive prank, it has now become altogether more serious.

Three hours later the other MIR's crew comes out on to the launch deck, trim in their boiler suits, and shakes hands with their own friends, the engineers. Viktor Brovko's face is a study in anxious concentration. One can almost see him performing a mental checklist of all the submersible's working parts. He embraces the three departing men, a proper Russian embrace with both hands hugging their shoulder blades. The sequence of the first launch is repeated exactly. Up on the submersible's roof the three step out of their shoes and drop them in a cardboard box marked in felt-tip '*MIR 2*', like prisoners entering gaol and depositing their personal belongings for safe-keeping during their sentence. They disappear inside; the hatch is closed and dogged; they are swung outboard and dumped in the sea. Lonya repeats his aquabatics. *Koresh* tows them away and casts them adrift. After a long moment the buoyancy tanks blow and in a cloudlet of whale's breath *MIR 2* sinks from sight. As it disappears news comes from *MIR 1* that it has reached the bottom after rather more than four hours and is now at 5,200 metres, some three miles below the ship in which we now troop silently down to lunch.

8/2/95

MIR 1 returned at 2 a.m. The retrieval was hallucinatory: woken from a deep sleep, up onto deck, staring out from behind powerful lights into a black wall of sky and sea. Then the *Koresh*'s navigation lamps far out giving something to focus on, marking the sea's bounds, adjusting the eye to differentiate swinging gleams from faint overhead constellations. Behind the *Koresh* a luminous puddle appeared like green wobbling jelly. We could now see that the tender was towing a cloud of glowing protoplasm that constantly swelled and stretched, shrank and dimmed, and occasionally put forth a bright eye. *MIR 1* had all its lights on. As it neared the ship I was reminded of a dying porcupine fish, *Diodon*, being rolled ashore by the waves; bloated and helpless, its back awash and at its stern an impotent whirring as of a tiny fin.

To describe its retrieval as merely the reverse of the launch would be to falsify it, although strictly speaking it would be accurate. What was left out would be the element of heroic mystery: that this benighted wallowing canister was not precisely the same object one had last seen disappear in sunlight thirteen hours earlier. Since then it had been to another universe and could not have returned identical in every way. Four hours ago that fat object had been nosing about canyons and outcrops never before seen. For a brief moment its halogen lamps had illuminated a geography that maybe last felt the sun 50 million years ago or perhaps had scarcely seen light since the planet formed. Then the lights passed, and all would be dark again for the next 50 million years. In the last thirteen hours, therefore, this small orange-and-white craft had been to a place without real co-ordinates, one that our recent forebears thought of as terrifyingly inchoate, godless, too primeval for any human connection, beyond morality, a leftover from Chaos. To witness the return of a vehicle from that strange universe to the diurnal human dimension is not completely real. Like the Kraken it rises mysteriously to the surface and in some sense it, too, dies. The boundless, slopping dark hems in the ship with, at the centre of a lit heart, the vivid drama of a man leaping out of the Zodiac on to the time machine's roof to attach the crane's hoist. It is unreal, an extension of sleep. We never quite know where we are at important moments. This might equally well have been an execution one had been summoned from bed to witness – even one's own – with the dreambound self hovering a little behind, always on the edge of nothing.

When the Anarchist climbs up to pop the hatch, normality rushes in together with an emotional gust of relief like fresh air, plainly visible in the crew's faces. The three time-travellers emerge stiffly, like William Beebe in that old black-and-white photo taken in the thirties, a tired, gaunt figure squeezing unaided out of his capsule's tiny hatch after a record-breaking dive, a maggot emerging from an egg. The co-pilot comes out first, then Bogdanov the geologist, then Anatoly himself, the captain being the last to leave his ship. As he gropes in the cardboard box for his shoes he raises a hand to the onlookers, who include his partner Natalya as well as the entire Orca team, calling up in Russian with a weary and not uncynical smile: 'There's fuck-all gold down there.' Then he climbs down the ladder and is absorbed into his applauding colleagues' upstretched arms.

At six a.m. *MIR 2* also returns safely. It, too, has found no trace of the submarine. Rumours fly about but can't be officially laid until the full debriefing, which will obviously have to wait until the MIR crews have slept and eaten. They say the Mysterious American's position – the putative 'debris field' – is nothing but scattered rocks. They also suggest the MIRs might actually have missed it or else bypassed it in a quest for geological samples. In scientific terms the mission was apparently a great success and *MIR 2* returned with excellent specimens. Was the Orca mission abandoned in favour of science once the dark waters closed above the submersibles? We'll just have to wait.

None of this would work in a novel, not just because the climaxes aren't supplied to order but because there's not much room in a conventional thriller for all the protagonists to have different purposes. But on the *Keldysh*, especially behind the opacities of the language barrier, there appear to be as many distinct intentions as there are individuals. Not even the Orca group is unified – by, for instance, a single-minded yearning for sudden wealth – variously protected as they are by scepticism or a bleak reckoning of the chances of success. Do even Mike and Andrea (who have been longest and most intimately involved with digging up the facts), absolutely believe that the submarine is down there with gold on board? Mike dreams of the farm he wants to buy and the debts he needs to pay off; Clive is having fun but is responsible to a serious crew of shadowy investors; Ralph would like to notch up another triumphant bit of derring-do. Quentin plans to spend any windfall on a new extension to his house, but he's not much bothered and certainly isn't counting on it. His involvement with Orca is less concerned with gold than with getting to know the entrepreneurial world of Clive and Simon. How else would a geologist meet people who knew how to tap into considerable wealth? A small businessman needs to know such things. One day he might want to form a brief partnership with Clive, perhaps, to exploit some zany, un-geological idea which crosses his mind while waiting at traffic lights or bathing his children. For Quentin is as inventive as he is exuberant. There, one feels, is a man who will make his own fortune rather than find somebody else's lying on a seabed. Andrea . . . what does Andrea want? Relief from penury, why not? And, like Mike, the relief of a proper climax after so many years of living with preparations for this enterprise, the reward for professional toil. I alone have no stake in any gold the expedition might find. It will make me not a penny richer. On the other hand there is the largesse of adventure, of being where one otherwise would not have been, meeting people one would not otherwise have known, and all of it a million times better than some leaden domestic scene.

Andrea has had quite an adventurous life, which adds a real weight of experience to what might appear the musty and academic profession of a researcher. Musty she isn't. Having read English and Philosophy at Manchester, she took up scuba diving to the point where she became a BSAC (British Sub-Aqua) club instructor. Her specialised hobby became diving on wrecks, and of all the Orca team it is she who has by far the most experience of wreck work. She is also a qualified suit diver, lead boots and all.

In the 1970s she tried to join the Royal Navy at their High Holborn recruitment office. She was turned down with unconcealed amusement. Deeply disappointed, she resigned herself to 'going commercial' (as she puts it) and applied for a job with

Green's camera shop chain which also owned several dive shops. They, too, casually turned her down. This time she was angry enough to enter a formal protest and demand to be properly interviewed. Something about her spirited complaint must have made them feel they ought to take this person seriously if only to discourage her from making a more public fuss. On interviewing her again Green's discovered she *was* rather impressive – so much so, they put her in charge of all their dive shops, both wholesaling and retail. When Green's was taken over by the Burton chain, the watersports part of the business was expanded. Then Debenhams bought out Burton and in a complete reversal this side of things was progressively run down and finally discontinued. Andrea moved over to become a sports buyer for Debenhams' Oxford Street store. Within six months she was made redundant.

She and a friend started a wet-suit factory in Battersea: Sea Wolf Ltd. They were using a new manufacturing technique whereby the neoprene was cut like pastry with a die rather than being laboriously tailored with scissors. Sea Wolf prospered, but a mistaken partnership resulted in Andrea and her business associate James being elbowed aside. In 1978, Andrea and James thought they might try starting an overseas marine salvage operation instead. Accordingly, they set up a joint venture with a partner in Sri Lanka, a business which lasted until 1983. During this time they looked for (but failed to find) HMS *Diomede* off Trincomalee. From the War Risks Insurance Office in London they bought a sunken British tanker, *British Sergeant*, for £400. She was lying in 70 feet of water off the East coast of Sri Lanka and offered good, straightforward prospects for salvaging commercial (i.e. non-ferrous) metals including the ship's manganese bronze propeller. Even the steel hull could in due course have gone to a local smelter. Unfortunately, Andrea and James's partner once again turned out to have plans of his own. As a result of a frame-up both of them wound up briefly and traumatically in a Sri Lankan prison.

They were, in fact, the innocent but handy victims of a complicated political scam. Their eventual release with apologies did not quite make up for Andrea's sudden lack of confidence in local business conditions. Somewhat gaunt and tottery, she flew back to London and from 1983 became a retained researcher at the Public Record Office, as well as at the National Maritime Museum and the British Library's Oriental and India Office collection. Some years passed before the day when Mike Anderson happened on her name at the PRO and began making his own enquiries about her suitability for his research project (for obvious reasons, CVs and references are not always easy to come by in the salvage business). As we know, Andrea's first job for Mike's company, Anderson Associates – then acting as the UK agents for Subsal Inc – was to try to find documentary proof that the cargo of gold Jock Walker said he saw loaded on to the *Aurelia* really had existed.

In its understated way, Andrea's quiet competence in salvage diving is probably as great as any Russian's on the ship, and immeasurably greater than that of anybody else in Orca. Besides which, she knows the documentation better than anyone and is a fund of technical information about related topics. Still more, though, she has flourished, after a struggle, in an aggressively masculine world which probably even today doesn't take kindly to women in diving suits. Her rejection by the Royal Navy all those years ago still galls her, but instead of making her bitter it made her determined. Again, mere doggedness might have turned her into a bulldozer, but she simply became a champion of anyone else who knows what it is to be mocked and dismissed. It is this side of Andrea, plus an excellent knowledge of the law and 'street smarts', that enabled her to do spare-time voluntary work for a gay helpline in London. She is a generous spirit; and talking to her I am aware that if there is one thing which cheers me about Orca it is the sheer diversity of its members, their widely differing backgrounds and qualifications. Is this heterogeneity a strength in a team like this, or is it a potential weakness? Who knows? But it is fascinating to uncover the varied paths by which they have all converged on this Russian ship at present ploughing its way down the Atlantic.

In the aftermath of the first dives a curious *tristesse* pervades the ship. The sonar lab is listless. Roman Pavlov and Brains prepare in silence for the ZVUK's signals to start again. Quentin believes people are more downcast by the failure to find gold than they had bargained for. I think it may have less to do with gold than with the underestimated strain of despatching six of their friends and colleagues to that other universe and getting them back again. The dives were the first in many months and *MIR 1*'s launch was not without its hitches. Not only had the hatch been recalcitrant but Little Lev in *Koresh* allowed the submersible's rear end to bump the side of the ship, causing superficial damage to the fibreglass moulding which protects the MIRs' main propeller. Then the crane driver raised his hook too far after release and jammed it in the block so it had to be dismantled between launches. This meant that had *MIR 1* aborted its dive it could not have been hauled back aboard immediately. In this swell that might have proved awkward. All this was less than perfect, and it had been watched and filmed by foreigners with their goggling eyes and lenses. The show hadn't been staged for the damned interlopers; it was more like a family scene being witnessed by strangers. Useless to explain that by the standards of any operation which involved deploying priceless gear at sea it, like the entire trip so far, had gone with miraculous precision. And this is perfectly true. To have reached the *Dolphin* search zone on the appointed day is a wonder; to have deployed all that equipment and retrieved it without loss or damage, a bonus; and to have acquired usable data of the target area into the bargain – just as planned – is downright incredible. Such things can only be appreciated by those who know the sea. It will not be understood by landlubbers who deal in airline and other daily schedules which occur with the predictability of TV programmes. They would just see things going more or less according to plan. They don't know in their bones that the sea has no plans, that we don't belong here, that every additional day successfully spent afloat is a blessing.

Orca members should not have turned up to the 5 p.m. meeting in the MIR lab. From the outset it was obviously something of a post mortem for the inner brotherhood. We stood around the lab bulkheads like well-heeled international riff-raff who didn't have to go home to a Third World dump like Kaliningrad. The Russians began with an unintended way of further freezing us out, with a birthday eulogy (delivered with much laughter) and presentation of a bottle of Georgian champagne to Little Andrej, who is 31 today. Thereafter, everything was equally in Russian which Anatoly with a slightly edged courtesy translated two or three times for our benefit as 'just technical points arising from the MIR dives yesterday, mistakes and problems which we must deal with before we dive next'. He added that there would be another meeting at 6 p.m. when we could all discuss where the MIRs had gone and what they'd seen. By now I was feeling such a grotesque interloper I eased out though the door together with Clive, Mike and Quentin, leaving Andrea sticking it out, her spectacles gleaming. What had emerged was that until yesterday neither of the MIRs had been down to 5,000 metres in the last four years. No wonder the ship had been twitchy yesterday. No wonder, too, that the ones who went down weren't worrying principally about Japanese submarines and gold bars: they'd been mainly keen to get back alive.

9/2/95

This morning the Anarchist was up on deck, reading intently from a book of poems and then considering what he'd read by staring upwards, beard jutting and beret thrown back. He has an admirable aura: cultured, self-contained, competent.

At this morning's usual 9 o'clock Orca meeting a sense of unity was conspicuously missing. It doesn't help that we didn't find the *I-52* on the first dives and no dripping bars of precious metal are about to be heaped on the *Keldysh*'s deck. People are vaguely dispirited, a measure of the optimism – not to say fantasy – they've been entertaining. Not quite three weeks ago I was wondering what, with hindsight, might have been obvious as the factor leading to disharmony among our treasure-hunters. This morning's meeting showed it to be the lack of a real leader, or perhaps a Project Manager, to represent Orca's anglophone element. This is no reflection on Clive, who has made himself extremely knowledgeable about every aspect of the targets' documentation as well as about the technologies involved in the search. But what he knows is perceived as being less important than what he is: the money-men's representative and a lawyer by profession. If we had had a professional salvor as our leader, the Russians might be paying us more respect. In a way, Andrea is the best qualified in that she has the most 'hands on' experience of working on wrecks in forty fathoms of cold dark water. But while it is fine for a woman to be a brilliant scientist, I suspect it would be less so from a Russian male viewpoint if a foreign woman were to lead a group of men she outshone in diving skills. Maybe I'm wrong about that; but in any case I think Clive's urbane, public-school brand of democracy which accords everyone a fair hearing strikes the Russians as evidence of weakness. The irony is that Anatoly Sagalevitch *is* Orca's director of operations and always has been, just as he is and always has been a shareholder in the venture. It is only that his evident frustration shows there to be a discrepancy between his title and Clive's function as a representative of the expedition's backers.

Ostensibly, this morning's meeting was held to consider how to choose the next targets in some order of priority – while the sonar data is still coming in and against the increasing shortage of time. Sagalevitch was being stern and headmasterly at the end of the boardroom table and clearly in control of what the ship was doing. Orca, though, were calling for more data, maps etc. and were visibly doing on their feet some thinking which might better have been done before and agreed in private so as to preserve the appearance of a united front. The various charts which have been re-drawn using our new bathymetry and side-scan data – already the most accurate maps of this area in existence – were spread out on the table. Orca had somehow intuited, or was determined to believe, that neither of the MIRs had properly covered the Mysterious American's target zone. Sagalevitch soon made it clear that not only had his MIR gone slap cross the spot whose co-ordinates Orca had agreed, but once all the delicate navigational adjustments had been made, the American's position lay about half a kilometre away in an area the sonar print-outs showed to be scrupulously blank. By now Andrea was visibly irritated by Orca's being wrong-footed. She began a feisty and pertinent question about how well *MIR 1* had actually investigated the agreed target. Anatoly shamelessly interrupted to ask Quentin to give his views on the sonar print-out but then almost at once launched into a completely extraneous aside to Clive about needing more money to prolong the search.

This was outrageous, but nobody appeared outraged. Clive did some excellent lawyerly prevarication about it being impossible at this stage to go back to the investors for a new injection of funds. He said he knew without asking it would be a waste of time. In my view he would have done better by stopping Sagalevitch in his tracks, and quite sharply. By suddenly introducing the money motif even as Quentin was talking, Anatoly – consciously or not – was surely pointing out that he didn't know who he ought to be dealing with on the Orca side: the scientist or the Keeper of the Purse. And this, of course, is precisely the hateful split he is all too familiar with in his own professional life back in Moscow. Poor Clive finds himself in an invidious position. Sagalevitch is bound at some level to despise him simply for being the investors' representative on the *Keldysh* for this leg. And if this little diversion was the heavy-handed ploy I took it to be, it was a way of making this embarrassingly clear. It's obvious that for all the purposes that interest Anatoly, he is now beginning to treat Quentin as the spokesman for the Orca group because he is the one member of the group who can talk serious science with the best of the Russians. The rest of us he probably regards as superfluous passengers aboard his ship – either representatives of a new world order that disgusts him or (as in my case) unskilled buffoons.

No doubt I am unfair. He must surely have respect and affection for Mike, who has not only been a friend for some years but is a considerable expert in his own right on salvage and maritime law. I couldn't begin to guess what he feels about Ralph; but they've been on numerous dives together over the years, especially on *Titanic*, so there's probably quite a bit of macho bonding, grace under 500 atmospheres, all that. It must be obvious to Sagalevitch that Andrea, too, is thoroughly professional and able, but historical research may not be a profession he's got much time for, especially since it's being put to use for so ignoble a purpose as gold-digging.

Later, when some of us retreat to Clive's cabin for an inquest and the solace of coffee, Quentin's reasonable line is to leave it to the Russians. They have so far shown themselves more than competent so why not leave them to get on with it as they think best? After all, Orca makes virtuous noises about this being a joint effort, and since Sagalevitch controls the hardware out here in mid-Atlantic, why not let the Russians do more of the thinking about where the *I-52* might be? Clive replies stoutly that co-operation is exactly what he's been insisting on right from the start, if Quentin will only cast his mind back, but bloody Sagalevitch wants it both ways. He wants to be able to whinge about Orca choosing the wrong targets to look at while reserving the right to complain that they didn't board the ship at Falmouth with the whole thing cut and dried and present him with a list of all the co-ordinates to be examined. Somebody volunteers that this isn't so much inconsistent as simply indicative of the man's deep resentment at having to preside over an expedition he scorns. 'Then he shouldn't have signed the contract,' says Clive truculently. 'We all know it's not what he'd ideally like to be doing, but this isn't an ideal world and he's got to earn a living like anyone else.'

'You're going to say that the least he could do is conduct himself with good grace,' I suggest evilly.

'No I'm bloody well not,' says Clive, who has absolutely no interest in moralities of any kind. 'He's a Russsky malcontent.'

At this moment, and not for the first time, I find myself

thinking about the loudspeakers in each cabin. When Quentin and I had opened ours one day in idle curiosity we had the impression that there was rather more circuitry than necessary. Surely listening devices would have gone out with the KGB's commissar? Maybe I, too, am becoming paranoid. But it strikes me that with all this technological ingenuity aboard, the Russians out of sheer habit might have ensured they kept one step ahead of these strangers in their midst. Sagalevitch is a street fighter. From a lifetime's experience of the Soviet regime, he's not a man who leaves his back unprotected.

Quentin suggests that the prospect of finding gold is still probably enough of an incentive for the Russians to make genuine efforts for as long as they can suspend disbelief in the whole caper. I know he sees no reason to take any more personal responsibility than he's being paid for – always a sound plan. Orca recruited him to interpret the sonar and keep an eye on the ZVUK procedures generally. As it is, his extra-professional abilities and charm are making him indispensable, the one thing he swore not to become. Had it not been for his patience and long hours of nerding, few of Orca's vital messages would have been sent when they were, and neither would we all have laughed so much. But Quentin can take care of himself. He spends a good portion of most days working away in his cabin at Geotek's business and not Orca's.

Later, I remark to Roman Pavlov (who has been telling me that no one aboard the *Keldysh* is under contract to the Institute in Moscow because the Institute doesn't give contracts, not even to Sagalevitch) that I hope nobody is relying on our finding gold. He says not to worry, they already have experience of gold-hunting (the Mexican venture). It's just a matter of the *Keldysh* paying her way ... If not even Anatoly has a contract with the Institute then it's hardly surprising he finds dealing with Orca difficult. The poor man doesn't make things easier for himself or for us by being *heavy*. His displeasure is heavy, his *bonhomie* and occasional good humour are heavy, his tactics are often those of a heavy, his consumption of vodka is not light. In his defence, his preoccupations are also heavy. His motherland is in a state of collapse, his wife died of cancer three years ago, his Institute is broke, the future of the *Keldysh* and his MIRs is in grave doubt, one eye is troubling him after a recent operation, he fears for his life back in Russia. And so on.

Schedules, messages, agencies, dates, contracts. I think there's not enough time to find these two wrecks, let alone salvage them. To be realistic is to remember that mantra about missing the *Titanic* four times, even with her precise co-ordinates. Why do Mike and company imagine that finding a possibly frag- mented World War II submarine can be done in a couple of weeks?

The geologist Misha (Mikhail) mentions casually (now!) that *MIR 2* did see a tin can the other day, 'sharp-edged and with very little rust' but he paid it no attention because it wasn't a rock. Andrea points out that if it really was sharp-edged it could argue World War II vintage, since rounded edges for things like petrol cans are largely a post-war development. It was appa- rently roughly gallon-sized. I hazard the idea that we ought perhaps to be seeing a lot of things like that on the seabed hereabouts – galley and other rubbish from all the US Navy craft like the *Bogue* patrolling the area for days. Andrea says she believes warships would have been under strict instructions never to dump metal rubbish in the water column in case an enemy sub picked it up on its sonar. I don't know; but I do know how people behave at sea, even when told not to.

Tonight the atmosphere lightens considerably. Quentin and

Roman Pavlov have been playing around with the rolls of sonar images down in the lab, correcting them for drift and cleaning them up electronically here and there. They've concentrated on the object that looked so likely from the first: the white lump about 80 metres long which the MIRs didn't visit because they were more interested in the now-discredited Mysterious American's position. They have subjected this image to various filtering techniques, emphasizing line and relief, and it certainly looks quite anomalous to the geology of the immediate area. The yearning eyes of the gold hunters can even pick out details. To them it's the *I-52*, bent but intact. That's her sail, there . . . How high's that bit, Quent? Twelve metres? That'd be about right for a conning tower, then . . .

Ralph comes down to the cabin and explains kindly that to an old hand who has spent as long as he has poring over sonar scans of the *Titanic* this is 'looking good'. If so, he'll need drastically to re-write his much-aired professional judgement that the *I-52* suffered catastrophic implosion and that we should be looking for a debris field. He has already begun this process: 'Of course, you gotta remember that Jap. hull was riveted, not welded, OK? We're talking World War Two construction here. It's not like *Thresher* and *Scorpion* [two US nuclear submarines which sank in the sixties and which had hulls designed for 500 metres.] Its maximum operating depth was only 100 metres. It would have sprung all sorts of leaks before the pressure could have built up enough to tear her apart. Also, she'd certainly have been badly damaged by those two Mk. 24 mines . . .'

We all gather around the blip on Quentin's computer screen and can practically make out the Rising Sun hanging limply from its stern in the stilly depths. Since people tend to see what they want to see, computer image enhancement, by making it still easier, is a boon to fancy. In any case everyone feels suddenly optimistic again.

Later Clive admits to having earned black looks from Sasha the Wireless Officer by whistling in the radio room. Superstition, wishful thinking, the fancies that flicker seductively about the supposedly hard edges of technological life, the virtually real ... They're all here in abundance. Pipe-dreams. Chimeras.

FIFTEEN

10/2/95

'The shit finally hit the fan,' someone remarks, playing laconic
for all they're worth. Last night at the 6 p.m. meeting Ralph was
rash enough to look sceptical about the green-shaded portions of
the map which represent the areas the two MIRs searched.
Headmaster Anatoly called him into his cabin afterwards and
'gave him a roasting' (Quentin) or 'shot me' (Ralph). At this
morning's session in the boardroom (Clive, Andrea, Ralph and
Mike), Ralph did his version of a *mea culpa*. 'It's true,' he said.
'I've not been on this ship for the last two years and I hadn't
familiarised myself with the work they'd done on the MIRs'
onboard sonars and I should have done. Anatoly was sitting
there with his six-guns drawn and I was sitting there with my
Winchester and crossed bandoliers ... I have to tell you guys,
when Simon gets aboard this ship at Dakar I really believe his
life is in danger. I personally could not guarantee his safety.'

There was a lot more of this 'Danger Man' rhetoric, repeated
often enough in the same phrases to suggest it might have been
used before, at similar junctures at dive sites around the world.
Poor Ralph's position is the immemorial one of being hoist with
his own petard. He has – how might one put it? – majored in
being Old Hand Ralph for a bunch of Limey greenhorns (or

something of that nature: he does frequently caricature himself), and is suddenly revealed as not having done his homework. This being said, he did have the courage and honesty to admit his error – one which, in any normal circumstances, would seem pretty trivial. Anyone with his experience would need to be a genius of self-restraint not to act loftily omniscient with a group of non-professionals for most of whom he evidently feels contempt. Still, his position is a bit equivocal. When he so curiously described himself to me as 'a perpetual bridesmaid', referring to his perceived role in life as photographic observer rather than scientific participant, he was being ruefully accurate. His mistake is to believe that by acquiring a degree of working knowledge about several disciplines he has graduated to the role of bride.

In this case he hadn't known the Russians had recently replaced the MIRs' onboard sector scanning sonars, or echo sounders, with a brilliant example of inventive ingenuity. They needed to improve the instruments' range, and the required equipment would normally have been vastly expensive. What they did was to take an ordinary Furuno commercial fish-finder, as fitted to any weekend angler's boat, do a little Roman Pavlov-style reprogramming, encase it in oil and bolt it on to the submersible. It probably cost them a couple of thousand pounds, if that.

Anyway, to an observer it often seems as though Anatoly is alternately sour and furious, leaving the Brits to be explanatory and appeasing. Ralph says Sagalevitch perceives Orca as 'a headless chicken', which is a harsh way to describe a killer whale. Clive, who is in daily consultation with Anatoly, refutes all Ralph's accusations point by scrupulous point. After all, Anatoly is himself directing operations so it is hard to see what could be seriously amiss. Probably the truth is that of a cultural divide.

And since Anatoly is a registered Orca shareholder it is hard to make sense of Mike's impression that both Sagalevitch and his partner Natalya doubt that Orca will fulfil all of its financial undertakings. Mike, who is beginning to look haggard and withdrawn, says he has literally spent hours with them this trip, both severally and together, and at the end of sociably vodka-laden occasions leaves with the feeling that at last they understand Orca isn't going to cheat them or renege on its agreements. Then the next day, he says, everything's back to the original position and he feels he has to start all over again from scratch. At first this sounds less like ill-will on Anatoly's part than cultural bafflement allied to all the other pressures he is being subjected to. But then one remembers that the Russians have a perfectly good understanding of the basic idea behind a contract since they themselves are always insisting on drawing up 'protocols'. These are basically documents designed to let them off the hook in case Orca later turns round and accuses them of not having fulfilled the terms of their contract. As soon as the search zone for *Dolphin* was agreed, for example, a protocol was drawn up defining the co-ordinates which all Orca members had to sign, as well as Sagalevitch and Bogdanov. One gathers that even among themselves the Russians constantly draw up these little documents for things such as equipment lent to one lab by another. It's a hangover of the Soviet system, no doubt, the arse-covering instinctive to bureaucrats the world over.

I'm sorry to see Mike retreat into his shell, other than at our daily ping-pong sessions. For an ex-policeman he seems easily injured, which might explain why he's ex-. He has done a lot for Anatoly in recent years, visiting him in Moscow, getting the *Koresh* built, trying to push business his way. It must indeed be hurtful (or plain infuriating) seeing Sagalevitch's apparent refusal to believe him – seeing himself, come to that, lumped in with the rest of us as just another amateur prospector. So . . . it has taken a little over a fortnight for a large group of adults to regress to that institutional hugger-mugger one first encountered at boarding-school at the age of eight. Gossip, rumour, wounded feelings, send-ups of third parties behind their backs, emotional overkill, people bustling self-importantly from cabin to cabin with the latest titbit, the currying of favour, the dread of displeasure: all the egoistic noise of individuals worried about their hierarchical standing . . . an edifice which collapses to dust the instant one sets foot on dry land. Extraordinary that so many people must live perpetually like this in offices, governments, bureaucracies, academia, churches, hospitals, armed forces, institutions and organisations right around the world. I was asked today in a rather pointed manner how I thought I might become 'more engaged'. Did they mean 'less disengaged?' I countered. Yes, dammit, that's exactly what they meant. Well, I said, the way I look at it is that I'm supposed to be a fly on the wall. That's my job description. I'm not paid to be a participant. In fact, I'm not paid at all. So my only responsibility is to take notes and try not to get underfoot.

So how interesting to visit Anatoly for an official interview at 2 p.m. I found him closeted with Clive, grimmish; but he was expecting me so there was tea and a plate of chocolates waiting. After Clive had left I asked Sagalevitch a string of technical questions about the MIRs and gradually the enthusiast took over and he began to sit a little lower in his seat.

His first sight of the sea, he tells me, was in 1958, when he was 20. He came to Moscow to work at the Academy of Sciences. At that time he was overawed by the pioneers of underwater exploration: by Beebe, Piccard, Cousteau, and then in 1960 by the *Trieste* dives. He never dared believe he might himself become a part of that world one day. As he says this he looks thirty years younger, almost a schoolboy. 'Maybe sickness,' he says, to explain his hero-worship. It's a knowing self-assessment. Millions of adults were reduced to school kids by the Moon landing in 1969; only dolts with hearts and brains of stone feel nothing for magic made real. Going to the Moon, going to the bottom of the ocean – what's the difference? If it was a sickness, it was surely a healthy one to catch. Gradually Anatoly himself learned to dive, became involved as an engineer in various research programmes, wound up meeting many of his heroes of the suboceanic world. He has met Jacques Cousteau, is friends with Peter Benchley, author of *Jaws*, and James Cameron who made the film *Abyss* and is about to make *Titanic*.

Russia turns out to have a long history of manned submersibles, with about fifty different types having been developed. The Ministry of Fisheries had a big fleet of them, so did the Soviet Navy. There are twelve in the Academy's history alone. Even the Shirshov Institute has had six submersibles. At this very moment, says Anatoly, there are more under construction, though their progress is frozen for lack of funds.

I find myself wondering – but not aloud – why it is that Britain, with such a remarkable and pioneering history in oceanography behind it, should never have shown the least enterprise in physically visiting the ocean depths. For an island race with the *Challenger* expedition behind it – one of the most fruitful scientific expeditions of the nineteenth century, and many would say of all time – it is surely odd that curiosity and our then-technical mastery should not have driven us to explore the seabed visually. Whatever skill we possessed seemed to go into designing submarines for military use, such as the *Holland I* of 1900, the start of one of the world's better submarine fleets.

But we left it to others to be pioneers of the true deeps (*Holland I* had a maximum operating depth of 60 feet, and even Second World War submarines were rated to no more than a few hundred). The reasons may just be circumstantial: lack of money, or the wrong stodgy person in power at the wrong moment. After all, in 1900 the Third Sea Lord had declared that even submarines were 'underhand, underwater and damned un-English'. There again, it may be down to something far more complex and cultural. How *do* nations choose what to specialise in? Sagalevitch, meanwhile, is being lyrical about his own designs.

'We put all our knowledge and experience into the MIRs,' he says. 'They were state-of-the-art, and still are. Apart from being so manoeuvrable, they're very comfortable to work in, especially compared to *Shinkei* and *Alvin*. And the rest.'

He ends by telling me that the dive he made two days ago with Bogdanov and Mikhail was long-planned, taking place exactly on the fifteenth anniversary of one all three made together in the Red Sea in *Pisces*. 'Time goes fast,' he says wistfully, no longer the schoolboy. 'Yuriy is sixty-one. I shall be fifty-eight.' He asks me about my own health. 'Heart? Blood pressure? Drugs? Seasickness? Because sometimes it is very rough on the surface.' Dare I begin hoping he'll expend a precious JUFO seat in a MIR on me?

I leave his cabin aware of having been in the presence of a powerful personality, one far too complex to get to know on a short trip even were it not for the stresses he is under at present. Our rapport will never be anything other than distant, which in this emotional bear-garden is no bad thing. Meanwhile, he dominates this ship like a capricious Bligh. The nominal Captain, Yuriy Gorbach, is a dapper, quiet fellow with a stateroom next to Clive's. He is a gracious man if one wishes to visit his bridge, and has a reputation as a Lothario. I should be interested to know how he and Anatoly co-exist in terms of the dynamics of command.

11/2/95

The trouble with modern treasure-hunting is that it doesn't *feel* like an exhausting activity whereby one gains riches by dint of superhuman effort. It's hard to shake off the R. L. Stevenson and Hollywood expectations: that at some point grizzled desperadoes with picks and shovels ought to do some really hard digging. Shared physical labour not only puts the idea of a common purpose beyond all doubt, it is an unequivocal and draining occupation. Filmically, the Great Moment occurs when the gang is too exhausted and dispirited to talk, reduced to grunting and going off to sit with black private thoughts in the shade of a rock, hats pulled fiercely over eyes, leaving one dogged fellow to go on labouring out there with his spade ... when suddenly there comes the hollow *clunk!*, the hoarse shout, the excited scramble as inertia is shaken off in a flash and the men come running.

This is how it ought to be. Instead, it's sometimes hard to remember on *Keldysh* that a hunt is going on electronically twenty-four hours a day, even as one is shaving or drinking coffee or staring out of a porthole. A small crew down in the sonar lab sits in front of a screen in shifts. It is wearisome and it is skilled, but it isn't labour. Later, there can be endless discussion and disagreement over blips on a print-out, but there is something invalid about debate and emotions which haven't been earned or grounded in toil. A group of scientists coming into a boardroom at 9 a.m. and 6 p.m. with neat rolls of sonar images is too bloodless a procedure to involve the nerve-endings. The gusts of animosity or assertiveness that play around the room from time to time feel self-indulgent and footling (and yet another reason why one never could believe in *executives*).

Today is Andrea's birthday. The Russians are shocked and intrigued to discover that she is about twenty years older than she looks. Maybe this, or gallantry, or the sense that some emotional repairs with Orca wouldn't be a bad thing, leads them to insist on there being a celebration after dinner in Clive's cabin. The place gradually fills and becomes cheerful. Two things lodge in the mind, apart from my own social woodenness. Viktor Brovko, the remarkable engineer who sits at our mess table, turns up with a present for Andrea of a sprig of lime tree in a pot, just coming into leaf. He apparently has quite a sapling growing somewhere below decks. I wonder if this is peculiarly Russian, an expression of deep yearning for endless *taigas* and deciduous forests, or else simply the refined sensibility of someone who values the sight of fresh, living green on board a ship. Andrea is very touched, as anyone would be by such a perfect birthday present.

The other unforgettable thing about the evening is Anatoly coming in with his guitar and an air of truculent roguishness – or maybe roguish truculence – to sing a song he says he has just spent the day composing (both words and music). This is not a birthday ode to Andrea but a curious, affectionate and satirical serenade to Quentin. It may be that something in Quentin's bearded and extrovert presence appeals particularly to the Russian character; or that he is the only Orca member who is a bona fide scientist with a doctorate; or it could be that Anatoly simply likes him. It hadn't occurred to me before but there is probably a category of people who have songs written for them, just as there are others who have their portraits painted. Most of us are resigned to going unserenaded and unpainted to our graves, wondering slightly about this small, élite category of

157

which Quentin is evidently one. Had he lived before 1828 and been a friend of Schubert's he would by now be an immortal, up there with Sylvia, Gretchen and the miller's beautiful daughter. However, instead of *'An Quentin'* or *'Quentin am Spinnrad'* he gets a Sagalevitch special called 'Inspector Huggett'. Why 'Inspector'? Anatoly is a jazz fiend and there may be a precedent I don't know about. In any case he pronounces it 'Hudjit' and sings with passion and ironic emphasis. He laughs sarcastically as he sings, staring into Quentin's eyes like a lover. The more it goes on, the more it is borne in painfully on Orca members that their enterprise is being not ungently mocked. It is, in its way, a work of rude genius and goes as follows:

> How do you think, Inspector Huggett:
> Where is a gold?
> How do you think, Inspector Huggett:
> Where can be sold?
>
> Golden adventure
> On this fantastic ship;
> Golden joint venture
> We go very deep.
>
> How do you think, Inspector Huggett:
> How and because?
> I'm very mad, Inspector Huggett,
> What is saying boss?
>
> Where's your science
> And where's your technique?
> How will you find?
> And how is it big?

May be couple ton, Inspector Huggett,
May be only one.
If I find gold, Inspector Huggett,
Get a lot of fun.

Drink all the wine
Around whole the world.
All girls are mine,
Because I have a gold.

I will buy a farm, Inspector Huggett,
On the end of skies.
I will buy a farm, Inspector Huggett,
Come to paradise.

Golden umbrella
And golden limousine.
My way is stellar
And I will marry queen.

I will marry queen, Inspector Huggett,
I will buy her ring.
I will marry queen, Inspector Huggett,
And I will be king!

My golden crown
On very stupid head.
Imagination grown
But brain's very bad.

I'm full of shit, Inspector Huggett.
How to be rich?
Where is a gold, Inspector Huggett,
May be on the beach?
Sure on the beach!
Sure on the beach!

Three weeks later, on the eve of our departure, Anatoly presents Quentin with a copy of this song inscribed 'To dear "Inspector" Huggett in memory of mad desire, never happen'. At the time, staring at a bulkhead with a fixed grin in order not to meet the singer's roving gaze, I remember that in American English – which is what Anatoly speaks – 'I'm very mad, Inspector Huggett' means he's angry. 'What is saying boss?' presumably refers to Clive. 'I will buy a farm' has to be Mike's ambition and 'Where's your science/And where's your technique?' refers to all of us. As I creep off to bed I find I'm pretty relieved after all not to be the sort of person who gets addressed in song. It seems to be rather a double-edged business when you discover you're a lightning rod for furious currents. Safer to skulk and take notes.

SIXTEEN

Things are happening but scarcely touch me. On all sides the
ocean lies, as it has lain day after day, calling to me. I stare long
hours into its rumplings as into a hearth, mesmerised by the play
of light. Sometimes it seems I can glimpse the bottom three miles
below as from an aircraft window: the hills and valleys, the
blackish outcrops among ochre dunes. At other moments the
ocean becomes a gigantic lens, the Earth's cornea, curved and
blue and staring into space. On such a surface the *Keldysh* is not
even a mote in the planet's eye. I yearn to jump in; I am too cut
off. The sea is well seen from a ship's rail but it is scarcely smelt
and little heard. Diesel fumes and funnel noise obtrude. Yet its
presence is insistent. It renders gold trivial, our expedition futile.

A small albatross once appeared; then a little petrel-like bird
on its unrepeatable flight path amid constantly shifting terrain,
darting into valleys and skimming temporary crests. Why am I
so bad at birds? I keep looking at bird books but can't memorise
anything. Why 'bad', though? How is it that a basically
eighteenth-century invention of taxonomy for natural scientists
should have turned into the drudgery of a moral obligation for
late twentieth-century lay people? This is not an argument to be
pursued very far, unfortunately, before it turns into a panegyric

for ignorance and the plain man who knows what he likes but can't put a name to it. Nobody as lazy as I am regrets more than I do the fact that things become more interesting the more one knows about them. This is itself a bore. It's even truer of people, who otherwise mostly look the same to me.

Afoot, then, are more hopeful-looking targets and, this morning, some sort of battle order for dealing with them. Tomorrow the MIRs will be launched once more. In one will be Quentin, Nik Shashkov and a co-pilot; in the other Clive, Burt Reynolds and his co-pilot. The two groups of targets are very far apart – up to 8 miles – and some others lying to the west will have to be dived on another day. In any case Clive's MIR is to set off about four hours before Quentin's, allowing him to get down to the seabed and find out if the big target is the *I-52* before the other MIR is launched. If it isn't, Quentin will dive on the other position and the two submersibles will slowly work their way towards each other. Quentin's sector also contains some good possible targets to look at, but what it really affords is a chance for some serious geology. Quentin couldn't be more excited by this prospect than a small boy about to be taken up in a helicopter for the first time. According to the scans there is an interesting basaltic ridge separating him from Clive's position. As it were.

Quentin and I spent some time with Nik Shashkov yesterday in *MIR 1* as it sat tethered to the deck. It's really like one of the early space capsules: a plain steel ball some 2 metres in diameter whose inner surface is largely invisible behind instrument panels, arrays of switches and controls. It's too interesting to be claustrophobic, which merely means I can't be a claustrophobe. Despite the restricted space I can see why Anatoly claims his MIRs are designed for comfort compared to other submersibles. The pilot occupies a well-upholstered seat in the middle. When he needs to peer through the biggest of the three viewing ports for close-up work he kneels and leans forward on forearm pads while his hands fall most naturally on to two small joysticks like gear levers. On either side of him are long strips of curved cushion which Anatoly calls 'couches'. The co-pilot occupies the left-hand one and the scientist or JUFO the other. Presumably they recline or huddle or assume a foetal position while taking exquisite care not to knock a switch. There are sick bags and piss bottles and a full medical kit including what Nik calls 'candles'. 'Candle' turns out to be the Russian for suppository (analogous to the French word *bougie*). We asked Nik what these particular ones were for and were rewarded with a hasty and bashful mime. Yes, yes, we said, we understand all that, but suppositories are only a delivery system. What do these deliver? But Nik didn't know or wouldn't say. Perhaps it's a drug for motion sickness. Or for a painless death when all hope is gone.

Both Quentin and I have the same kind of apprehensiveness about going down in a MIR, complete with proliferating scenarios of all the possible ways in which something might go wrong. It's worse for him, and not just because he's going down tomorrow and I'm not. He is a working oceanographical geologist who has been sending down pressure cases full of instruments to deep seabeds for the last fifteen years or so. He knows exactly the terrifying hydrostatic pressures involved, the precision of engineering needed to make even a simple protective case watertight, the frequency of failure. He has personal experience of the thousand and one unforeseen ways in which beautifully-designed pieces of equipment can fail. He is full of awe for the technical feats involved in building these submersibles. He's also unsettled to learn that at 5,000 metres he will notice a slight optical distortion of his viewing port because the acrylic slab – which looks to be about 20 centimetres thick – will bulge slightly inwards despite its taper. It's less than reassuring to be reminded that at 500 atmospheres solid materials can be extruded like toothpaste, as it is to learn that the entire steel sphere shrinks overall by about six millimetres. Obviously this is allowed for, just as Concorde is engineered to lengthen by several inches with the heat of supersonic speed, an allowance which even had to be designed into the cabin carpet. (Ralph tells me that the Lockheed SR71 'Blackbird', which used to be – and probably still is – the world's fastest aircraft, leaks fuel like a sieve on the ground and has to be refuelled in the air before going to its operational altitude and speed. Again, the leakage was designed in. At 2,000 m.p.h. everything expands and joints seal properly).

Still, the essence of the MIRs is not just that they're obviously brilliantly engineered but that there are two of them. With a spare submersible and the Russians' improvisatory genius, surely *something* could be done if one became stuck on the bottom? We know that one of the pilots' chief fears is of becoming entangled in a wreck. 'We should be so lucky as to find a wreck,' says Quentin bravely. I discover I'm not looking forward to the solemnity of watching him park his slippers in the cardboard box marked '*MIR 1*' and ease himself down the hatch. He faithfully promised his wife he wouldn't go down. Later, in the cabin, he looks at a packet of photos of his three boys playing on the sands at Weymouth last year. His eyes fill with tears, just as he predicted. 'I'm a real wimp when it comes to looking at their pictures,' he had said sometime during the second week. 'I couldn't have looked at them after only a couple of days out of Falmouth, I'd have been weeping like a baby.' Not only is it charming, and rare, to find an Englishman moved to unconcealed tears at the thought of his absent family, but it makes his present predicament still more affecting. He promised Kath he wouldn't go down in a submersible, but he's going all the same. He has no choice but to go. It's not a question of being macho, or even afraid to admit that he is afraid and thus obliged numbly to go through with it. The occasion has brought out of him that root certainty we all carry: that this isn't a dress rehearsal, that we have to take our chances when they're miraculously offered, that this is what he wants to do. 'For fifteen years I've been looking at samples brought up from seabeds. Now I've got the opportunity to see it with my own eyes. I'm a geologist: it's as simple as that. There are plenty of grand old marine geologists in the world who are better and far more experienced than I am but who'll never get the opportunity to go down. It's a one in a million chance. Imagine if I turn it down and then in a year's time I hear the MIRs have since done fifty dives and made important discoveries. What will I think? What a bloody fool I was not to go, to have played it safe. Playing it safe's a modern suburban disease. To hell with insurance. To hell with insulation. I want to see those rocks. Oh, and find that submarine too, of course.'

And if the worst does happen? What of the family? Here the adoring father and loving husband comes up with an authentic bleakness which is not in any way a denial of love but an admission of how things are. 'They'd get by,' he says. It's true, of course. 'They'd go on. They're not badly set up.' For the rest of the evening Quentin vacillates between doubt and decision. In a silence he'll suddenly catch my eye and softly go 'Pssss . . . !', the sound of the high-pressure leak which signifies the end, our standing private joke. Then he'll say 'Gotta do it, you know. I've got to go.'

'So much for the departing husband's solemn oath to his beloved wife,' I observe, playing Devil's Advocate as the game requires, a reassuring kind of flirting with arguments which pretends that he still might call the whole thing off whereas we both know the proverbial wild horses wouldn't stop him going.

'Bastard!' he laughs. 'That's really rotten. You know how to put the boot in.'

'No, no, they'll be all right. We'll pack the kids safely off to the Moonies and I expect Kath'll ... They don't have workhouses any longer, do they?'

'Completely below the belt ... '

'You won't feel a thing, you know. Ralph says you might just have time to hear a click.'

Away from these private moments are the public discussions about what to do if the submarine is found tomorrow. As soon as the first MIR starts talking to *Keldysh* on the acoustic telephone the US Navy will hear every word. The recordings will be duly processed and minuted and a report will reach someone's desk in Norfolk, Virginia. Somebody will look at the co-ordinates and say 'That's just the *Keldysh*. That Coastguard Orion got a positive visual ID the other day.' The *Keldysh*, of course, has been buzzed and eavesdropped on for the last thirteen years on oceanographical cruises around the world. Her activities and sound-prints are minutely known.

But if a MIR finds the *I-52*, how best to preserve for as long as possible the fiction that the *Keldysh* is here in this unpromising spot to do some geology? Well, don't start shouting over the intercom things like 'We've found her!' or even 'Target positively identified'. I suggest to Quentin that he use the phrase 'rocky outcrop' exclusively to refer to the sub. It has the merit of lending itself to elaboration. 'It's about 80 metres long, I'd say.' Or, 'It's fractured into three main chunks, which explains the sonar image, plus there's some scattered debris.' Or even, with incredible luck, 'There's also what looks like mineral deposits in the outcrop's lee. Could be a nodule field.'

This might fool them for a week. But the moment the MIRs start going to and from this 'rocky outcrop' day after day, possibly accompanied by metallic sounds of cutting which are not just those of manipulator arms putting specimens into bins, plus conversations which seem not entirely about geology, and those dossiers will be brought out again in the Norfolk office. A message will go to the Naval Ocean Research and Development Agency at Stennis Space Center asking what's so interesting on the seabed at these co-ordinates? Stennis probably won't know, which with any luck would delay Orca's unmasking for a further week. NORDA isn't concerned with salvage so wouldn't be likely to know what any professional salvor might. But somebody somewhere will eventually come up with the name of the *I-52*, and that will be that . . .

It all feels like counting chickens well before they're hatched. But tomorrow they might just find the broody hen, so it's best to be prepared.

Mike and Andrea tell me that if we find the sub, I'll have to muddy the co-ordinates and distances a bit in my account because to know that it was – for example – 9 miles from the official sinking position would be very useful to the salvage trade. This is because so few wrecks have ever been found at this depth and dating from this period that almost no figures exist for average errors. The *Titanic*, for instance, was found 5 or 6 miles away from the original search zone based on its given sinking position. To be able to make a general rule that co-ordinates as established by ships and aircraft in the Second World War were 79 per cent accurate, say, would enable interested parties to draw search zones of more limited diameter. There are good figures for shallow-water wrecks, but finding deep-water wrecks is a much younger science and nobody in the salvage business wants to hand out free information. Neither does Orca, especially if we find the submarine but can't reach the gold and have to go away for six months in order to have special tackle made. In this paranoid atmosphere it's easy to visualise Ifremer's smash-and-grabbers just waiting over the horizon to sail up and drop their 50-ton pliers.

There's nothing like gold for obliging people to think ahead while worst-case scenarios skitter in front of them. Except an impending descent to 5,000 metres in a Russian submersible, that is.

Downstairs in the ZVUK lab Roman and Brains turn out to be lively and subversive in off-duty mode. Brains has worked for the Academy of Sciences for over twenty years. He tells of the bureaucratic frustration of life in the Shirshov Institute. One scientist came up with a brilliant invention for some piece of equipment and kept trying to get the Institute to patent it before the West could steal it and make a fortune out of it. This, the scientist insisted, was becoming daily more urgent the less money the Institute could lay its hands on for its research projects. 'Absolutely,' the Secretary would agree, and did nothing. Finally the frustrated scientist got bored with sending minutes and protocols and went up to see the Secretary in person. He waved cheerfully to the receptionist, marched into the man's office, leant across his desk without a word and cut his throat for him. '*Swit!* – like that. Dead Secretary.' Brains and Roman collapse in laughter. What happened to the scientist? Nobody knows for certain. As a rule-of-thumb for dealing with bureaucrats it can hardly be faulted.

It's not just the language barrier one increasingly regrets aboard the *Keldysh* but the mutual diffidence we feel in trying to evaluate people when we all suspect everyone else of being at least as sophisticated as ourselves. Living in the sticks in Southeast Asia has taught me that much: the tougher and more needlessly stupid the conditions people are obliged to live under, the sharper and more subversive their wit often is, and the more inventive their ploys for whizzing freely about behind life's wainscoting. I yearn to tell Brains that his demolishing humour is appreciated for what it is, part of a survival strategy, just as I'd like to tell him that the necessary virtue of 'make do and mend' which helps him and his colleagues do first-rate science on a tiny budget really appeals to a vestigial Protestant streak in me.

The ZVUK sled has been hauled in and now sits dripping on the after deck. The stays of both vertical stabiliser fins have torn away. One fin was flapping against the frame and interfering with the sonar returns. Now the ship is retrieving the navigation transponders which were dropped the other day and will re-lay them for tomorrow's dives. The submersibles' hangars are full of activity as the machines are readied and everything is double-checked.

This morning some of the crew caught 'a large blue fish with a rounded head' which I didn't see and which sprayed blood over the ZVUK winch. It was apparently about a metre long. I'm surprised there isn't more fishing going on. Although Sasha the radio man has a rod and squid hooks he never seems to cast it. Instead he leans at night over the rail outside his wireless room, gazing down from on high into the pools of light cast on the sea by various deck lamps. At the sonar-towing crawl of under two knots I should think squid conditions were perfect. 'Kalamar' he says wistfully, but doesn't cast. I assume it's forbidden to trail lines and spinners when scientific equipment is deployed. By day the flying fish skitter and plane away among the wave tops, sunlight flashing on their aerofoils. To skip so breezily between mediums looks light-hearted and they always make me happy.

Quentin comes up from below to tell me of his growing rapport with Yuriy Bogdanov, the grand old rock-hound. He rather respectfully (for the geologist is maybe not quite as approachable as his George Brown/teddy bear appearance suggests) asked his advice on his forthcoming first descent in a submersible. 'I've known people who've gone down for the first time,' Quentin told him, 'but they never seemed to get much work done. I don't want to waste the opportunity so what do you recommend?'

Bogdanov was surprisingly firm. 'Nothing,' he said simply. 'Just enjoy it. I didn't achieve anything on my first trip, either. It's a great experience, so have a good time.'

So now Quentin feels free to go down and whoop and goggle and lollygag, and all with a curious balaclava borrowed from Andrea which he intends to fold up as a pad between his forehead and the icy rim of the little porthole. Bogdanov is impressed that Quentin is the friend of a friend of an American geologist – actually a geochemist – who has long been an idol of his own. I, too, am impressed that Quentin should never have noticed anything odd about this American's name, given the man's profession. It is Gary Klinkhammer. I quote him what Ruskin wrote in a letter in 1851, peevish at the growing rationalism currently sweeping the natural sciences:

If only the Geologists would leave me alone, I could do very well, but those dreadful Hammers! I hear the clink of them at the end of every cadence of the Bible verses.

Quentin is so pleased with this he rushes off to e-mail their mutual friend to forward this quotation to the Gary in question.

Later, he tells me there is an excellent Turkish geophysicist who uses airguns for seabed profiling. His name is Mustafa Ergun.

SEVENTEEN

13/2/95

This trip is wild; you never know what will happen from one moment to the next. At about 9.30 last night the *Keldysh* picked up a message from the Norwegian Coastguard saying there was a yacht called *Wanda* 120 nautical miles from us which had sent out a very faint mayday and would we stand by for an official request to go to her assistance? At breakfast this morning Andrea, who knows everything, explained none-too-patiently that of course the yacht wasn't Norwegian but the Norwegian Coastguard happens to have jurisdiction down here . . . He *does*? Here we are, a thousand miles west of Senegal, and it doesn't seem obvious to me that we should be in Norway's bailiwick. Still, come to that, what are US Coastguard Orions doing based in the Azores and overflying this area? Exactly whose coasts are they guarding?

In any case we were too far away to divert. But Quentin and I have let our imaginations flash up some quite interesting SOS scenarios. Had we diverted it would have scuppered today's MIR dives. Would we have abandoned all those expensive transponders now hanging above the seabed in a complicated pattern? Or would we have left them and picked them up later when we returned with the half-drowned lone yachtsman whom we can already see: a bearded Norwegian named Bent Persson? He would have to be kept aboard the *Keldysh* for the next fortnight at – possibly for – the doctor's pleasure; but what could he be told about this oceanographical research vessel remaining on station day after day while its submersibles brought up a steady stream of gold bars? 'You're not listening, James,' says Andrea crossly. 'I've just explained that the Norwegian Coastguard has jurisdiction here. It doesn't mean that the *Wanda* is Norwegian, nor that there's only one person in her.'

'Bent. Exactly. I can see the poor fellow clearly.'

But Andrea is not easily stopped when in explanatory mood. She begins with something like 'Under the terms of the Merchant Shipping (Peacetime) Act of 1967 ...' and I take refuge in imagining Bent clinging to the keel of his upturned yacht and wondering whether his last radio message got through to anyone with a grain of sense or conscience.

Naturally there's a certain amount of tension in the air today as Clive and Quentin prepare to go down. The first two Orca members, in fact, to be putting their lives where their money might be. It's generally thought that Clive's MIR has a real chance of finding the submarine: his is the most likely-looking sonar target yet. As the investors' representative, Clive could reasonably argue that none of this would have happened without him. But as the researcher so could Andrea, and both she and Mike have rather selflessly elected not to go down on this leg since they're not leaving the ship at Dakar and will have plenty of opportunity to dive on the *Aurelia*. Still, there's a feeling of the Orca team having suddenly been split between Those Who Go and Those Who Are Left Behind. I definitely feel left behind.

Another scenario, which nobody but an unsuperstitious ghoul would consider on this, the thirteenth day of the month, hours before his two friends are due to dive: what happens if a MIR is lost? Not physically lost, since with all those sonars and radars and transponders plus the second MIR that would be difficult. But yes – supposing the worst occurs and there's a catastrophic accident? Everything would stop. Orca would be aborted, all that investment would be forfeit. Quite apart from the three deaths, which would surely take the heart out of even the most avid gold-hunter, the remaining MIR would at once be 'grounded' while rigorous tests were done on the wrecked one to establish the cause of the accident. These would have to be carried out in Finland, where the MIRs were built. The psychological blow to Anatoly and the crew would be devastating. The aura of 'jinx' would confirm all their resentment at having been forced into vulgar commercialism in order to survive.

In any case the *Keldysh* would at once sail for Europe, abandoning an area for which it had produced the best bathymetric and sonar maps ever made: in other words with data of potential value for any other salvor who wanted to try his hand at the *I-52*. Orca might be able to sell it, of course. I'd bet the *Keldysh* would never return; but since there are so few submersibles in the world rated to 6,000 metres it's likely no one would, not for a mere two tons of gold (assuming nobody else knows about the *Aurelia* and her alleged cargo).

10.30 a.m. We have just watched Clive in his borrowed blue Soviet Union jump-suit climb aboard *MIR 2*. When he changed beforehand he seemed not the least bit nervous, but who knows? He's not the sort of person (either as the son of a famous psychoanalyst or as a professional lawyer) to let himself appear vulnerable. Actually, he looked vaguely heroic in the bright sunshine when he climbed up the curved ladder around the

MIR's midriff bulge and onto the top. As he shuffled out of his shoes he waved up at Quentin and me and shouted: 'Don't hog all the Madeira!' – a quality remark in the circumstances. His curly head disappeared, the hatch closed, he was swung into the sea. Lonya lithely performed his unhitching, *MIR 2* gave a great sigh of light green turbulence and was gone.

Down in the cabin Quentin says that ignorance is bliss. Yesterday Clive had asked him 'What's the pressure like down there?'

'Oh, about 7,500 pounds per square inch.'

'I see ... On *every* inch, is that?'

I think Clive's a good deal more witty than ignorant. Before going down to the uttermost parts of the sea it is stylish to show disdain for pressure. It's a way of getting his own back after a surfeit of Ralph's right stuff and Quentin's correct stuff. Not having that compulsion to visit in imagination every atom of the steel shell, the molecules in the acrylic windows and the glass droplets in the syntactic foam; not having to stretch his own skin around the outside of the sphere so as to sense each ounce of increasing pressure, Clive is maybe a little protected against a sense of imminent disaster. Moreover, he is plainly an optimist by nature. Things tend to go pretty well for chaps like him, so why shouldn't he be? He's off to find a submarine, not to worry about the million-to-one chance of getting killed doing it.

Well, old Clive will now be about half a mile beneath us as I write this. It's a weird thought. In the adjacent cabin, through our communal bathroom – which with both doors latched back is more like a lobby between us – Quentin is furiously rattling the keys of his computer in what he describes as 'therapeutic nerdism'. He'll be making his own dive at about 2.30 p.m. but doesn't yet know where. Clive's MIR is diving on target 19 first. If it turns out to be the *I-52* Quentin will abandon target 1 and join him there. The day has been allowed to acquire a make-or-break feel to it, which may be an error. Both Mike and Andrea have said they are convinced the sub will be found today, and that if it isn't we will probably never find it. Since both of them have been connected with the sea, salvage and diving for many years I take this as an experienced judgement. None the less, I think it's a mistake to make public declarations of the sort which leave you nowhere to go. If a blank is drawn today they will be in an equivocal position tomorrow. There will still be two targets to be looked at, plus the whole northern part of the search zone yet to be mapped with sonar. They will find this a dispiriting task if they've really given up hope. Yet what kind of fantasies does this suggest these supposedly hard-headed professionals have been entertaining? That within three weeks of leaving Falmouth we would have found a submarine which disappeared in three miles of water half a century ago, and be hauling up her cargo of gold? Just like that? It's all very interesting. Aspiring salvors with their dreams of daring ventures to bring up gold from the deep should not underestimate what an emotional business it is, how it unexpectedly forces people to acknowledge their own characters, their often paltry or peculiar motivations (no, it *isn't* just for money – it never is), to recognise how other people's temperaments are an integral part of the enterprise and no less important to the outcome than the expedition's financing and provisioning and all the rest of it. The only thing is, this personal aspect is so hard to predict in a group of people, most of whom only met each other weeks or days before boarding the ship. How ludicrous we all are; as unstable and opaque as the sea on which, it sometimes feels, we are aimlessly adrift.

Midday. In two hours or so Quentin will be suiting up. Like

the aircrew aboard carriers he has entered a pre-flight bubble: still in the world and functioning, yet apart. In a way he has already started the journey and is somewhere on the ocean bed near Clive. I restlessly wander the ship, watch the flying fish, rigorously censor out of my mind the premature image of Quentin's blue suit climbing the ladder and descending through the hatch, up the ladder and down the hatch, up the ladder and down the hatch as though trapped in a loop of film. Sometime before dawn tomorrow the loop will reverse itself and he'll be climbing up through the hatch and descending the ladder. Then after a pee (eighteen hours!), he says he wants Madeira for breakfast and to be reminded that he needs to phone his business partner Pete with a list of terse and vital messages: an old-fashioned voice-to-voice link which we know works and I can't think why we don't always use. Among the vital messages will be one to arrange air tickets from Dakar to London for himself, Clive and me.

14/2/95

Russians are just like Filipinos: they really want to know if I, too, celebrate St Valentine's Day 'in my country'. Who else would remember these pregnant trivia?

After watching Quentin disappear beneath the waves in *MIR 1*, I spent yesterday afternoon chatting to 'The Cossack', Lonya, who is 28, has a daughter of 6, and lives in Moscow when he's not aboard the *Keldysh* and dicing with death in the Zodiac. He loves it at sea. He speaks excellent English, was briefly a tank commander in Afghanistan and thinks the current war in Chechnya is lunacy. He says he earns about $600 a month on the *Keldysh* but makes up for it by being a partner in a series of construction companies in Moscow. Why a series? Because to encourage free enterprise such companies are not taxed for their first two years. On the last day before this concession expires, Lonya dissolves his current company and starts another. Moscow sounds perfectly mad, although part of the madness is at least readable in that people tend to stick to blatant identities. *Mafiosi*, for instance, only drive BMWs, whereas the merely rich prefer Mercedes. Lonya is a fount of educated sense and subversive cynicism. He tells me many ex-KGB officers have gone into fiscal enforcement (a bit like Italy's *Finanza* police), charged with the task of making more people pay higher taxes by firmer and corrupter means. Despite having relatives in the United States he denies the slightest interest in moving there. 'America is not my country,' he says firmly. 'I was born in Moscow. Moscow is my town. All my friends are in Moscow. I can get by.' Indeed, he gives off an aura of competence. He is tall and slim with a small blond moustache and – as people aboard of both sexes notice – cuts a dashing figure indeed, standing practically naked in the Zodiac as it leaps and prances among the waves, holding only a knotted rope tied to its prow. Youthful and heroic, Lonya provides a most necessary element of swank aboard this ship which, intellectually dazzling as its complement no doubt is, tends towards middle-age and stolidness. Chatting of this and that, he matches my own enthusiasm for Mikoyan, the brilliant Russian aircraft designer, by fetching magazines from his cabin full of cutaway drawings of the Mig-31 interceptor.

I ask him about the Anarchist. Lonya says his name is Sergei, and he not only reads poetry but writes it as well. What is more, from time to time he composes his own scientific reports in verse to relieve the monotony. My admiration for this man grows daily. If I ever do get a trip in a submersible I hope Sergei will be tending its hatch so that his calm, bearded face will be the last thing I see before it shuts and the first when it opens again.

Later, Lonya introduces us and I ask Sergei which poet he was reading up on deck the other day. He gives a shy smile. 'Joseph Brodsky.' Definitely my sort of people. A shipload of wizard technicians who read Brodsky and write their reports in verse ... I somehow can't imagine this on a North Sea oil rig, though with loners one never can tell.

Not a night for sleep. I was conscious of the empty cabin next to mine. By midnight I'd listened to enough spectral voices in the MIR lab; the acoustic intercom between Control and the MIRs, miles away beneath us, and the hollow echoes off the seafloor and the water column a couple of seconds later. Such ghostly sounds must be peculiar to communication under water, where radio is virtually unusable. Water readily absorbs radio waves, and even the low frequency radio used by the military for talking to its submarines fizzles out a few metres below the surface. The MIRs use a Finnish acoustic intercom called Comec, operating at 8kHz. The system uses considerable power. The transmitter takes the voice and bumps the frequency up, while the receiver lowers the frequency back down again. They say if one were swimming about outside the ship with one's head beneath the surface these conversations would be clearly audible in the water column as a high-pitched burble. None of this technical ingenuity prevented communications from being bad for other reasons (which certainly seems all of a piece with this trip's experience in general). The two submersibles were miles apart and often screened behind genuine rocky outcrops. There was little pleasure to be had in the dead of night listening to Control trying to raise Quentin's MIR over and over again and hearing nothing over the hissing loudspeakers but the ghost of the query flitting eerily past us after a 15 kilometre round trip. The sadness and emptiness of the deep which contained a silent friend was not edifying; better to go out and stand at the rail and be buffeted by wind.

I had a shower at 4 a.m., put on an anorak and went back on deck to see *MIR 1* return. Clive had meanwhile got back in one piece (but without having found anything that wasn't geological) at 1.30 or so. Out on the deck above the bridge it was extremely dark despite a bloated moon the colour of beeswax candles setting an inch or two above the horizon behind a droopy eyelid of cloud. Dark, too, despite splendid starfields overhead across which the masthead lights swerved like mad meteors. I paced from one rail to the other, searching for the luminous jellyfish in the black waters which would signify the monster emerging, but it was dawn before it finally surfaced maybe half a mile away to port. It was a moment of relief which gradually turned to impatience since it took *Koresh* nearly an hour to herd *MIR 1* safely into *Keldysh*'s flank. The submersible was swung aboard, Sergei himself officiated and at last Quentin climbed down, tousled and owlish in the early light and with a grin that wouldn't go away. He came and sat in my cabin and said to no one in particular '*Fucking* hell,' then repeated it four times fervently like a mantra. It sounded more articulate than it reads. He had clearly binged on a rich banquet of experience, although his MIR had picked up nothing more significant than a bottle.

Mike and Andrea are notably sober this morning, for predictable and predicted reasons. It strikes all of us as unfair that sonar images which looked suggestively like hard targets of a non-natural kind could so readily turn into undistinguished areas of pebbles and boulders or sudden juts of basalt. At the morning meeting it is agreed we should go back to 'mowing the lawn' with the ZVUK for another two or three days, polishing off the remaining northern sector and re-scanning the area where Quentin's MIR found the bottle. This is because they also spotted some other things including a piece of reddish fabric and some possible aluminium sheeting. They filmed the fabric but we won't see the video until six o'clock this evening. Quentin does say that in his experience it's suggestive to find three man-made artefacts so close together on a sea floor at this depth. The hope is they'll be the edge of a debris field, of course ... *The* debris field.

Andrea examines the bottle down in Ralph's video lab. She knows little more about bottles than I do but because of her professional relationship to knowledge she adopts a formal, descriptive approach to the object which, in any case, we're all looking at. 'Well,' she begins, 'it's, er, 30 centimetres tall. Dark greenish brown. Poor quality glass if you'll notice – lots of bubbles and flaws. Blown rather than moulded. The neck has a slight bulge in it and its bottom isn't flat but turned inwards ...' I am irresistibly reminded of a sketch the late Peter Cook did for a *Private Eye* record many years ago, purporting to be Arthur Negus and John Betjeman examining an *objet d'art* which turns out to be the flesh-and-blood Lady Minerva Threbbing sitting on a lavatory ('A rather large, seated figurine ... Late nineteenth century, you can see from the varicosy legs by Edmundo Varicosi who was active – extremely active – in this part of the world ...') I can add nothing to Andrea's description other than to suggest its shape is that of a Bordeaux rather than a Burgundy, but the fact of the matter is none of us has a clue. For all we know it's a Silesian stout bottle. We tentatively agree that it almost certainly dates from no earlier than 1850 and no later than 1920. But since it's the only likely artefact we've yet found Orca members perform terrific mental gymnastics in order to provide it with a plausible connection to a Second World War Japanese submarine. Later, someone will advance the theory that it might have been taken aboard the submarine by one of the three Germans as a gift to the Japanese commander from the U-boat's captain. In their desperation the most ordinary treasure-hunters can betray the fantastical inventiveness of second-rate novelists.

As the result of their dives Quentin and Clive have acquired a distinct mystique. *Been there, done that.* I'm definitely envious. Clive is either playing it cool or he was relatively unmoved by his experience. He certainly hasn't said, with Quentin's happy incredulity, '*Fucking* hell! What a *blast*! Those holothurians! After that, bungee-jumping would be a real yawn.' Both had the sense to keep written accounts of how they felt and what they saw at various depths. Quentin has read me a few representative paragraphs of his. I do think literate and emotional scientists make the best company in the world. His pilot, Nik Shashkov, had amazed him by taking nerdism to extreme lengths – or extreme depths. At about 2,500 metres the Russian had produced a laptop computer and begun rattling the keys in some navigation programme he'd invented. A thousand metres further down he terrified Quentin by suddenly opening the MIR's tool kit, selecting a screwdriver and a soldering iron, unscrewing a control panel and doing a little ad hoc rewiring. This is undoubtedly evidence of the Right Stuff, though the real thing is a little more prosaic than Hollywood likes to believe. Quentin, meanwhile, was wiping a trembling hand over his viewport and surreptitiously licking his fingers to see if they tasted salty.

'And did they?'

'Yes! I was petrified! Then I realised it was my own cold sweat.'

As infinitesimally the window bulged towards him.

This story gets wackier by the day. I've just been called to the bridge to listen to a nicely-spoken Frenchman on Channel 10 informing us in English that the *Keldysh* is currently in 'Navarea II', a danger zone they use for testing missiles. This fellow is speaking from the 'B. E. M. *Monge*', which turns out to be a mysterious white ship covered in bulbous radomes and golf balls shadowing us on the horizon. Anatoly explains over the radio that we're doing 'scientific fieldwork using towed sonar' and cán't be interrupted in mid-experiment. There's a pause for consultation. 'OK,' comes the reply at length. 'You may stay in the danger zone if you insist, but at your own risk.' When Quentin wakes I shall ask him if his own craftily-worded codicil to the insurance policy Orca has taken out to indemnify itself can be amended to include Exocet attack. In any case we ought to have a grandstand view since the 'window' of maximum danger opens at 9.45 p.m. and stays open until 4.00 a.m. tomorrow. *Il ne fallait que ça.*

Others are more suspicious when the Frenchman's parting shot is to wish us luck with our transponders and submersibles. There's a general feeling of 'Never mind Norfolk, Virginia. It's the bloody French we've got to watch. Their Navy's probably working for Comex [a big Marseilles-based salvage company], trying to chase us off the *I-52* to snaffle it for themselves.' Up on the bridge Ralph and Anatoly look at each other and Anatoly says 'I never mentioned submersibles.' Sometimes even salvors can take paranoia too far. Apart from the fact that the white *Monge* will have been listening-in to our transponders and the MIRs talking – they could hardly have failed to hear – there aren't that many oceanographic vessels in the world, fewer Russian, and only one *Keldysh*, which is internationally famous for its submersibles.

5.10 p.m.: But I start this sentence after a ten-minute stint on the bridge deck watching a French anti-submarine warfare aircraft with hardly a single marking on it make low passes over us. It then made some distant wide turns, probably dropping its own transponders, before heading away vaguely eastwards – presumably back to Senegal or some other Francophile country on the far coast of Africa. Even this seems to me no cause for panic. If they're going to begin testing missiles in a few hours they're surely obliged to establish that the area's clear of shipping. Personally, I'm glad they know where we are.

And now Anatoly has called an emergency meeting at 6.30 p.m. The long and the short of it (as we wearily foregather around the familiar chart in the familiar boardroom) is that he is going to capitulate to *force majeure* or, as Quentin calls it, Frog-power. It emerges that the *Keldysh* has since been advised by the French military to keep out of the area altogether for two days, and for irregular periods subsequently. Orca members are pretty much astounded by this. It will effectively ruin the rest of our plans for the *Dolphin* site. Time is already short because the unexpectedly stiff wind and high waves have slowed down the sonar scanning. If we're aiming to reach Dakar before the end of the month we need every hour we can get. There is, as Clive tries delicately to remind Anatoly, such a thing as a contractual period of time to be spent on this site. Quite right, says Mike with unexpected spirit. We're in international waters here, the French are hardly going to risk sinking the most famous etc., etc. Basically we should tell them to piss off and there would be nothing they could do about it.

Someone: Oh no? You don't think they might make things hot for us in Dakar if they wanted?

Someone else (not absolutely on the ball): How do you mean?

But the thought of Senegalese customs giving Orca special attention when dealing with the precious manipulator arm flown out from Aberdeen, plus the warehousing and clearance of sundry stores including critical electronic gizmos, is enough for the majority. Orca agrees with Anatoly to a rescheduling of the ZVUK scan, which now can't start until 4.00 a.m. when the French have stopped playing war games. It also agrees to reduce part of the target zone decided on this morning. Once the meeting has broken up and we're in Clive's cabin drinking the fast-vanishing remains of our case of Madeira the gloves are off. Apparently (and I'd certainly never heard this) the *Keldysh*'s officers knew all about these impending French exercises way back in Kaliningrad. Accusations of perfidy abruptly switch from the French to the Russians. *They knew all along* . . .

If it's a rich diet of soul-food for paranoics, it's good cause for amazement in writers. The longer this trip lasts the more I wonder who really knows what's going on. There is a constant sense of hidden agendas, of Anatoly playing games with Orca, of Orca having long since out-thought Anatoly, of every contingency coming as a temporary panic but of nobody being really surprised. Is this the way salvage operations are usually conducted? Mike and Ralph and Andrea would presumably say No, very firmly; but I increasingly suspect they are. In fact, much as the professionals would like to refute it, there probably isn't such a thing as a 'normal' salvage operation. I bet they're all like this, heavily plotted and run by characters who fancy themselves as can-do action men but who spend a lot of time shut moodily in their cabins, dreaming and scheming and spending the fortune they have yet to find.

8.45 p.m.: Did I say this trip was wacky? We've just received a three-line fax from the blanc *Monge*: 'Operation Navarea II has been cancelled. You may resume your work at once. Thank you for your co-operation.' So, end of that little crisis. You wouldn't need to be a genius to work out that the missile exercise would certainly have involved some sonic modelling by the French, and almost the last thing they would have wanted was a full-blown oceanographic vessel hanging about, listening and recording on every wavelength. The *very* last thing would have been the *Keldysh* retrieving some of their equipment accidentally-on-purpose with one of the MIRs.

EIGHTEEN

For the benefit of anyone who fancies the idea of getting together an expedition to search for something, I can now formulate a modest law: that no two people on any quest are ever looking for exactly the same thing. They may agree that they are, and they may fervently believe that they are; but they are not. Behind every grand project all sorts of unacknowledged caveats, designs and sub-desires are held in abeyance. Thus even a seemingly simple hunt for lost gold is to some extent a *pretext*. It is hardly surprising that differences and fractures become apparent between the participants, in an atmosphere emotional enough to affect the outcome. And now, three-quarters of the way through this first leg, this shipboard enterprise sometimes feels less like a single-minded salvage operation than a floating conspiracy: a conspiracy to conceal the varied agendas of secretive hearts beneath an ostensible quest for ingots.

The interesting thing about gold is its simplicity. It is desire, shorn of ifs and buts and concentrated in a single block. It is even more basic than money, which is a theoretical construct. Most people probably still operate on an interior Gold Standard. If you say 'I'm looking for some gold' no one will ask, Why? They'll ask Whose? or How much? or Where? An entire mythology enwraps it. It explains everything from base greed to noble quest. Like love, gold is its own explanation and its 'accursed hunger' (Virgil's *auri sacra fames*) sanctions all behaviour. People who believe themselves to be down-to-earth – Mike Anderson, for example – become impatient if one wonders aloud whether gold mightn't be something of a metaphor for pure longing, unattainable happiness, an epitome of that quasi-mystical economy of losing-and-finding which hovers behind our lives and seems to motivate all we do (jobs, loves, shopping, power). They will respond in plain-man, Johnsonian style by taking one conversationally to a bank vault, throwing open the door, kicking a heap of ingots and saying 'There, dumbo, you think that's a metaphor? That's half a million Troy ounces of 99.9 per cent fine. Try lifting a bar if you don't believe me.' But no; what we're hefting is nothing but a lump of dream taken from a heap of promise.

Such thoughts quite easily crowd in at sea as we lose the hard edges of life on *terra firma*, of the solidity we agree to accord things and purposes. Searching for gold lost beneath the waves fattens little worms of paradox and doubt. The blank, unmappable void which separates us from it is also that which sustains and keeps us afloat. It sets at naught our finest and most scientific calculations. If we do find gold, it will be chiefly through dumb luck, as every scientist aboard recognises. And is it really there, anyway? Anatoly asked that very question only this morning, suggesting that maybe the *I-52* had brilliantly tricked the *Bogue* and the *Haverfield* on that June midnight nearly half a century ago. But this only poses other conundrums (such as if the *I-52* did escape being sunk, what happened to her, seeing that she never re-appeared?). The question, Is the gold really there anyway? means something different. The sheer effort, ingenuity and expense of this enterprise lend a weary implication: Will it be what we hope it is? And once more it is possible to wonder exactly what would constitute an entirely satisfactory outcome to this expedition. 'Gold bars, of course, you idiot,' asserts the plain man with his customary truculence. 'Perfectly satisfactory, thanks. I'll take them, and you can have your speculations, and welcome.' But will the gold really have that exact quality needed to assuage everybody's desire, leaving nothing over? Or else is the void at present separating us from it more a version of libido, something fluid and unlocatable like sexual desire that tries, but never wants, to be satisfied? In short, is this entire quest a prolonged dream of pleasure, gratifyingly risky? Such are the ever-imprecise (but always accurate) co-ordinates at which treasure-hunters may be found, and at which they are excited to be.

15/2/95

At 6 p.m. we watch the videos made by Quentin's and Clive's MIRs. In terms of plot Clive's is the weaker since Quentin at least brought back pictures of the famous bottle being retrieved, as well as of the piece of reddish cloth they saw. (It's a pity Nik, his pilot, decided against retrieving the cloth itself. He was worried it might billow or tear and possibly cover one of the sensors on the outside of the submersible.) The most significant artefact of all – the piece of aluminium or whatever it was – was neither filmed nor collected because they overshot it and the swirl of sediment in their wake created an opaque orange fog in which it became lost when they turned back to look at it. These tantalising fragments apart, the seabed hereabouts looks unexciting on a small screen. No holothurians (sea cucumbers) were filmed, only an abyssal shrimp. A good few tracks are visible in the sediment, but otherwise things are on the desolate side. There is little deep current in this area and the deposition of sediment takes place at a very slow rate. Outcrops of pillow lava relieve the monotony: strange rounded nodules in the characteristic shape that molten lava takes when instantly cooled by sea-water. It all happened 50 million years ago. Quentin gives us a running commentary on the film we're watching, which leads to a short seminar on the formation of turbidites. One is never absolutely certain with Quentin that one's leg is not being given a tweak. He has been known, when offered a crumbly chunk of rock to identify, to classify it as fubarite. There is no reason at the time to doubt this deadpan piece of scholarship. Only later does one discover that the geologists' acronym FUBAR stands for 'Fucked-Up Beyond Recognition'. (I did check afterwards and found that turbidites really are bona fide sedimentary forms.)

Watching these short bits of video footage does not in any way salve my envy or otherwise diminish my desire to go down and see for myself. They are, indeed, a perfect demonstration of the camera's complete inadequacy to capture an experience. Since people nowadays tend to know the world via a little rectangular peephole – the twentieth century's camera obscura – it's hardly surprising they become bored and dissatisfied. What we were watching was actually momentous: the very first footage of a place never before seen. Yet it unreeled before us like something we might have goggled at a hundred times before from a suburban sofa, hardly more interesting than shots of a desert filmed at night by torchlight and at walking pace. Was it because Quentin is a geologist that he had come and sat in my cabin with his ecstatic grin, saying *Fucking* hell' like someone still in the grip of a powerful dream? I don't believe it. Something happened to him which was entirely dependent on being there and doing it, and what is brought back on film and tape bears the same relation to the event as the banalities of speech and writing might bear to a mystical experience. Certain things can only be lived, not eavesdropped.

16/2/95

Andrea is gloomy at breakfast. We're now coming to the end of our surveys of the *I-52*'s sinking zone and so far have nothing to show for it but a single bottle. She's worrying the evidence, shaking it, going over it again and again to see if we can be overlooking some glaring piece of data. She is the most painstaking person I have ever met, so that hardly seems possible. She has – how do I have the impertinence to say it? – the air of someone momentarily oppressed by the thoroughness of their own character. She begins talking about the Mysterious American and the unsatisfactory way in which the matter has had to be left unresolved. She says she can imagine meeting him in London afterwards and taxing him with his co-ordinates and watching his genuine amazement as he says, hand to brow, 'Thirty-nine degrees fifteen? Did I really say thirty-nine? Oh God, how stupid. I meant *forty*, of course.' The honest mistake, in other words. Or she can envisage our scepticism and refusal to pay him his $6,000 bonus as goading him into a fuller confession of his co-ordinates' provenance. 'What do you mean, the sub's not there? It was certainly there when the US Navy sent an ROV down to photograph it. You don't imagine they moved it for fun?' That sort of thing.

So this morning poor Andrea seems hung over by a private, itchy sense of unfinished business, unsolved mystery, data which can't be explained, the whole vague and slippery world whose physical actualities so wilfully refuse to conform with all the hard information on file about them. More than that, I suspect the episode of the American's co-ordinates, with its secretive aura, has begun to seem typical of something she perceives as radically unsatisfactory about the whole way in which Project Orca is being conducted. It is no use pretending she's happy about Clive's and Simon's roles. A casual observer, dumped aboard the *Keldysh* for a day, would be excused for thinking that where Orca is concerned Clive is the boss, the decision-maker who also acts as chief liaison with Anatoly and the Russians, operating through a series of Delphic meetings in his stateroom. Despite Orca's repeated avowals of the importance of democratic decision-making, the putative observer would probably never suspect that it was Mike and Andrea who were the original instigators of this project; that with the exception of Mike himself nobody outranks Andrea in terms of the length and depth of her involvement. Nor might they guess that Andrea is the only member of the Orca team with professional, hands-on experience of marine salvage. Not even Mike, for all his theoretical knowledge of the business (that irony again!) has actually dived on wrecks. On being informed of this the imaginary observer might well become a considerable admirer of Andrea's patience and discretion, of the way in which she is more often to be found in the cramped seclusion of her cabin working on the data than bustling about making executive noises.

Andrea's preferring to retire with her files has become more apparent as time passes and tensions increase. One of the reasons is that research is her job and, as already suggested, something might still lurk in the records that everyone has miraculously overlooked. But a still better reason is that she often feels her patience tried sorely enough to make withdrawal a judicious necessity. Initially, I believe, she and Mike relied on being old colleagues and now and then commiserated bitterly with each other over the manner in which their project had been so smoothly 'hijacked by the money-men'. They would even find an occasional ally in Ralph, who was also keeping himself to himself in his commissar's cabin while making pungent observations about Orca's 'unprofessionalism'. But Mike, too, began to retreat into himself as the leg progressed. These days when outbursts do occur, they tend to concern specific issues. It is not just Anatoly who has noted the Orca team's lack of professional salvage expertise. Even Quentin's presence aboard has been questioned by certain Russians because although his credentials as a geologist and sonar expert are impeccable, the fact remains that from a salvor's viewpoint he is basically an academic. The contention is that sonar work in salvage operations is a specialised subdivision of a skill, and being able to detect basalt outcrops on a sonar trace does not necessarily confer an instinct for spotting wrecks, which comes only from long practice. (Since I know no better, this sounds plausible to me.) The resentment being expressed is equally for the manner of Quentin's appoint-ment. It has been claimed that Clive and Simon met him, liked him, and signed him up on the spot as Orca's sonar expert without first consulting Andrea and Mike, who arguably would have preferred someone from within the salvage profession for their pet project. As the trip goes on, therefore, more and more of what are perceived as Orca's failings are blamed, at dissident moments, on 'the money-men's high-handedness'. 'So much for conferring and consultation,' someone remarked one disgruntled evening. 'About as democratic as a bulldozer.'

But in Andrea's case there is another motive for unease, one of more private origin. Hearing her accounts of an adventurous and mostly penniless life, it is impossible not to feel affection for someone who has had self-reliance so thrust upon her, whether or not it is what she wanted. Anyone may graduate in philosophy; far fewer have the knack of living their lives in a resourceful, independent and fatalistic fashion. I particularly like the way Orca's sole qualified salvage diver is also the streetwise and sympathetic person who used to help run a gay helpline in London. Years of being privy to the miseries and indignities that a society carelessly inflicts on the victims of its orthodoxy have given Andrea an admirable briskness with the establishment and its myrmidons. On this trip, at any rate, this surely cashes out as a mistrust for what it is that Clive and Simon represent, as well-to-do public school boyos with City connections. In her scrupulous way she resists *ad hominem* attacks, being friendly towards both of them as individuals. But she would be less than human if, as Orca's representative female aboard, she did not see them as domineering.

It really isn't a matter of personalities. I don't think Andrea knows Simon at all well; and as for Clive, she can easily see his charm while appreciating that, in his bohemianism, he is hardly anyone's model of establishment orthodoxy. But I suspect she remains wary of the class; and it would not surprise me to discover that she mentally rolls Clive and Simon into a single composite – as it might be *Slive* – whose loyalty to Orca's nameless investors is greater than it is towards the Project's originators. In the final analysis Slive is shifty, an old-school-tie adventurer who cuts corners with a knowing wink and whose real agenda is never quite revealed. Under the suave guise of openness he manages always to give the impression of keeping something up his sleeve. He is not someone you would instinctively rely on at thirty fathoms, and neither would one necessarily trust him in a boardroom. 'Slippery' is another word one could imagine in connection with Slive (though it is never used about either Simon or Clive).

So, do class and gender, too, have a bearing on whether long-lost gold is finally stacked up on deck in a wet heap? That terrible British handicap? It is something to consider. I also wonder whether Anatoly's resentment of us collectively may include a simple level shared by all the other Russians, which is that we foreigners are representatives of a triumphant ideology, most of us without even the claim to being as good at our jobs as they are at theirs. Communism was no personal fault of theirs, any more than capitalism was of ours, but the net result is that the Slives of the world are calling the shots. In such a context even a useless drone like myself can stroll about their ship, smiling benignly, a representative of the new order, a sort of Burlington Bertie of the sea-lanes. Again, this might make them no less professional; but who is to say sheer bitterness might not have its practical consequences?

18/2/95

Yesterday was devoted to politics. That is to say, to working out where we think the search for this elusive submarine might be extended in these few remaining days, and then selling the idea to Anatoly. The factors which must be juggled include the following: 1) We have to leave the area and head for Dakar by or on the 23rd at the latest. 2) We have already begun eating into the search time allowed for *Marlin*. 3) The Russians could 'write off' that time debt on *Marlin* by making a quick excursion for their own benefit westwards to Yuriy Bogdanov's black smoker site on the Mid-Atlantic Ridge. 4) It would be hard explaining to the investors how we gave up on *Dolphin* after only four MIR dives and with a central strip still left un-sonared running slap through the centre of the target area (a sonar fault in the early days of the operation). 5) It will take until tomorrow to complete all the scanning that seems essential. The turns at the end of each strip 'mowed' are now taking seven hours because more strands have snapped on our second-hand sonar cable and it has to be treated with extreme delicacy. If it breaks, *Marlin* will probably have to be abandoned altogether even if they did manage to retrieve the ZVUK.

This leads, at 6 p.m., to a final 'targets' meeting in the

boardroom with all the sonar print-outs laid the length of the table. The truth is, there aren't any really hopeful-looking targets left, though there are a few anomalies which are pretty certain to be quirks of geology. But at this stage anything is better than nothing. We want another twin MIR dive before abandoning the zone, if only to check more thoroughly the area where Quentin and his crew found the cloth, the bottle and the 'aluminium' sheet. On the other hand we can hardly expect Anatoly to send down his beloved submersibles just to roam about in the hope of seeing something interesting.

Sagalevitch, however, seems quite benevolent tonight in a satirical sort of way. Being no fool he realises exactly what the deal is and is obviously resigned to it. The Orca cause is made marginally less implausible when Quentin says that because of navigational uncertainty his MIR may never actually have found Target 1, which from the start was the most hopeful-looking of all. The upshot is we'll finish the remaining sonar scans, put down the transponders tomorrow, and have a final dive on Monday 20th.

Later that evening Mike talks about how difficult it is to interest potential investors in this sort of salvage work. His experience as an ex-Vice President of Salvimar and Subsal have not left him with much respect for either the knowledge or enterprise of 'money-men'.

'Do you know, I explained the technology of the thing and exactly what we'd be doing until I was blue in the face. And *still* someone asked me, perfectly seriously, "What happens if a monster comes and swallows up the submersible?" Honestly! I'm not joking! He really meant it. You've no idea how little your average punter knows about the sea. They expect to find a bottom covered in seaweed at 5,000 metres. They don't know the most elementary things about biology or physics. The truth is, they don't *want* to know. They don't want to make the effort and they don't feel they need to. Venture capital groups and pension fund managers tell themselves they haven't the time to understand the technology. They want to read a single-page outline and be able to grasp it at one go. They don't even know where to *file* a salvage project. The marine salvage business is in real need of funding, but I'm blowed if I know how to get potential investors to understand the technology, even at the simplest level. Your average primary school kid would be quicker at it. Until he grew up and became a money-man, that is.'

If potential investors could witness the blank we have been drawing in our search for the *I-52* it's easy to see why they might lose interest, regardless of whether they understood the technical stuff. As noted earlier, it's a very high-risk business and as such would hardly attract pension fund managers. To get it in perspective (using someone else's figures): it took fifty-seven days of sonar work to find the *Titanic* – a vast hulk lying on a bare seabed without rocks to distort the scans. It took a total of 487 days to find the *Central America*, using three different kinds of sonar simultaneously, twenty-four hours a day. (So far, its salvors have allegedly retrieved a single ton of gold in an extravagantly costly operation which has lasted three years.) And here we are on the *Keldysh*, having just completed our fifteenth day of sonar scanning of the *I-52* search zone and already running short of time, cash and patience.

NINETEEN

19/2/95

I am to get a dive after all! Andrea will be in one MIR tomorrow, and I in the other. To take proper stock of this honour all I need do is remember that to date there have been more people in space than have been down to 5,000 metres and below. I have to find some way of dealing with my excitement. I go up on deck and notice that in the old MIR tender (which the *Koresh* replaced) someone has set out tomato seedlings to catch the sun. They are planted in dried milk tins. They remind me of the lime branch which Viktor Brovko has growing somewhere below in full spring green. The sight of fresh leaves in the middle of the ocean is heartening and one can see how the Noah myth of the olive twig came about. The idea of a new universe brewing up over the horizon is almost believable. As it is, I'm reminded also of my bamboo hut in the Far East and my friends' habit of planting flowers around it in dried milk tins. Viktor told me the Russian word for lime is *lipa*, which also happens to be the name of a Filipino version of poison ivy, *Laportea meyeniana*. These connections with my other life feel like good omens for tomorrow. On all sides of the ship the rocking dazzle winks and beckons, just as the waters of the Elbe did for Anselmus in E. T. A. Hoffmann's *The Golden Pot*. Only in this case the swell is considerable and the lively breeze kicks up fluffs of foam from the crests which form and collapse and leave their faint marblings on the flanks of newly-heaped water. These are not ideal diving (or towed sonar) conditions, but since I'm not seasick I shan't mind being thrown about by a bit of surface noise.

In the evening there is a party in the sonar lab for the exhausted ZVUK team who have been on twenty-four-hour shift duty for days, staring at screens and charts and print-outs. Their part is over for this leg and they can now stand down. It is not long before they can't stand up. Anatoly brings fat bottles of vodka and his guitar. The benches have been cleared of computer terminals and are spread with roast chicken, cold sausage, and plastic bottles of *sheila*-and-tonic. *Sheila* is the Russian version of poteen, or the Americans' moonshine, or that Italian stuff – usually produced by monks – which is basically super-refined grappa, about 96 per cent pure ethyl alcohol. Not methyl, one hopes, though being aboard a ship of scientists gives confidence. Apparently there are several stills down below, each producing a *sheila* which its maker can identify by taste; subtleties of flavour which connoisseurs can easily recognise. The stuff reminds me of Dylan Thomas's description of grappa in one of his disgruntled letters from postwar Italy: 'It tastes like an axe.' Tonight the Russians claim boisterously that it is 'for men only' – something of a rhetorical gesture seeing that at the moment there's not a woman in the room. It's a reminder that this isn't supposed to be a pleasure, exactly, so much as a macho ordeal. Thankfully, since I'm diving tomorrow I'm legitimately restricted to apple juice and watching things develop. The ZVUK team are pleased that my awful stainless steel hip flask (a Christmas present) which I tied to the sonar sled has come back up impressively crushed, though still watertight, while Quentin is sad that his can of

Heineken fell off, thereby losing him a chance of winning a $20 bet with Ralph that it wouldn't implode but would become slightly wrinkled.

Three of the men connected with the sonar and winch teams resemble Rasputin: tall, skinny, bearded and with pepper-and-salt page-boy mops. They are splendid company, even though under the influence of *sheila* their little English falls apart and my non-existent Russian is stillborn on apple juice. Soon Anatoly starts singing to his guitar: this time not a satirical poem at the expense of 'Inspector Huggett' but Russian folk songs in which everyone joins. They are all in E minor and couched in terms best described as heroic misery. The nearest Rasputin translates as they go. 'From Baikal-Lake this . . . My father in prison . . . My brother in Siberia in? Yes, han'cuff . . . My mother sick . . . My sister get baby no father . . . ' He takes me passionately by the hand and examines my face anxiously through the *sheila* fumes. I want to tell him that it's perfectly all right; that we, too, have people like that. We used to think of them as problem families though nowadays I expect they're called 'differently-advantaged progenitive units' or something. I can tell by the tears in his eyes that Rasputin and I understand one another perfectly. Not long afterwards I sidle off to bed. Tomorrow I'm to spend up to eighteen hours among the roots of the sea looking for a Japanese submarine. I hear later that the party became a lot wilder after I left, which I'm quite used to hearing, and that the folk songs switched to a major key and became hilarious and thigh-slapping.

20/2/95

8.00 a.m.: Briefing. I'm to be in *MIR 1* and launched at 9.30. It all seems oddly casual from inside the MIR lab. My pilot is Viktor Nishchcta, whom I've not met but often noticed because he's a dead ringer for my old Filipino friend Romy Parreño. So I start out by thinking I already know this total stranger and – in another incarnation – have spent many an evening in his company drinking ESQ rum and eating stewed dog. But better still, my co-pilot is ... the Anarchist! I will now solemnly undertake to think of him by his proper name, Sergei Smolitskiy, but it may not be easy. To be going to the seabed with this wonderful figure who writes his reports in verse is pure icing. I've just been handed a flameproof jump-suit rather too small for me so will wear Quentin's overalls with the Geotek logo that shows up so well on Ralph's videos. We do our bit. If there's a *crise* three miles under the ocean in which flameproof clothing would be useful, I doubt it mattering much what I wear.

A morning of astounding summery beauty. I suit up and stand talking and being photographed out on the MIR deck as part of Ralph's visual record. Clive and Quentin are about to present me with half a one-dollar bill to take with me (and which has already been down with them) when Anatoly suddenly snatches it, tears it up and drops the fragments over the side. 'Very bad luck, taking money to that place.' Never take pornography into a cathedral, his tone says. While this piece of superstition is being aired the *Keldysh* is joined by two elegant seabirds: narrow albatross wings with a central dark band, white body with a long thin tail more like a single trailing plume. Possibly some species of tern, but I know I shan't have the inclination to look them up. We haven't seen a bird for a fortnight, and here out of the blue come two glaringly obvious omens which I'm taking as inspirational rather than valedictory.

One thing I only discover much later is that *MIR 1* is already being referred to as 'the writers' MIR'. Viktor Nishcheta graduated in literature first, then went and took another degree in electronics, wise man. Thus we all three of us have pretensions to being connected with quills and ink and possibly even soulfulness. I therefore determine that any published account of the next eighteen hours or so will be exactly what I wrote at the time and not embellished with fragrant *aperçus* as they occur to me later. If there *is* a later. Actually, amid the gallows humour with Clive and Quentin my main apprehension is whether or not I shall last out the dive without having to pee. This must be far worse for Andrea. It was blushingly made clear to her yesterday that the MIRs are equipped only with 'male' pee bottles, and would she be embarrassed to, er, well, in front of two men? The Russians are oddly prim and she replied cheerfully and stoutly that *her* worry was of being a source of embarrassment to them, she being perfectly capable of dealing with her own bladder in whatever company. She is splendid. These things have to be thought about.

10.10: Inside *MIR 1*. Our hatch man removes the conical polythene ring that protects the polished steel face of the rim. The hatch closes on a blue tropical sky and Viktor locks the lugs from within with the central wheel. All exterior sound ceases. Isolation begins. Viktor and Sergei are busy with the pre-dive checklist. It's very hot and cramped and sweaty.
10.15: We're swung out over the side. Even the crane's groaning hydraulics are inaudible. Departing faces: Quentin, Clive, Andrea in her blue jump-suit. She'll be diving in about half an hour. Blue water rushes up over the viewing ports, which are angled downwards. Swell, rocking. Colour and light values are those of a theme-park aquarium. Silvery bubbles, shafts of light as a window rolls partially clear. No fish.
10.30: I've missed the moment when Viktor took on ballast and we began to sink. So many switches being clicked, acoustical

telephone crackle from the loudspeaker, general hummings and whooshings.

113 metres. The blue outside my little viewport is of a glowing dusk. It has lost the surface milkiness like rosemary in bloom and is now more the colour of delphiniums. This was the maximum operational depth of most Second World War submarines; 377 feet and there's still light outside. I don't know why that's so affecting.

218 metres. Past twilight to late dusk. Surprised there's any light outside, but there is. Wish I'd been able to do this before writing *Seven-Tenths*, especially the 'Reefs and Seeing' chapter. I also wish they'd turn the lights off inside. The sea's intense violet colour is strangely piercing and I think would steep even the MIR's interior. It's a quality of light I've never quite seen before. It doesn't exist on the earth's surface and perhaps can't even be produced artificially. It does something to the mind which feels like faint genetic meddling. The crew are fettling up Clive's computer, now programmed by demon nerd Nik Shashkov to help us navigate. The Anarchist is wearing his beret, which is the king of its species with a wick on top as thick as a slug of goose shit. From time to time he fluffs out and then preens down his magnificent beard, using the back of one paw like a cat. He catches my eye and smiles. Nothing bad can happen with the Anarchist aboard.

265 metres. I remember that an emperor penguin was once recorded at this depth on an eighteen-minute dive. A bird looking for fish at 870 feet.

10.37: *300 metres*. Midnight outside. In other words still not absolutely lightless. I really got that wrong but there's so little on record to go by. No sensation of falling, though there wouldn't be since we've long since reached our terminal velocity of 30m./minute. Silence. A tiny bead containing us, sinking into night. Like Quentin before me I think of the *I-52* beginning to break up at this depth. At nearly 1,000 feet its rivets would have begun popping and welds tearing. Watertight bulkheads imploding. Black water slamming into every secret recess and compartment, including wherever the gold was kept. Bodies in fragments; some open mouths. We cruise serenely on past, having scarcely begun.

364 metres. The first phosphorescent grains stream upwards beyond the viewport. It's like night diving in the archipelago, familiar and reassuring.

400 metres. It is no longer possible to distinguish the black overhang of syntactic foam (somewhere above us like the MIR's eyebrow) from the surrounding sea – i.e., to my eye all ambient light has gone. Possibly not to someone thirty years younger, though, and certainly not to squid and all the other biota of the Deep Scattering Layer which migrate up and down the water column daily. Viktor sucks toffees and exchanges jokes with Sergei who strokes his beard and plots our course.

10.55: 800 metres. For me this represents some kind of grand climacteric, a psychic barrier, in that it's the point Beebe and Barton reached – half a mile or so – in 1934 off Bermuda. Beebe was my boyhood hero. He was then 57; I'm now 53. It has taken a long time. Luminous granules still drift upwards, sometimes eddying around the viewport's frame like the lone snowflakes that presage a long storm.

871 metres. Now a few green banners slide past; faint phlegm studded with stars. The crew are communicating with Control about the computer, joking. Their voices and laughter are beginning to echo as they bounce around the water column.

922 metres. Not banners, but sacs containing fiery points. Siphonophores?

11.04: 1 kilometre. Condensation beginning to bead around the edge of the hatch overhead. Hope it *is* condensation. Quentin said that on his dive Nik Shashkov ran his finger around the connectors where they enter the sphere, then licked it to taste for salt. It's too late to worry. Anyway, water has been known to leak around the edges of *Pisces*'s windows at low pressure, though it stops as you go deeper. They, like the MIRs', are not conventionally sealed. This dry seating of tapered acrylic into steel is technically known as an 'interference fit'.

11.11: *1,210 metres.* More jellies sidle upwards, one like frozen smoke, another a snake outlined in green dots like a Greek constellation. Hoffman's Anselmus again and Serpentina and tokens of nameless love. A slow, upward shower of fragments of light.

11.20: *1,461 metres.* The sphere is cooling rapidly. I've just put on another two pairs of socks.

1,517 metres. Oh, the far constellations that enwrap us all the same!

11.42: *2 kilometres.* Still a few sparks and jellies.

11.50: *2,240 metres.* The wandering granules seem to be sparser. As always, one wants to know what it is one *can't* see. Astronomers have their hypothesis of 'dark matter' to account for interstellar stuff they can't observe and without which their sums won't come out right. Down here in this placeless place one wonders about the mass of creatures which don't operate at our wavelengths, that must rely on infra-red and pheromones and sounds, to whom this world is no 'darker' than that of a bat. Placeless, because no matter how still and suspended the layers seem through which we're descending, each molecule of water making up this 'place' is in motion and sooner or later does get its chance to see the sun. They say it takes 250 years for deep water to come to the surface and another 250 for it to sink back down. Everywhere these huge, slow, invisible wheels turning.

Caught up in them, we ourselves are nowhere: just at a set of co-ordinates which not even Sergei could precisely define with Clive's computer on his lap.

12.10: 2,730 metres. In the last 500 metres we've had lunch: a plastic box each of rolls, cheese, salami, a gherkin and a steak sandwich. Plus hot, sweet coffee in a stainless steel thermos. Apples, chocolate and peanuts to come. The language barrier has been partially solved. The Anarchist speaks German about as well as I do, Viktor marginally less so. All three of us know peanuts as *Erdnüße*, so communication is possible. I'm really sorry I can't understand their jokes with Control. '*Wörterspiel*,' says Sergei regretfully. No decent pun could survive translation via two languages.

2,891 metres. The granules seem to have stopped but a faint ghost just passed us like a wisp of interstellar gas.

12.20: 3 kilometres. There's now a long echo when Viktor talks to Control. Acknowledging their last reply, he always signs off with a double press of the 'transmit' button on the microphone. We can hear the two pings clearly on the loudspeaker, like the soundtrack of one of those submarine warfare films. Three kilometres is a meaningless measurement; it could as easily be three thousand. Despite the communications, the glowing computer maps, the sonograms and all the bright switchgear, we're surely lost. Descending without the sensation of descent, beyond reach. Quentin said that passing 100 metres had made him sad for the submarine: that in some unfair way he was stealing a march on that doomed object of half a century ago, soon to be full of water and the collapsed bodies of nearly a hundred young men. That was 300 feet or so. Maybe as a significant figure 300 is to him what 47 is to me: my father's age at his death, the sense that each year by which I go beyond his span is a way of leaving him behind. How fascinated he would have been to sit in this tiny capsule now – he who barely lived to see Sputnik and maybe the dog Laika but not (by seven years) the first Moon landing. And his son – this half-recognisable man now his senior by six years – scribbles and jots and gazes at 3,480 metres, drifting down into nowhere and belonging to a time zone we could call Primordial Galactic, where years as humans recognise them thin out and vanish in a long oblivion.

13.05: *4 kilometres.* Extremest night for considerable stretches, but sporadic dim spores still straggle past. Something bursts against one of the camera brackets outside the viewport and for a frozen moment resembles the tenuous envelope of a supernova millions of light years distant. I suddenly find I can remember the name of the people from whom my parents bought the house I grew up in, in 1948, when I was seven. They were the Harbrows. A name from nowhere, to nowhere, and for no reason. Viktor's voice, enquiring about the Furuno sonar, bounces and fades away as through an endless gallery of metallic baffles, lost on the edge of no known universe.

13.15: *4,212 metres.* Viktor turns on the exterior lights to test them, making of the solid blackness a milky violet fog with a light upward snow of particles. These all appear to have red right-hand edges, a trick of the viewport looked through at an angle. I also remind myself that the optical properties of the tapered acrylic block change as it deforms under pressure (here about 7000 p.s.i.). Lights off again. The visual equivalent of sudden silence.

13.23: *4,400 metres.* Polythene bags of thermal clothing are pulled from various holes and compartments. Struggling into a one-piece padded suit without knocking one of the vital switches is like trying to get into a sleeping bag while lying in a crystal coffin.

13.28: *4,507 metres.* Still an occasional spark keeping us company. The Furuno gives 271 metres to the bottom. It's very cold.
13.55: Exterior lights on. For the first time Viktor kneels forward and leans at the controls beside me. We stare out through the milk. Faintly, faintly, a green lunar surface forms below. An asteroid is swimming upward to meet us.
13.58: *4,828 metres.* Touchdown. Level sediment. A tiny crab scuttles. Otherwise nothing stirs but the heart. Either tears or condensation on my window. I wipe vigorously. I'm looking out over a patch of planet never before seen. Since we're in a sphere, Viktor and Sergei are also looking out of their ports at a view which scarcely overlaps; three people in a single eyeball but with three distinct visions. Nor have the inhabitants of this planet ever seen such lights as the MIR sheds as it squats among the million wormcasts, blazing with energy at all sorts of wavelengths. Everywhere are the tracks of living creatures. A large white fish comes in slowly, head down, from the edge of our penumbra to investigate. It's probably 2–3 feet long with a heavy catfish fore-end and an eel-like tail. Close up, it somewhat resembles a large albino tadpole with scales. It has eyes with two dark markings in front of them which might be infra-red or other sensory organs. Is it attracted by our light? Sound? Smell (molecules of hydraulic oil)? Viktor moves a joystick and we glide off just above the surface at a brisk walking pace. Hardly any motor noise. More like ballooning. Large, blackish-red holothurian with fleshy plume on its back, *Pseudostichopus.* Beautiful red prawns, some the size of langoustines and with jewelled eyes whose retinas sparkle in our lights, beetle past in mid-air (so it seems) on feathered oars. A white/grey starfish. Again I think of night fishing on the sediment beyond the reefs, familiar and friendly.
14.30: There are a lot of floating particles in the water column.

Quentin's wrong: it isn't just muck kicked up by the MIR's propellers (as he explained some of the 'snow' on the video pictures of his own trip). Down here we're at the benthic boundary layer, where water column meets seabed. Much of the suspended matter drifting past our lights is resuspended partly as a result of the almost imperceptible current but mainly because of the activities of the various fish and animals. It's a slow, infinitely languid world. The particles are known as 'nephels'. (The word derives from the Greek *nephele*, meaning a cloud).

14.55: We're going round and round on the spot in a whirling ochre fog of our own making while Sergei tries to work out where we are. Occasionally we tack off in one direction or another into the clear, sometimes coming upon our own skid marks in the sediment like UFO tracks on some benighted American desert and giving a similar superstitious jolt that perhaps we aren't alone down here.

16.05: Our target turns out to be a dune. They're very steep, with sharp crests one imagines would have been slumped and flattened by currents and general erosion. Not so. A black, straight line appears ahead – looking amazingly like the edge of a submarine's hull if you happen to be keeping your eye open for one – and the sediment falls steeply away into an abyss. Once we're inside the valley we lose the signals of our navigation beacons which were laid in a pattern of three over this area before we came down.

How benign it feels here! I should like to come and live in a perspex igloo to watch just how the shrimp and fish and floating jellies and echiurid worms co-exist, minding their own business so successfully in this most un-barren place. Almost no scientist ever gets to see what my eyes are so greedily devouring. How, for instance, did Heezen and Hollister write their great descriptive textbook *The Face of the Deep* as early as 1971? So many species remain unidentified, so many behaviours unexplained. Everywhere in the sediment are spoke burrows: a central hole surrounded by a 'clock face' of grooves made by the worm whose burrow it is when it flicks out a tentacle or proboscis and hauls in anything which happens to have settled on that patch. But how does it know where it has flicked before? The intervals of the spokes don't form a precisely regular dial, and some are shorter than others, but none ever seem to overlap. Why not? Come to that, there are many tracks in the sediment which are dead straight. How does an animal make a dead straight track in total darkness? No one knows.

16.17: I wonder what it smells of out there.

16.21: I like the silence. Ralph says he plays *The Ride of the Valkyries* at maximum volume on his dives, blasting it into the water column to 'freak them out a little up there'.

16.25: Viktor says, as if to set my mind at rest, '*Wir haben Pipi-Flasche.*'

16.30: Freezing, streaming metal surfaces. My toes, pressed up against the sphere, ache with cold despite three pairs of socks. The temperature out there is currently 2.31°C. There must be a pocket of particularly cold water; it's normally a pretty uniform 4°C.

17.00: *It isn't the sea.* 'The sea' means nothing here. It is not where we are.

4,938 metres. Neither does it feel like an 'abyss' or the bottom of anything; it feels like a planet taking place in the head. Nor does it feel contiguous with the nearest continent, unlike Madeira with Cornwall. You can't imagine this surface ever becoming fields or underlying the low, earthen towns of Africa.

18.00: Another matey snack. How does the time go so fast? Viktor drinks only UHT milk from the carton (Lancashire Dairies. Little did it think, the day it was packed in Clitheroe or somewhere, that it would be drunk at 4,791 metres beneath the Atlantic.) He explains that what he *really* likes is UHT milk and Pepsi, mixed 50/50. Is this bizarre admission designed to encourage further confidences? We have a brief conversation about Boris Yeltsin's future and gang warfare in Moscow, where both he and Sergei live.

19.05: No submarine anywhere. We encounter an obviously modern tonic water bottle. Otherwise nothing but the plains and dunes of this marvellous land. I can't believe we've been down for nine hours though it's true that, if asked, I wouldn't be able to guess how long had elapsed. More than twenty minutes and maybe less than twenty years. Not an instant's self-awareness, so not a moment's boredom. The sphere, despite having shrunk 6 millimetres overall seems to have expanded. It's now a large room, a gliding observatory, in which I spend long hours quite alone.

19.41: My birth-year, by chance. I've never encountered a landscape which has conveyed such a strong impression of happening *inside* the eye. Notions of some impartial, objective, 'scientific' gaze have never seemed flimsier, less likely. The darkness, our wandering spark of light, the randomly unrolling view of a world happening without me and yet in me, the clear bursts of memory it triggers so that lying on the sand beside a holothurian I saw the name of a schoolfriend I'd loved when we were both about eleven – 'one of those sterile but exquisite attachments of boyhood, when nothing is done, nothing even said; and everything taken for granted,' as Norman Douglas puts it. A name I'd thought clean forgotten. Yet there it suddenly was, as though incised in the sediment. No wonder this land feels so benevolent: it's been here all along, and so have I. More and more I can't *not* believe in a form of genetic memory. Those millions and millions of years spent in this land before we were driven ashore by predators: surely they must have left their mark? Something that may not even show up as a collection of codons in our DNA but which the complete genome gives off like a whiff of brine?

19.57: This seafloor is really riddled with echiurid worms. I suddenly remember digging for lugworms at Swanage when I was eight. I also remember a far more recent claim that all sorts of radioactive waste including plutonium gets locked safely into the sediment around the various outfalls of Sellafield. British Nuclear Fuels Ltd.? Nirex? Whoever made the claim didn't know – or hoped the public doesn't know – that echiurid worms like *maximillaria* simply kick it all out again.

20.20: Too much sweet coffee. Having a pee at 4,872 metres, the first in eleven hours, is fabulous. Sooner or later someone's going to say what a pity it was that I didn't happen to dive on a more photogenic site (no black smokers, not even the foothills of an underwater alp). The point about alps is that they are more impressive thought about than viewed by torchlight. You can't see things at any distance under water. Water so readily absorbs light that the sea's topmost 10 metres filter out roughly 90 per cent of daylight. Down here maximum visibility with all our exterior lamps on is indeed about 10 metres. There are no panoramas on the seabed. The very nature of sea-water is to make one concentrate on detail: a patch of minerals, the tightly sinuous track of an enteropneust, a single spoke burrow, the light organ of a shrimp. To some extent the observer in his submersible *becomes* a microscope, peering through a thick acrylic lens set in a narrow tube of illumination, with the entire ocean's surrounding black rigidity forming the body of the instrument. It is said of the nineteenth-century poet Annette von Droste-Hülshoff that she had a peculiar optical condition which gave her extraordinary close-up vision. Her friend Levin Schücking described her 'almost conical eyeball, such that when she closed her eyes one could see the pupils glitter through her delicate lids'. She would wander the shores of Bodensee examining minute shells and grains of sand whose details were lost to any normally-sighted person. They were her worlds within worlds which enraptured her and afforded such a contrast with an outwardly uneventful, even grey, life. Maybe seabed studies should be approached in a similar manner, as being the more intense and focused for their apparent restrictedness, the more ravishing for their seeming drabness.

20.45: A sack lying draped over a worm hill. We back up, hoping to see Japanese characters on it, for there is writing of sorts. Close up, I can see it's English. '*Kartoffeln*,' I explain. They laugh. It's one of the sacks of spuds the *Keldysh* bought in Falmouth.

20.51: I'm not misled by the shadows things cast: the inch-long sperm (some creature's fry) swimming tremulously past one of our halogen lamps makes a boa writhe across the sediment. Fish hang in twos: the animal above, its shadow staggered below, both moving together and apart with the MIR's passage. I'm used to this after years of seabed spear-fishing by torchlight, knowing how shrimps can look like lobsters, how monsters duck behind rocks as you pass over them.

21.36: *4,978 metres*. We've been recalled by Control; our search is over. I feel sorry for Mike. I feel sorry for expectations. I feel sorry for those vanished men in their craft which might almost have dissolved completely away for all we've found of it. But what a land in which to leave your dispersing molecules! No coral, no pearls, but a sea-change all the same. The ballast pump sounds like old-fashioned windscreen wipers labouring. And now the place which doesn't exist begins to fall away, or we fall upward. Black milk floods back to fill the dwindling hole our light leaves. An appalling sense of loss as the features disappear according to their size. The privilege of having seen it is unaccountable. I doubt my luck ever to visit these regions again. Now everything's gone and the brief glare of our unnatural light withdraws, leaving the 50-million-year darkness as before. '*Auf Wiedersehen, submarine*,' says Viktor.

21.55: 'It took them five years to find the *Titanic* and she was 16 miles from where her coordinates said she was,' Sergei says consolingly. Everybody is always quoting this, usually with varying figures. Neither he nor Viktor believes the submarine sank. They tell me so as the outside lights are clicked off and we embark on our three-hour rise to another world. Maybe she faked her sinking; maybe she was badly wounded and crept away after the Americans left her to die elsewhere; maybe she reached the African coast or even Japan ... Maybe she did. I'm afraid I don't give a damn.

22.20: I am wondering why Beebe's description so differs from mine – at least in his finding that once all light had gone there was nothing but 'chill and night and death'. For the last twelve hours I've not thought at all about death in the sense that he means. For the first half-hour I considered in an academic sort of way the possibility of dying, but that was very different. Chill there certainly was: the MIR's steel hull conducts the ambient temperature most efficiently. But death? And then I think of how it must have been for Beebe, a true pioneer, the first man ever to go as deep as half a mile, way past the remains of light and with only interior lamps trained through the windows to reveal what was in the water column immediately outside. Although he wrote so well about light and the excitement of entering a strange place, he can never even have glimpsed that timeless land and its creatures far below him, nor felt its infinitely slow rhythms move in his blood. Nor did he have manœuvrability, but dangled helplessly on the end of a cable like a plummet on a string. If that cable had snapped, he would have gone. So it was different for us, with the comforts of a further sixty years' technology, eating our sandwiches on the bottom and touring effortlessly about with our headlights on. It was a different realm we saw. Death was there, all right, though not as an absence of the human, of light, of warmth.

23.05: Silence. Only the loudspeaker's hiss. We stare into space, dozing with our eyes open. My hand aches from writing and cold. The Anarchist has peed; I'm determined not to again.

23.27: But I wish we'd get a move on, all the same. This is the only part of the trip when I've become conscious of time. Watching the red LED display of the depth meter going steadily backwards, but not fast enough.

00.45: Exterior lights on.

00.49: Surface. Immediate rocking and tumbling in the swell. Does nothing for bladder. Or handwriting. The lights brighten and fade as they plunge in and out of the surf, reflecting off the bubbles but barely off deeper water. No sound from outside. A bright white foot waves at my viewport. Lonya's? Now *Koresh* is towing us: helical clouds of bubbles stream back from its screw. We rest in a violent, tossing pool of *Keldysh*'s deck lights and suddenly the foam falls away from the windows and we are hanging over the sea.

01.28: *MIR 1* secured. Outside I glimpse Viktor the engineer, Anatoly, Quentin and others. Cape Canaveral. The depth meter reads -29 metres. Had we been over the 5,000 metre mark? Who cares? The hatch is hard to crack: the air inside is still much cooler than out, so it has to be lifted against a slight vacuum. Ears pop. Stiffly I emerge, carrying my pee bottle in a plastic bag.

Before going to bed I write: It didn't feel like the bottom of the sea, the bottom of anything. The communications lag, the capsule, the navigation difficulties; everything suggested space travel. But I can now see why seventeenth-century scholars like Thomas Burnet in *The Theory of the Earth* thought of the sea as godless, frighteningly ugly in the 'unfinished', primordial sense of jagged reefs and cliffs and coastlines. With late twentieth-century eyes I turn all this into its unique virtue. Where I have just returned from is wonderful beyond anything I've seen before, and partly because it is so spectacularly ungodded, too remote to be anthropomorphised. This is why I can't assign a time to it but am tempted to borrow the naturalist Philip Gosse's term *prochronic* for the 'pre-time' that existed before the Creation story in Genesis. It was so alien and peaceful as to make one profoundly calm. Untouched, unfashionable. Here were no lovable cetaceans for people to have mystical blurts over. In its salutary insistence on the primordial nothingness which is the real groundswell beneath all our lives it was notably benign and reassuring. There was nothing to fear, nothing that would not return a level gaze: something nearly indistinguishable from affection.

04.07: It won't let me sleep, that land three miles beneath my bunk. It seems to fill every available space. So dark down there and yet so many eyes. What is it? A unified intelligence busy with tiny acts stretched over aeons? (When you get home, check that stanza towards the end of Stevens' *An Ordinary Evening in New Haven*):

> It is not an empty clearness, a bottomless sight.
> It is a visibility of thought,
>   in which hundreds of eyes, in one mind, see at once.

But what has it done to me? What were those names doing on the bottom? Why have I started remembering people from forty years ago in such detail? Slanted afternoons, the words of pacts, the nape of someone's neck. I have been moving through a bath of solvent which has thinned away crusts and membranes which had built up around certain memories. I don't understand why this should have happened.

TWENTY

And this morning I wake after only two or three hours' sleep, still high. Full of energy, I feel like a boy who has just heard he has passed some notorious and crucial examination. There is the same sensation of his whole past having been summarised; that from now on he will be moving in a slightly different sphere; that even contingency is on his side.

I return my rinsed pee bottle. Nobody is about. The MIR lab is locked. I have to go around by the deck to where the submersibles are lashed down in their garages. I climb up to the hatch of yesterday's magic carpet and hang the plastic bag on its lip. *MIR 1* doesn't look travel-stained. The side panels are off, revealing the hydraulics amongst whose pipes Lonya tied my two net bags full of polystyrene coffee cups. The cups are now craggy thimbles an inch tall, their air spaces collapsed, the plastic hard. If you send ordinary cedarwood pencils down to 5,000 metres they shrink to little dowels as hard as teak with lengths of graphite protruding from either end. It would be interesting to take down a football-sized chunk of balsa wood. It would probably compress into a hardwood marble.

The Russians I meet in the corridors on the way to Andrea's cabin shake my hand, beaming. Andrea and I embrace as aquanauts. In no describable way we are both a little transfigured by our experience. *MIR 2* went even deeper than *MIR 1*, but with equally negative results in terms of finding lost treasure. If Andrea's pleasure in her dive is tinged with private disappointment at not having found the submarine, it doesn't show. Ralph very graciously presents each of us with a gunmetal medal of twin dolphins separated by a trident above a relief of *Trieste 2*, the badge of the Deep Submersible Pilots' Association. He explains the iconography thus: the dolphins represent aquatic mammals, the trident represents Neptune's kingdom, and *Trieste 2* is the manned submersible with the all time depth record (though apparently a place 897 metres deeper than the 'deepest' spot on Earth has recently been found by the unmanned Japanese vehicle *Kaiko* but not yet dived on). Overnight I have become one of the boys and acquired a little bit of the Right Stuff of my own, though happily not enough for me to be put through the authentic badge-awarding ceremony as Ralph lovingly describes it. These DSPA badges are backed by two sharp metal prongs, and the proper ritual should involve the awarding officer hammering the badge into the proud neophyte's chest with a blow of his fist so that it sticks in. Circumcision, hazing, initiation ... after which, presumably, the chrysalis breaks open and the new man steps forth in his gorgeous plumage. Andrea says firmly that nobody's going to make a new man of her by hammering spikes into her breasts, thank you very much. Ralph seems to accept that doing things precisely according to the gung-ho book would perhaps be a little unseemly in the case of these two Limeys of a certain age and uncertain inclinations, but one can see he's disappointed. Still, there's always 'Crossing the Line' for him to look forward to, when Simon will get his come-uppance.

In the mean time Anatoly has played a nifty trick. Even as I was going down yesterday he summoned Clive to his cabin to ask how he would feel if the *Keldysh* headed straight for the Mid-Atlantic Ridge as soon as the MIRs were up and the transponders collected. Clive, still with a good deal of vodka in his veins after the previous evening's carousing in the sonar lab, was in no fit state to fight, especially as there was a faint suggestion in the air that Anatoly had been indulging Orca with these last MIR dives. So Sagalevitch and Bogdanov have got their way after all. The various Orca folk, recognising the inevitable when they saw it, gave their consent – almost by way of apology for our having found no gold, perhaps. It's perfectly obvious Anatoly had long ago decided that by hook or by crook the *Keldysh* was going to do some proper science before it sailed for Dakar, and I've no doubt the charts were already out on the bridge and the helmsman given his course before Clive ever set foot in Anatoly's cabin. In any case everyone is very pleased, except maybe Quentin who is still anxious about catching his flight home. But he, too, is a geologist at heart and the MAR site is a definite attraction. Schedules have been rearranged and Yuriy Bogdanov is giving a pre-black smoker lecture tonight at six. It's an ill wind that blows nobody a seminar in Russian at drinks time.

Anatoly, too, shakes me warmly by the hand. 'My writers' MIR,' he says. I feel a little overwhelmed: not merely gratitude for what was perhaps the greatest experience of my life but real admiration for a man who is in a class of engineers like Brunel. The sheer elegance of the MIRs' design (they don't have to go around dropping weights everywhere like the French and American submersibles), the versatility and manœuvrability with which they outperform all rivals, is wonderful and – remembering that by next year they may be laid up from lack of funds – slightly melancholy.

I'm still not sure where I am, nor where I've been in the last twenty-four hours. At least I share that dazed wonder with William Beebe. After he'd set his record with Otis Barton sixty years ago, he wrote in *Half Mile Down*: 'If one dives and returns to the surface inarticulate with amazement and with a deep realisation of the marvel of what he has seen and where he has been, then he deserves to go again and again. If he is unmoved or disappointed, then there remains for him on earth only a longer or shorter period of waiting for death.'

We are now steaming hectically westwards to MAR and the geologists' Grail. We have abandoned the area we pinged and ploughed so thoroughly these last three weeks while debating endlessly events that took place there so long ago. The wreath Orca planned to throw into the sea to exculpate itself from accusations of grave-robbing remains unthrown. There was to have been a service held for the benefit of Ralph's video record as well as to appease the spirits of all those young men. May as well save it for the *Aurelia*, is the feeling. After all, we're still none the wiser as to whether the area really *was* a graveyard.

And in the evening, after the lecture, Clive is waylaid by Anatoly who springs on him yet more extraordinary news. He and Natalya have been ordered to leave the ship at Dakar and return to Moscow. The Institute is flat broke. Yuriy Bogdanov will take over for the second leg as the expedition's head while Nik Shashkov will be in charge of underwater operations. This crisis in funds means that even if the liner is found – say towards the end of the sixteen-day search period – the *Keldysh* will not be able to follow through to take advantage of the contract's generous provisions for bonus payments. If they stayed on-site any longer they wouldn't have enough money to return to Kaliningrad and settle their debts, which include paying the crew. *They say . . .*

This throws Clive and Mike into serious grown-up mode so Quentin and I take our drinks on to the deck over the wheelhouse to watch the sunset. It's hard to think Anatoly's absence will greatly damage Orca's chances with *Marlin*. It might even improve matters since his changeable and often grouchy moods create an unsettling atmosphere. (That being said, nothing will alter our admiration of the man as the designer of the most beautiful machines we have ever entrusted our lives to, and which are serious in a way a Rolls Royce or a Rolex could never be.) If *Marlin* is found it will be up to the Institute whether they proceed at their own cost with the recovery operation. According to the contract they have to get $7 million's worth of gold up on deck in order to earn their $2 million bonus. For their part, the Orca investors can also agree to proceed beyond the remaining sixteen days on-site by paying the *Keldysh* at her normal daily charter rate. But switching to this rate also renders the bonus clause inactive. In any case, it may prove impossible to contact all twenty investors in time to solicit their agreement for such a switch.

Obviously – belatedly? – Anatoly doesn't like this provision. Which is to say, he can now see he'd probably have been better off being paid at the conventional charter rate from the outset rather than allowing himself to be seduced by jam clauses. Maybe it will be better if he does go back to Moscow because there at least he'll be able to negotiate in person at the Institute. He needs to ask them for money so that *Keldysh* can proceed according to contract (a request not likely to be granted). He also needs to guarantee a sum large enough for the ship to be refitted in Germany in July, otherwise her certificate of seaworthiness expires and she will be impounded indefinitely in Kaliningrad. He does say that if they find *Marlin* he will fly back to rejoin the ship for the salvage operations. Well, who wouldn't, with the prospect of picking up gold bars in the manipulators of the submersible he's designed?

On top of all this it turns out that the Shirshov Institute as a whole is in hock to Inmarsat to the tune of $84,000, of which the *Keldysh* owes $18,000. As phone bills go it's on the steep side, and various Earth stations are closing down on us as the news of our insolvency spreads. Ironically, given all the mock-Francophobia caused by the *Monge* and rugby, only France is still open to us and all our calls are being routed through a station there. 'Well, *Vive la France!*' Quentin and I touch glasses, but a trifle distractedly. I'm still lifted by the effects of yesterday's dive and don't really give a damn about communications and contracts, and he's worrying about his family and the flight home. There is something oppressive about all these background shenanigans, most of which concern trivia which in a few weeks' time will be quite forgotten. We must endeavour to rise above them, I tell Quentin, and remind him of the sterling example set by Emperor Hirohito in 1945. Shortly after a second atom bomb had been dropped on his country he was obliged to apprise the people of Japan's surrender. He began his announcement with a phrase whose panache surely outdid anything even a Briton might have managed in terms of understatement: 'The war situation has developed not necessarily to Japan's advantage.' This cheers Quentin no end and he resolves to put a braver face on his own trifling problems.

After dinner we return to our station over the wheelhouse, this time with Clive and Mike, bringing with us generous new rations of Spanish wine that were passed out yesterday as well as a plate of cheese and a box of biscuits. The biscuits, to judge from their flavour, were probably baked in Riga in 1983, but who cares? Above us wheel the most flaming constellations, the Milky Way as thick as cream, planets like soup plates and the

heavens additionally slashed and tinselled from time to time by
meteors. The wind is following and we sit in an unusual stillness
where normally one would be punched and buffeted. Calmly the
Keldysh speeds on towards the Mid-Atlantic Ridge. The touching farewell trio from Act 1 of *Così fan tutte* comes to mind, not
least because of its well-wishing:

> *Soave sia il vento*
> *Tranquilla sia l'onda*
> *Ed ogni elemento*
> *Benigno risponda*
> *Ai vostri desir*

But what are our wishes? Well might Mike, Andrea and Clive
be crestfallen, considering the failure of 50 per cent of their
project and Anatoly's impending defection. Unexpectedly, Mike
breaks his own reticence as well as silence to wonder aloud about
friendship, what his relations with Anatoly and Natalya might
ever have meant in the context of their frequent implications that
he's trying to swindle them; yet unbitterly, with puzzled
resignation. It is true he is very straight, which can pass for weak
when compared with the devious thug which Anatoly sometimes chooses to be. So he sits broodingly and drinks little and
gives off a sense of injury. Sometimes, as now in the blanching
light of galaxies, he looks like Dennis Waterman well after the
series ended, drawn and pallid. Something has happened to Mike
on this trip. His variable enthusiasm, always subject to changes
of mood, seems now to have settled into outright resignation. I
suspect he invested too much fantasy in this single project, not
least dreams of serious money. It is sad to see things going
wrong for him – such a reversal in barely a month at sea. Not for
the first time we have the feeling that our own game has been

caught up in a foreign one which nobody can second-guess. In the face of that it is best just to drink wine beneath this blazing sprawl of stars, phosphorescence at bow and stern, heading somewhere new.

22/2/95

And the notion of having been hijacked into someone else's plot is much reinforced this dawn. There, hove-to not a mile away, is another ship, the *Professor Logachov*. She is a geological survey vessel run directly by the Russian Geophysical Institute. Orca's suspicions bubble and seethe. How long ago was this rendezvous arranged? What is to happen? (But just think how scared we'd be if we had a couple of tons of Japanese gold under our hatches! *The Russian Mafia*. Why mightn't they be?) Both ships just sit there in the long swell. The slowly climbing sun bleaches the darkness out of the water and moods lift as menace fades. We are not just anywhere, but directly over the MAR site Yuriy Bogdanov recently discovered. *Koresh* is launched and takes Anatoly, Bogdanov and Nik Shashkov across. They claim to have had no idea there was another Russian ship here. What, both our radar and radio are on the blink? So this is no rendezvous but a genuinely fortuitous meeting . . . ? Who knows what to believe? But in any case time is short, and Bogdanov and co. need to do a quick deal with these other compatriots of theirs because the *Logachov* has some long cables deployed (sonar? coring?) and she'll have to haul them before the MIRs can be launched – it would be far too dangerous otherwise. The *Keldysh* now starts getting under way to drop transponders, and according to Little Andrej the *Logachev* is helping by providing us with exact co-ordinates and triangulation with transponders of their own. It's all a very strange sequel to the *Dolphin* operation, a sort of opaque parenthesis taking place on another level which, one suspects, always was the realer of the two.

I can't help feeling that the search for the *Aurelia* will be no more successful than that for the *I-52*. If I hadn't seen it for myself I would never have appreciated quite how difficult it is to find a large object on a seabed. When I first heard the immemorial story, it seemed almost unbelievable that both MIRs had failed to re-find the *Titanic* even after they'd already dived on her and established her position to within a matter of yards. Now it's all too credible. In a submersible one only sees whatever falls within that tiny puddle of light as it crawls blindly about. It's like looking for a contact lens on a beach by peering through the sleeve of a matchbox. No doubt in fifty years' time such methods will seem ludicrously unsophisticated and crude, but at the moment there really is nothing better and besides, as an experience it could not be improved on. I now realise I was quite apprehensive lest our MIR find the submarine. I'm still unsure what effect it would have had, coming on that huge black coffin locked down there in the cold and dark. It would have towered frighteningly over our little capsule, chill with gloom, a battlefield relic quite out of place among the timeless echiurids busy with evolution. Luckily (though only for me) it didn't happen. Wherever the *I-52* is, it has passed to another dimension. But seeing it through the slit of a matchbox would have squeezed the heart.

23/2/95

I awake as I slept, under the clear-headed influence of the deep sea, that drug still flowing in my veins. On my mental retina I see from the edge of our penumbra a fish approach, very slow, in slightly head-down attitude. Its tail ripples. This lost and peaceable place is not just prochronic but pro*photic*, pre-light.

'Let there be light!' (and fans of the *Creation* will hear a blazing chord of C major), but it never penetrated here. No sunlight. None here, ever. Only eternal, cold blackness whose denizens perfectly well organise themselves at other wavelengths and to different rhythms. What I visited was the heart of a slow, timeless egg undergoing a Darwinian process of germination. Millennia after the human race has been extinguished some life-form will be evolving in these regions, rising in the water column a few centimetres every thousand years until it colonises the euphotic layer, decides it's bored with being part of the marine food chain, and makes its way up a beach ... The whole laborious process starts once more. *Next* time, though: Not consciousness, not writings; not the dire vanities of longing and regret or the empty fervours of prayer. No capricious deities with their tacky rewards and endless punishments.

And love? What about that supposedly quintessential trait which *Homo sapiens* thinks will let him off the hook of eternal damnation? On that distant, nearly unreachable planetary surface it is a miracle to see the slow fish moving into the pool of light. The busy machine ticks on like a waterproof watch movement, with a precision of spoke burrows and navigation in a dark which is not dark to those that live there. Lacking the pained self-interest of human lovers, these creatures are at least open to that dissolved benignity drifting everywhere, in and out of cells, through the pores in the sediment, in brains and palps and flagellae. The watchers in their armoured chariot were nobodies down there, and nothing. At most they signified the briefest of events: split-second interlopers goggling through acrylic corneas and busy with an economy of milk cartons and urine bottles. And yet they did sense the benignity of which they were a part. They did see the hidden wellspring of all planetary life. It is not something they will forget.

Yesterday I went down to visit Goldenhands (that is his nickname in Russian) in his workshop. One of the pins came out of my watchstrap during table-tennis and got stamped on and bent; I needed to borrow a small hammer. He was there among his lathes together with my fellow-aquanaut, Sergei Smolitskiy. He and I embraced like old comrades. His beard smelt of limes. He was beautifully inlaying a knife handle for someone's birthday present. (Passing note: no fewer than thirty members of the *Keldysh* crew have birthdays in February, according to Anatoly. What's so erotic about the Russian May? Is it the end of winter?) Goldenhands did my pin in a jiffy. He was machining a new something-or-other for one of the MIRs out of a block of solid metal. The skill in that shop, the same whether making birthday presents or ship's equipment, epitomises the whole attitude and way of life of this remarkable team. I discovered to my amazement that Goldenhands is 78: amazement because this upright, white-haired man who does exercises on deck each dawn could pass for a healthy 60, but chiefly because probably only on *Keldysh* would one still find a man of that age to whose skill people entrust their lives. He tells me he still gets a MIR dive now and then.

And at breakfast this morning Anatoly came and put his arms tightly around Goldenhands as he sat next to me. While he hugged he told me: 'Today is his birthday. He was born in 1917, the year of the Revolution. The Red Army was founded in 1918 and it's Red Army Day today, only now it's called Defenders of the Motherland Day. This man fought in the Second World War in the Siege of Leningrad.' The respect and affection in his voice are unmistakable. These two men hugging half over my plate are true veterans of another world order. I was born two months after the beginning of that infamous siege in which more than a million people died. Once again I feel I've intruded into a family.

I am excluded not only by chronology but by an altogether softer life for which I suppose I ought to feel thankful. Still, I am also glad never to have been spoken for by the fatuous Ronald Reagan with his superstitious, Cotton Mather rhetoric of Evil Empires. Wrapped together, these two Russians are as though comforting one another, affirming that the world's largest country remains the Motherland, that harsh experiences and acts of extraordinary suffering and heroism retain their validity no matter what the vagaries of political fashion. Comradeship alone remains unironic, untouched by all contingency and reversals of fortune.

Watching the MIRs being swung out to dive on Bogdanov's vent site is different this time. I now know first-hand the sensations, sounds and movements the crews are experiencing, as well as their excited anticipation. *MIR 1* contains Anatoly and Bogdanov and a co-pilot, while *MIR 2* has on board a stranger: a gaunt young geologist from the *Professor Logachov*. Lonya performs his usual death-defying leap from the rubber Zodiac on to *MIR 1*'s curved orange back, lands badly, obviously hurts himself. The swell is considerable, the height differential between the two craft see-sawing violently. A tall wave breaks over him as he disconnects the crane's gear from the slot. His crouched shape can once more be seen under the water, a green shadow. Quentin, taking pictures, remarks how this could never happen in British science nowadays: a risk like this would be considered unacceptable by the Health and Safety Executive. How would we do it, then? Oh, we wouldn't. We'd have to wait for a flat calm, which in this part of the ocean might mean a month. At a typical $38,000 a day that would probably blow an entire year's research budget, and all for lack of a bit of courage. Balls-out science is no longer for us. An era has passed and it's hard to see how we'll ever again be in the forefront of oceanography. Or any other scientific enterprise that entails risk. A querulous nation of couch potatoes endlessly worrying about their safety ... (This is one of Quentin's favourite themes). At which point Lonya limps past, one ankle already strapped up. He certainly won't be doing *MIR 2*. 'It's nothing,' he says crossly when someone asks, obviously impatient with himself for a lapse in his balletic concentration. Even as he speaks his replacement is being swung over the rail in the Zodiac.

Later, we go up above the bridge to toast the setting sun with our last bottle of Blandy's Madeira. The sea is difficult, choppy. Indulgently we watch the efforts to retrieve *MIR 1*. Little Lev appears to disgrace himself by letting the tow-rope become snarled in *Koresh*'s propeller. This leads to a long delay made all the more pleasurable for us at the thought of the discomfort of the wallowing submersible's occupants. Ours is now the *Schadenfreude* of fellow-professionals. When eventually *MIR 1* is retrieved I run into the jump-suited Bogdanov on the companion-way. His face is that of a happy schoolboy. 'So many black smokers!' he says. 'So much geology!' A slightly green schoolboy, it has to be said, after rocking violently in that swell for an hour.

After supper we see for ourselves what fabulous specimens they've brought back. Great blackish lumps veined and marbled with glittering minerals and metallic deposits. There is even part of an actual chimney. One of the planet's nostrils, it is a craggy flue with an oval hole right through it lined with a crystalline green salt. Quentin, like Bogdanov, is beside himself. 'Don't touch, don't touch ... ! I've never seen such ... Heads of departments all over the world would give their left bollocks to see what we're looking at ... You've no idea how rare specimens of this quality are ... Moon rock ... ' I don't touch, but I can sniff. One sample is pungently sulphurous, like anthracite cinders or fresh coke. Another smells of wet dog-blanket – again, probably sulphur. The excitement intensifies with the arrival of *MIR 2* bearing more sections of chimney, a basket-load of rust-coloured mussels and a perspex drum containing jars of various shrimps, small fish and crabs. Scientists and engineers mill around, all talking at once. It turns out that Viktor Brovko the engineer, our table-mate, himself designed and built the impeller system which enabled these specimens to be 'hoovered' up undamaged by means of a flexible hose. When no one's looking I lick one of the mussels, then wonder if it is radioactive.

Among the dazzled scientists is Sasha, the geologist from the *Professor Logachov*. He obviously can't believe his luck. Two days ago he was an ordinary geo-nerd, hove-to above this 'secret' MAR site, sending down probes. Suddenly he found himself whisked aboard the *Keldysh* and packed off in person down to 3,000 metres in one of the famous MIRs to see these black smokers for himself, returning with armfuls of unique treasures. He wanders about in a daze, a grin tacked across his face, shaking hands with total strangers and taking for granted that tonight everyone in the universe is a fellow-geologist. His eyes have the look of one whose retinas are still showing an interior film shot 10,000 feet below the deck he's standing on. He wanders up to me with a dark wet lump like a piece of coke in his hand and asks in Russian what sounds like '*Serpentinitye?*', breaking off a blackish-greenish fragment and giving it to me. When I murmur something in English he beams and says stumblingly 'Magnese silica 'ydrate?' No priest ever treated a wafer with greater reverence. Eventually he is hustled away like a child who has been allowed up long past his bedtime for a special occasion. Anatoly and Bogdanov have to run him back to his ship in *Koresh* and reach some sort of amicable agreement about how to divide the scientific spoils, then return so that *Keldysh* can at last set sail for Dakar.

So out of a general feeling of disappointment has come this extraordinary last-minute research bonus. Clive remarks in best lawyerly fashion that had it not been for Orca the *Keldysh* and its MIRs would never have been here. As far as science is concerned, all is forgiven. We may not have found a Japanese submarine but we revisited Yuriy Bogdanov's longed-for site, and the films and specimens he has collected will lead to a major article in *Nature* and he will be famous. He is, of course, already well known in international geology; but it looks as though the site he discovered is quite different geochemically from the TAG sites already investigated several hundred miles to the north. From other points of view, too, this discovery will probably have far-reaching consequences. Marine molecular biologists have long been wondering about the genetics of vent communities. On the face of it, the biota living around each vent seem to be specifically adapted to the peculiar local conditions: high temperatures, the presence of free iron, concentrations of hydrogen sulphide or whatever. Now, with the discovery of this Atlantic site, it may be possible to do DNA studies to see if its organisms show a direct relationship to their Pacific counterparts, or whether they are merely brilliant examples of convergent evolution. (After the expedition was over it was confirmed that Bogdanov's site had yielded some new animal species, some brand-new minerals and an unknown type of black smoker.)

It is astounding, in retrospect, to have been present on deck when the dripping specimens of a scientific 'first' came back. It was like being on a research vessel in the heyday of nineteenth-century oceanography – the *Beagle*, perhaps, or the *Challenger*. It didn't matter that it was late at night. People appeared on deck in their dressing-gowns, seized their specimens and bore them off to their labs in a state of high excitement. The frail, elderly biologist known to us as 'Ms Zimmer' left a nylon fur slipper behind her on the soaked and oily deck when she grabbed a jar and sprinted for her microscope. Off they all went to preserve, sort, examine. Some of them would have sketched the objects, for the Soviet system for training natural scientists was in many ways still close to the old ideal which made people into true observers and recorders, and reserved instruments as tools.

For my part, I have borne away to my own cabin the fragment Sasha gave me. It sits in a plastic envelope, a softish chunk of unidentified hydroxides, something created by the chemical machine on which we are afloat. Bent over *MIR 2*'s collection tray tonight, sniffing, I caught the waft of something reassuring. I want to say 'benign' yet again, but the word is too full of intentionality and too contaminated by anthropomorphism. One needs a word to describe a sense of *process* (and emphatically not *progress*). The infinitely slow machineries of life I saw three miles down, the faint gas of chemical reactions which fills the little plastic envelope: they both are part of this common process which is not quite optimistic, yet not completely neutral, either. Then it strikes me. What I have been seeing and smelling and touching these last few days is, quite simply, Evolution. And Evolution smells like wet anthracite and dog-blankets and has the salt, rusty taste of a mussel shell found near a hydrothermal vent.

TWENTY-ONE

24/2/95

This leg is all but over and we are on a course for Dakar. All day the *Keldysh* has been galloping Africa-wards, headlong into the trade wind as though through knee-high undergrowth, all flying mane and bursts of thistledown. Her bronze hooves thrash. The horizon is empty, the tropic sky feathered with cirrus. Up on deck I read a novel by 'Abram Tertz' in the shelter of the roaring funnel. The wind whips the pages.

Those blackish, purplish lumps unloaded from the MIRs last night looked credibly like gold and were received as such. They had the aspect of undistinguished fragments of information that our species might need in order to prolong its tenancy of this planet, but undistinguished only in the manner of one of those identical-looking pieces of sea or sky in a jigsaw puzzle; otherwise crucial. By contrast the Japanese gold Orca was hoping to pile on deck seems truly academic, an irrelevant and even unhealthy trafficking with the past. Move on, move on, hums the rigging. Move on, hums the current recharging the MIRs' immense, oil-topped batteries. Move on.

Well, we have moved on; have abandoned one search zone and left our sacks and bottles down among the holothurians somewhere over the horizon astern. This is not meant to sound an incriminating or ironic note about scientific vessels jettisoning rubbish. 'There is nothing on earth we can't turn to our advantage,' reflects Abram Tertz's Little Jinx blackly, and this is as true for other biota as it is for us. Animals inexorably shape other animals' lives. Bat guano falling for centuries on a cavern floor supports a rich crop of bacteria, and slowly the nitrogen they fix leaches out via groundwater to feed the neighbouring forest, which in turn feeds the local population. In the same way, human refuse on the ocean floor often provides nourishment or else forms habitats supporting colonies of unseen creatures. For a century the major shipping routes were marked by steamers throwing overboard millions of tons of clinker raked from their furnaces. Today, long-established clinker habitats cover large areas of those routes and support carpets of sessile encrusting organisms where before there were few or none. Something will take refuge in our bottles, too. Just as we did.

As any diver knows, wrecks provide a marvellous habitat for all sorts of creatures. One particular cargo vessel which sank in 1,500 metres of water has recently been found to support the only known colony (other than around an undersea vent) of the three-metre long red worms that metabolise hydrogen sulphide. In this case the H_2S comes from a decaying cargo of coffee. With the exception of very large crude-carrying tankers foundering off a coast, the ships which sink seem to spread remarkably little pollution. When one thinks of the thousands of steel-hulled vessels which have sunk in all the world's oceans over the last century in peacetime and in war, frequently with exceedingly toxic cargoes, it is notable that they appear to have left so little mark they are often impossible to find even with the most sensitive equipment. At some point a week ago, one or other of our submersibles was quite likely within a few hundred metres of the *I-52* – probably far less. Yet there was no discernible trace of its presence anywhere on the seabed, no horrid stain of man-made vileness pooling across the sediment like the area of dead soil surrounding the mythical Javanese Upas-tree.

It is right that the sea should not be treated as a dustbin or an infinite oubliette for the human race's refuse. But when people look with horror at polluted coastal waters (such as Santa Monica Bay) and ravaged shallow seas (such as the North Sea), they forget that seven-tenths of the planet's surface is covered with water whose *average* depth is 3,800 metres (or 2.36 miles). This inconceivable body of diluent is itself a chemical machine of vast complexity whose workings we have scarcely begun to understand. By far the greatest pollution danger to the oceans comes in fact from the land, in the form of a steady stream of agricultural and industrial run-offs, street drainage, plastic refuse and synthetic hormones such as oestrogens. It does not come from the occasional well-publicised toxic cargo.

The panicky guilt which maintains that almost everything our species does 'ruins' the planet betrays its essentially religious origins in the Genesis myth of Eden. Here, for example, is a Greenpeace manifesto I was handed in Falmouth and forgot about until today. I shall read part of its sermon into the record for the interest of future social historians because, being a perfect expression of a fashionable attitude, it would otherwise be ephemeral. It begins with the premise that the Earth is probably about 4,600 million years old. Since this is an age too great to be imagined, the Greenpeace vicar makes it homely by humanising it as a middle-aged person of 46. On this timescale, then, modern humans

have been around for four hours. During the last hour we discovered agriculture. The industrial revolution began just a minute ago.

During those sixty seconds of biological time, humans have made a rubbish tip of Paradise.

We have caused the extinction of many hundreds of species of animals, many of which have been here longer than us, and ransacked the planet for fuel. Now we stand, like brutish infants, gloating over this meteoric rise to ascendancy, poised on the brink of the final mass extinction and of effectively destroying this oasis of life in the solar system.

This is a pure, unreconstructed religious view of mankind as sinful such as might have been heard thundering from almost any nineteenth-century pulpit, complete with references to Paradise and a general tone of exuberant hysteria. What is notable is that at the last gasp of the twentieth century this kind of superstition still believes in a pre-Darwinian notion of the world as a static Eden which we have lately had the temerity to foul. It is a rhetoric that makes it more, not less, difficult to think straight on the subject of pollution since it implies that everything which occurs 'naturally' cannot pollute (*Homo* clearly being an un-natural species, even though 'brutish'). We patently need to find another, unmoralised, word for this activity; or else what are we to say about the huge mass of complex chemical soup constantly pouring out of volcanoes, undersea vents and natural oil seeps just as it has for millions of years? Greenpeace demonises chlorine as 'the Devil's element' (again the religious imagery) even as marine algae, microbes and plants everywhere are busy churning out a stream of organo-chlorine compounds, among them banned or restricted substances like chloroform, carbon tetrachloride and various dioxins. Dioxins, in fact, occur naturally in every fire ever lit, especially in forest fires. There have always been dioxins in the environment, even in the Garden of Eden. And as for radioactivity, you risk a heftier dose of radiation by walking through an Edinburgh street lined with granite buildings than by strolling on Mururoa Atoll or along the beach at Sellafield. But if this cannot properly be considered as 'pollution', how are we ever to balance the environmental budget?

The Church of Greenpeace may see this as a moral issue but its crusade looks a little different when viewed from outside. In our professed, new-found concern for all creatures great and small (leaving conveniently aside the daily mass executions in the name of global hamburger chains and fried chicken franchises) can be glimpsed the panic of a species thinking chiefly about its own welfare and the future of 'The Race'. It may be this that makes a middle-aged sceptic notice something unfortunate in the statement by Chris Rose, Greenpeace's director of campaigns, when he refers to the necessity for 'carrying out acts which are legitimated by the moral deficit they address, rather than the means which are used'. It is a cruel irony that this no doubt well-intentioned and thoughtful man should be exactly paraphrasing Hitler and any number of totalitarian monsters of the recent past. It's good old ends and means again.

So despite my being by inclination a natural scientist and as saddened by the idea of extinctions as anyone, it turns out that the Church of Greenpeace and I have little to say to one another on this particular topic. A few days ago I read on the seabed not just the names of people I had loved long ago but also an old message *en clair*: that things evolve according to contingency. There is no blueprint, no model, no plan for how the Earth should be. Since *Homo sapiens sapiens* is just another species, everything he does is natural. However it all turns out is fine, because that, too, will only ever be temporary. No matter how we make our own planetary bed we will still have to lie in it, and it would have been our grave in any event. It doesn't *matter*.

That's the whole of it. We are lost among galaxies, like any old holothurian on its patch of sediment, and there's no problem with it.

An 'official' party down in the MIR lab at 7.30 p.m. Quentin and I are a bit late, having been trotting to and from the radio room in the usual ritual of attempted communication. The line only went down once: in view of our unpaid bills it's a miracle he got one at all. So we sidle into the packed lab in the middle of a speech by Anatoly in his Lugubrious Headmaster mode. People are munching sausages and pizza as they listen to this summing-up of the last six weeks, tumblers of vodka at the ready. It has not been an altogether bad term, Anatoly is saying. The new boys (and girl) settled in well. There were some notable academic triumphs, especially among the Sixth Form scientists, who should be congratulated. On the games field, too, everyone pulled their weight and it was inevitably a keen disappointment that the season should have ended with defeat when the school took on Japan. The game was gallantly fought, as one would have expected, but in the final analysis the wily Easterners were just too strong for us and retained the Gold Challenge cup. The school came away honourably but empty-handed ...

Dutifully, we all drink to this. There is a five-minute lull in which to annex a sausage and a glass of something drinkable, then the headmaster is up again for another speechlet and a toast. Then another ... And another ... People's drinking rituals are really most odd, from culture to culture. The Russian ritual is as strange as any I've encountered because it's so unsettling. Just when you think you can relax and start talking to your neighbour, you're interrupted by the whole party being brought to a halt for a formal expression of banal sentiments and a skull-cleaving swig of spirits. Formality and alcohol are an uneasy mix.

There are highlights all the same, among the more memorable of which is Anatoly proposing the toast 'To beautiful women' and being answered quick as a flash by Andrea's voice saying loud and clear 'I'll drink to that!' Quentin and Clive collapse at this splendid piece of subversion. Anatoly vaguely smiles: a headmaster who has missed the joke but is used to having the last laugh. At some point the proceedings turn into prize-giving time. Orca members file past the Head (now rather rumpled about the eyes with drink) and are each presented with a signed certificate of their dive, plus souvenir photographs of *MIR 1* and the *Keldysh*. This feels like a generous and good-natured thing to have thought of, and we all drink to it.

I have never liked parties. I hate the noise and I hate standing up to drink and I hate the way my face aches from maintaining a grin while bawling pleasantries at people who need plastic surgery but who would be best served by simple beheading. And one of the reasons I most hate parties is because everything is muddied and unclear. Terrible things are said which seemingly have no effect. People lacerate each other equably. When it is Ralph's turn to be picked on by headmaster Anatoly a scene develops, a public performance which could not have been without years of preparation.

The initial impression Ralph gives tonight is of being in his element. This tall, bearded figure dressed for the occasion with leather pouches at his belt and glittering black cowboy boots is, as we know, a veteran of many *Keldysh* cruises, a veteran of MIR dives (a qualified co-pilot), a veteran of hanging his hide out with the boys but what the heck, it was kinda fun even though it got hairy now and then. He is Old Hand Ralph, but as such presents something of a puzzle. His familiar manner with so many of the crew seems compromised by his being unable to speak Russian. If this is the man 'with more MIR dives than any other Westerner', whose recent career has been so bound up with the *Keldysh* (especially when filming the *Titanic*), why hasn't he learned a bit of the language? And does he not act in the United States as the Shirshov Institute's banker? It's odd. Mike Anderson is making a real effort to learn Russian, which is appreciated. But then, Mike is a trier. The inheritor from his Scots father of a Presbyterian ethic, he knows that nobody gets anywhere in this world without work. Ralph, on the other hand, whatever his stock, comes with a Californian attitude: that what you are has less to do with what you know than with what you can sell yourself as. Blarney, in other words. Or at any rate play-acting, since tonight he is a curious composite figure with his cowboy boots and holstered electronic gizmos; as it were, a cross between a sheriff and a spook, Old Hand Ralph from the Skunk Works. He is right there up front, exchanging *badinage* with Anatoly across several intervening heads.

Anatoly, meanwhile, has shed his headmaster's guise. Now he is a boss brigand inviting a minor foreign clan leader to step just a little further inside his cave. I vaguely sense what's going to happen, but not how, and I can't watch his victim's face because poor Ralph doesn't seem to notice anything amiss. Instead I fix my eyes on his dazzling boots. Now Ralph himself tries to propose a toast but he is speaking in Californian which nobody really understands, including me, and people continue talking. He resorts to some still louder joshing to make sure we all recognise we're good friends anyway. Then he makes a tactical error. He chooses this moment to make a serious announcement. What he wants to tell his comrades in the MIR team is that they have all been adopted as honorary members of the Deep Submersible Pilots' Association and that the normal fees have been waived by the Association in recognition of the Russians' extraordinary contribution to deep submersible pioneering, which is internationally acknowledged and appreciated. This means – Ralph explains – that they'll be getting their gunmetal badges and newsletters completely free, and there'll be a package waiting for them in Dakar full of insignia and citations and whatnot.

Meanwhile, the vodka has flowed and people are talking to each other and still nobody understands Californian so this news of American goodwill goes unheard. I'm sure Ralph organised the whole thing with the DSPA as a surprise, and might well have paid the membership fees himself, for he is a kindly and generous fellow. He now appeals to his old friend the brigand to help him out and interpret for him, and at last the brigand has his chance. He raises his hands, effortlessly achieving everyone's attention. His gang falls more or less silent, sausages to mouth. He announces that he has to do an important piece of translation, and nods to Ralph. 'In Dakar . . . ' Ralph begins. '*v'Dakari*,' interrupts the brigand jovially, with a throwaway gesture to show how easy this translating lark is to a man of his calibre. The gang roar. 'In Dakar . . . ' Ralph tries again, louder. '*v'Dakari*,' copies the brigand. Things are going all his way. The gang are falling about, especially his women. 'Listen, fellas,' Ralph bawls, grinning hectically through his beard, 'in Dakar . . .' An artist might have left it there but the brigand has all the gossamer touch of Nikita Khrushchev, whom he is beginning oddly to resemble. Vodka really does something to the eyes. '*v'Dakari*,' he intones with heavy emphasis. It's a riot. Nevertheless, Ralph proceeds gamely in the general din. Words like 'insignia' and 'waived' can be heard above the general hubbub. They are not understood. 'All charges are waived by agreement of the DSPA, you guys,' he roars hopelessly, looking around for pleased comprehension. At length, the brigand tries this foreign vocabulary on for size and decides to wear it mockingly.

'Waives,' he calls, waving. The whole thing is degenerating. By the time it's explained that the MIR group is being honoured, all for free, interest has shifted right away from the message and on to the medium, the hypnotic brigand who holds everyone in the palm of his hand – at least, to judge from the way the gang are acting up he does.

What is really happening? (God, how I hate parties.) Is the gang being sycophantic towards their chieftain who invented the wonderful steel chariots for galloping about the seabed? Or are they indulging him out of the sheer relief of knowing he'll be leaving the ship in a few days? Or is this Russian solidarity in the face of an *Amyerkanyets*? Or did they think it was high time a self-appointed old friend was reminded that he ought to learn to converse for himself in his old friends' language? Or is it just a lot of drunks having a lot of laughs because that's what you do at parties? I suddenly notice the brigand has left the room at the height of his popularity and guess he's gone to fetch his guitar, so I ease out on to the MIR deck and watch the dark sea racing past. After a while a disconsolate Ralph comes out. I wonder how he will deal with his public battering and imagine it would be in character if he pretended nothing had happened. I am wrong. He begins with a touching and rather elegant ellipsis.

'You're a poet, I've been reading your sea book. There aren't big bucks in poetry, I guess. Same as me. You think I couldn't have gone the whole Hollywood route? Sure, you make a lot of money, but it's not for me. Smearing lenses with vaseline to make raddled old dolls look like dewy young virgins. I guess both of us have chosen to do things we want to do, enjoy doing, interesting things with some fun and excitement thrown in and to hell with the big bucks . . . ' He doesn't glance at the MIR he's standing next to. 'Toly shouldn't have done that. He just kissed it off. That was a real generous offer by the DSPA. They know these guys haven't got a cent between them. You should have seen it when *Keldysh* was in the States. The first Russian ship to be allowed up the Potomac in fifty years. July 5th, 1989. She moored at the old Ford Motor Company export dock in Alexandria, Virginia, a stone's throw away from the Pentagon. Like it's about four miles. Can you believe these folks weren't allowed to open the hatches in case they launched a sneak missile attack on the Pentagon or the White House? It's true. But our guys made a real fuss of this ship and its crew. Anatoly was meeting all sorts of people and being honoured, too. He was the first Russian to be elected an Honorary Member of the prestigious Adventurers' Club. I'm a member, so I know. Hell, we had US admirals coming aboard in regular suits, Naval Intelligence officers dressed to look like ordinary human civilians, you could see their eyes taking photographs of the MIRs. What I guess I'm trying to say, we pushed the boat out for Anatoly. He shouldn'ta just kissed the thing off like that.'

In his wounded way Ralph is perfectly right, of course. I find myself really liking this able, hurt man who has an odd sweetness and who can sometimes be seen gesticulating frantically to be let out of the caricature he has found himself in as camouflage turns imperceptibly into prison. He does shoot some beautiful and stunning images and he has a vulnerable eye. I think he knows his vulnerability extends a lot further than his eye, too; but an ex-Marine is not about to allow such things to be spotted so he has done an excellent job of being unnaturally intrepid. Tonight it took a friend, and a foreign brigand at that, to be ruthless enough publicly to dent Ralph's 'fustest with the mostest' aspect and it was not something I am happy to have witnessed. There are times when Anatoly is dark and savage and suspicious and his lower lip juts and it's not just the vodka talking. His *bonhomie* is as heavy as his anger. The protective shells, even of old friends like Mike and Ralph, are there for the crushing when he's in crushing mood. I'm quite sorry to be getting off in Dakar because I shan't have begun to know Ralph by then and I have the feeling he would repay knowing. Shipboard alliances. My surmise was right after all: treasure-hunts have far more to do with personalities than with technology. A female marine biologist emerges with a blast of folk song to dump armfuls of empty bottles over the side. The waves sweep them away and tomorrow is already over Cairo and racing towards us across Africa.

25/2/95

This morning Ralph's own account of the party is not at all stupid, and it's also generous. He blames himself for trying to make that sort of announcement on that sort of occasion.

'I was trying to talk to Anatoly's boys in front of Anatoly, giving them a bit of good news. He doesn't like that. It's better if he can call them into his office and tell them in person so he can imply it's something he's fixed up for them himself. Everything for his people has to come through him. It's part of the old Soviet System.'

And of course he's right. Last night's brigand was nothing if not an *amo*, a *padrone*. In any case Ralph has safely gone back to being a Marine today. There's a meeting at 2 p.m. for a preliminary discussion of the *Marlin* search zone. Anatoly says something to Ralph and I overhear: 'You talked to him, Toly? Outstanding.'

'We move on,' says Anatoly, twinkling heavily, 'to Gold Number Two.' Some fairly up-to-date bathymetry of *Marlin*'s sinking zone has been assembled, enough to indicate that the seabed at 1°S 10°W is steeply shelving and full of ravines. 'Like an underwater Grand Canyon,' as Ralph puts it, shaking his experienced head. Still, it's generally agreed it ought to be much easier to find a large liner than it was to find a submarine. There is a distinct air of enthusiasm among those at the table who will be going on the next leg, especially Yuriy Bogdanov and Nik Shashkov. It may look like an old *Dolphin* search zone meeting but several of us are already back numbers: Anatoly himself, Clive, Quentin and me. The only thing on the agenda now is *Marlin*.

TWENTY-TWO

Thomas Hardy's poem on the sinking of the *Titanic*, 'The Convergence of the Twain', depicts the punctual coming-together of the tragedy's two protagonists – the lump of ice and the liner – as inexorably planned by Fate, a.k.a. 'The Immanent Will'. There is something exemplary for Hardy in the way the proud maiden voyage of the liner (whose technology would nowadays be described as 'state-of-the-art') is ended by the mindless agency of the natural world. So much for human hubris, the old grouch implies.

The convergence of the *Aurelia* and the Italian submarine *Michelangelo* in February 1943, though involving a certain element of chance, was a far more intentional affair, being mostly determined by some interesting circumstances of war. I was, of course, due to leave the *Keldysh* at Dakar before she sailed on her second leg to look for the wreck of the *Aurelia*, and therefore had no particular need to become involved in search zone meetings for a sonar survey I would never witness. Nevertheless, I had eagerly read Andrea's files on the sinking. They struck me as having been compiled with the thoroughness and eye for detail I had come to expect from her, but she was not satisfied with them. Since by now we had reached the stage in the voyage of merciless frankness she was able to tell me that the research was only as good as Orca had allowed, in terms of time and money. She was acutely conscious that she had not been able to dig around properly on the Italian side of the story and that we were too reliant on Allied documentation. Above all, she had only got so far in her research into the gold itself, its provenance, its true destination, its very existence. This latter was no fault of Orca's, to be sure, but she still felt her incomplete knowledge reflected badly on her professionalism.

From the time the Canadian pensioner, Jock Walker, was put in touch with Mike Anderson back in the late 1980s, practically all investigation had centred around trying to establish the presence on board the *Aurelia* of the gold consignment supposedly destined for the Bank of England. As a preliminary move this made complete sense. Without reasonable certainty that the ship was carrying gold there would be no hope of attracting investors for a salvage operation. By the time Orca had 'been formed (with, as will be recalled, the *I-52* 'thrown into the pot' as the sweetener for the riskier proposition of the liner), everyone was 95 per cent satisfied that the gold had been on board. In fact everything still rested on the lone word of the liner's ex-Fifth officer, much as the alleged 2,000 tons of silver on board the *John Barry* were down to the assertions of her purser. The precise quantity of gold remained uncertain. Andrea's researches had led her to several dead ends. Most awkwardly of all, the Bank of England appeared to have no record of the attempted shipment. The rest of Orca's files were devoted to the actual sinking, being particularly concerned with the various rescue missions by Royal Navy vessels and RAF Catalina flying boats. The theory was that with so many different craft being vectored into the area of the torpedoing, it ought to be possible from the various records and logs to establish the position where the ship sank with reasonable accuracy.

It soon became obvious that this data would lend itself to the usual – probably heated – discussions about compass bearings, time zones, dead reckoning, wind speed, currents, and so on. Pretty much of a replay, in fact, of the *I-52* search zone meetings. I found myself far more interested in the broader patterns of a war which by then, in one way or another, had affected most of the world, and how these had conspired to bring fatally together a Canadian liner and an Italian submarine off the coast of West Africa. Since I live in Italy it was possible to start some research of my own once I had flown home from Dakar. I make no apologies for having become interested in the background of this sinking, and at such length. The losing side in a war seldom hears much other than the victor's accounts, and most Italians seem to know remarkably little about the role of their own submarine service during the Second World War (with the possible exception of having some idea about the extraordinary performance of their two-man chariots, the famous *maiali*, which did such damage to Allied shipping in the Mediterranean). Nor is the *Aurelia*'s fate widely known among the British. Without the belated revelation that she may have been carrying gold, it would probably have stayed that way. In any case I soon became caught up in accounts of Italian submariners which, as with all such records, leave one amazed at the skill and bravery of men who fought a war beneath the waves – a war, it should be added, not just against the elements and the enemy but against the inanities of a politics beyond their control. Some of the most authoritative accounts of this war have been documented by Giulio Raiola, to whose excellent book *Timoni a Salire* I am heavily indebted for much of what follows.

The first thing beyond the Italians' control was the conduct of their submarine warfare, which was subject to the overall strategic command of their German allies in the person of Admiral Karl Dönitz. Warfare (much like treasure-hunting) confirms the consequences of clashes of temperament as well as of arms. In their own ways the best German and Italian submariners were brilliant; the problem was that they seldom worked really well together. For whatever cultural or climatic reasons it turned out the Italians disliked the freezing North Atlantic. Unfortunately, this was exactly where the Germans wished to concentrate their efforts, having decided that the most valuable deployment of their huge submarine fleet lay in attacking the Allied convoys bringing crucial supplies of food, fuel and munitions from the US to beleaguered Britain. Dönitz's tactical masterpiece was the 'wolf pack' or *Rudeltaktik*, in which large groups of submarines would shadow a convoy and carry out mass attacks while surfaced at night, firing torpedoes and co-ordinating their movements by heavy reliance on radio (such a tactic obviously being impossible if the submarines were submerged).

This method turned out to be unsuited to the Italians who wanted to evolve their own, individualistic, methods. Dönitz somewhat grudgingly accepted this, and by the end of autumn 1940 was entrusting them with a more freebooting role. After the spring of 1941 no Italian submarine actively served north of Cape Finisterre in Spain. The submarines of the Italian fleet, which was of very modest size compared to the Germans', henceforth tended to operate as 'loners', often over immense distances (going as far afield, for example, as the Indian Ocean and the South American coast). Mostly far from all help and supplies, such deployments required another kind of bravery and obliged the crews to be even more than usually self-sufficient and ingenious.

As the war spread, bringing in Japan and the US, the routes east of the Cape of Good Hope represented the British Empire's point of maximum vulnerability, its lines of communication and support stretched perilously thin. Yet the Axis powers never really took proper advantage of this. Once again they failed to co-operate militarily. Their new allies, the Japanese, showed little inclination for joint operations and were downright unenthusiastic about turning Asian waters (by a 1942 treaty considered as everything lying east of the 70° meridian – more or less the frontier between India and modern Pakistan) into an extension of the European theatre of war. They had marked down that vast region for their own.

Irreducible geographical and political factors had much to do with the operating difficulties experienced by the Italian submarine fleet. An Italian port could only usefully serve as a home base for submarines confined to the Mediterranean theatre, the dangers of the Straits of Gibraltar being notorious among submariners of every nation. Tidal currents flow through this bottleneck powerfully enough to stop a submarine in its tracks, even to send it *backwards* with engines at Full Ahead. To avoid these currents it was advisable to hug the shore; but the shelving, rocky seabed was highly treacherous to a submerged vessel groping its way in the days before reliable sonar profiling. In any case sonar pinging was hardly compatible with stealth. The British presence in Gibraltar meant that the Allies effectively controlled shipping through the Straits. Axis submarines were obliged to make the passage furtively at night or else submerged. In either case the risks were horrendous.

For operations outside the Mediterranean, therefore, the Italian submarine fleet was based at Bordeaux, in the comparative safety of the Gironde estuary. Their headquarters there were code-named 'Betasom' ('Beta' being the naval code for the letter

'B' for Bordeaux, and 'som' being the first three letters of the Italian word for submarine, *sommergibile*). Released from joint operations in the North Atlantic, Betasom's submarines were modified for maximum range to prepare them for long-distance missions. Even the largest fighting craft (as opposed to cargo-carrying submarines, like the counterparts of the *I-52* which were later used for runs to the Far East) faced severe problems with these long missions. Precious storage and living space was taken up with extra fuel tanks, which in turn upset the submarines' buoyancy, trim and performance. For maximum efficiency they had to run on the surface, leaving them vulnerable to air attack and the weather.

In September 1941 Romulo Polacchini took over Betasom's command and promptly dispatched five of Italy's most renowned submarines to the Caribbean on their first mission in American waters. They were the *Torelli, Morosini, Tazzoli, Finzi* and *Michelangelo*. At the exact opposite of hunting in wolf packs, their tactics became known as *la guerra corsara* – pirate warfare – and entailed lurking in the navigable channels between islands like seventeenth-century buccaneers, awaiting their prey. This tactic proved most successful, and was adopted by German submarines in the same theatre. Between them, these Axis craft sank a great tonnage of tankers and cargo vessels.

However, the technological tide was beginning to turn at last. The Allies, stimulated by the devastation inflicted on their ships in the first two years of the war, began producing anti-submarine inventions that slowly swung the advantage the other way. Among these was a radar specifically designed to spot a submarine on the surface. The sub was usually unaware it had been seen, especially at night, and was hence highly vulnerable to the dropping of flares and sudden air attack. The Germans replied with their 'Metox' device for detecting radar beams but the Allies promptly changed their detectors to operate at micro-wavelengths of around 10 centimetres. (It was most likely the latest modification of the 'Metox' which the *U-530* transferred to the Japanese *I-52* to help her through the Allied blockade to Lorient in southern Brittany.) The Allies also produced 'Huff-Duff' or HF/DF, high frequency direction-finding, which enabled a ship or aircraft to get a bearing on an unwary submarine's radio transmissions. And once an Allied ship had found a submerged submarine on its sonar it could use its new 'Hedgehog' depth-charge launcher: a multi-barrelled affair that could launch twenty-four depth charges ahead of the ship, thereby avoiding the drawback of the old stern-launchers which had interfered with the sonar contact.

By the end of 1942 the new Allied technology was proving a real threat. Anti-submarine aircraft such as the Sunderland were patrolling the farthest reaches of the Atlantic (based on Ascension Island), while the approaches to western Europe – in particular the Bay of Biscay – were now lethal for any submarine trying to enter or leave Bordeaux on the surface. Betasom (and Italy) sustained a heavy loss when Primo Longobardo, the famous and eccentric submariner who had commanded the *Torelli* with great success, was himself machine-gunned to death in the action during which his new command, the *Calvi*, was rammed and sunk.

In other theatres, too, the tide of war was beginning to turn against the Axis powers. Large numbers of Italian troops were being taken prisoner in North Africa. The private diaries of several Italian submariners reveal pessimism, even premonitions of the defeat which for them was less than a year away (Italy signed the Armistice in September 1943). The same diaries lament, too, the passing of a certain gallantry that had often informed their harsh but heroic warfare out in the lonely wastes of the high seas. Victorious submarines would often surface after a torpedoing, not only to obtain visual identification of the ship they had attacked but to help the survivors. This seldom meant taking men aboard the submarine since space was so limited, but it might well entail helping exhausted swimmers to right overturned lifeboats and giving them compass bearings for a landfall. All the principal navies did this, no doubt influenced by an ancient tradition which made for a brotherhood among seafarers facing a common, non-human enemy that so often triumphed. But in 1942 the deepening war, its more powerful technologies and higher stakes, all conspired to introduce a new ruthlessness. Nothing did more to bring this into the open than the sinking of the *Laconia*.

On the night of the 12/13 September 1942, the *Laconia* was torpedoed by the *U-156*. She was a large (19,695 tons) Cunard liner built in 1922 and, like all such civilian vessels, had been requisitioned for the duration by the British Admiralty. Built in the same year as the *Aurelia* and of similar tonnage, the *Laconia* was likewise carrying Italian POWs – 1,800 of them. These were the luckless charges of some Free Polish gaolers later to be described as 'common criminals dressed as soldiers'. When the *U-156* surfaced next to the sinking liner its German commander, Hartenstein, could hear the cries of survivors in the sea around him. What he didn't know was that they were so few: that upwards of 1,200 Italians had already drowned like rats because their Polish gaolers had not stayed to unlock their cages deep in the hull. When the details of the sinking became known to the British High Command, Churchill sent a message to the First Sea Lord: 'The reports of the 650 survivors from the *Laconia* and of another ship show that a great tragedy has taken place ... '

But the incident's repercussions were even more tragic. The *U-156* promptly became the object of a hunt by Allied air patrols operating in the area. This came to an end when she was spotted by an American B-24 Liberator, surfaced and helping torpedoed survivors into their rafts. The bomber's pilot, Lt. James H. Harden, was at once presented with a moral dilemma, added to which he was far out in the Atlantic and getting low on fuel. He radioed the US air base on Ascension Island, Wideawake, and asked what he should do. There was a long delay while Wideawake contacted Washington but at length the order came back to Harden: 'Sink Sub'. The bomber, which by now had barely enough fuel to return to base, launched what ought to have been an easy attack. Harden believed he had sunk the *U-156*, although in fact the submarine got away to tell the tale.

The Allied bombing of their own survivors and the German submarine rendering them assistance provoked Dönitz to draw up and issue his notorious 'Triton Zero' order:

1. Any attempt to rescue the crews of sunk ships, whether in the sea or in lifeboats, to help right overturned lifeboats or to supply food and water, is absolutely forbidden. Rescue is contrary to the basic rules of war, which are to destroy enemy ships and their crews.
2. If this seems hard, remember that the enemy has no compunction in bombing our German cities, our women and children ...

As Giulio Raiola remarks: 'It was a grim decision; but by now Betasom had already issued similar orders and in general, at this stage of the war, the Allies behaved in like fashion.' None of this prevented crews on both sides lamenting such an edict. Certainly it was deeply unpopular at Betasom and individual commanders went on disobeying it on numerous occasions.

The sad affair of the *Laconia*, together with the wider consequences for submarine warfare, had a direct bearing on the imminent sinking of the *Aurelia* by the *Michelangelo*, as we shall see. In the mean time, the Immanent Will was taking the first steps to ensure the paths of these two vessels would cross. Gianfranco Gazzana, already a rising star among young Italian submarine officers, was given command of the powerful and already successful *Michelangelo* in September 1942. On 6 October this potent combination began the first of the two missions that would put Gazzana's name into the record books as the most successful Italian submarine commander ever. The battles between the North Atlantic convoys and German wolf packs were about to reach their climax in the next few months. No Allied merchant ships were now to be found on routes anywhere between Canada and Ireland without an armed escort, and usually they were part of heavily-protected convoys. But elsewhere there were opportunities for lone, buccaneering submarines. The routes around the Cape and the southern coasts of Africa still offered unescorted merchant ships that mostly had to rely on sheer speed to evade attack. The fact was they were unescorted because the Allies simply had no naval protection left to give. All available warships were either engaged in the North Atlantic or being used for vital work elsewhere – such as the preparations for Operation Torch, the North African landings, which began in November 1942. So a good many German and Italian submarines were sent to the South American coast, to the seas off Cape Town and to the Indian Ocean in search of the rich pickings still to be had. Between September and the end of the year, German U-boats alone accounted for sixty ships totalling more than 400,000 tons in the waters off southern Africa.

On her first mission with Gazzana the *Michelangelo* was also dispatched to prowl the routes west of Africa to see what she could find. With her was the *Tazzoli*, under the command of Gazzana's own ex-instructor, G. N. Battisti. The *Michelangelo* sank the 7,000-ton *Empire Zeal*, Battisti rescuing the ship's captain, McPherson, and the radio officer in flagrant defiance of standing orders. He handed them both over to Gazzana who took them aboard the *Michelangelo* and offered them the run of his submarine in exchange for their paroles. As the alternative was for them to be locked in the tiny officers' lavatory, McPherson and his RT man willingly accepted this deal. Although his radio man refused to talk, McPherson, an older and more philosophical man, told Gazzana he had been on his way from Durban to Trinidad, empty. He also admitted that the area was much used by isolated shipping, which the Italian already knew. Shortly afterwards the *Michelangelo* sank another cargo vessel named the *Andreas* and another five survivors were rescued. She then returned to Bordeaux, where Captain McPherson thanked Gazzana personally for his gentlemanly behaviour and promised to write an official letter to the British Government about their humane treatment. Gazzana returned the compliment by thanking his prisoners for their good behaviour.

Part of the point of relating this story is to show that Gazzana was, like most submarine commanders, an individualist. He was not a man who felt he or his command were bound by obedience to brass-hat strictures on how they ought to behave at sea. He was quite evidently a gallant and humane man, within the terms of being a commanding officer fighting a war that was politically little to his taste and maybe already lost. This needs to be said in view of the accusations made after he sank the *Aurelia* on his next voyage.

That, his second and final mission with the *Michelangelo*, began on 20 February 1943 when he left Bordeaux with orders to carry his *guerra corsara* to the coast of Argentina, engage isolated enemy ships and report any convoys he saw. The *Michelangelo* sailed fully provisioned for three months, with plans for refuelling and reprovisioning in the operational zone.

The dispatches radioed between Betasom and the submarine show Gazzana had no problems on the first few days of the outward journey, a route he had taken many times before. Suddenly on the 26 February Betasom radioed the *Michelangelo* with orders for an abrupt change of course, diverting it from the general direction of South America and towards the coast of Africa.

These surprise new orders required Gazzana to meet up with the *Finzi*, which had left Bordeaux nine days before him, and take on enough fuel and supplies to enable him to sail the *Michelangelo* on around the Cape and into the Indian Ocean. On 3 March Betasom radioed a precise position for this meeting between its two submarines; and we leave Gazzana for the moment as he heads towards this rendezvous, a point roughly 550 miles ENE of St Helena and remote enough to be comparatively safe from Allied air patrols.

The *Aurelia*, meanwhile, was in Durban taking on board a mixed cargo of humanity, 'military baggage', 800 tons of precious and heavily-rationed sugar and, of course, an unknown tonnage of gold. As Andrea's investigations had revealed, such shipments of gold from the Empire to replenish Britain's war chest were commonplace, and so far as can be established were remarkably successful in running the gauntlet of enemy attack, thanks mainly to their being carried in complete secrecy and generally aboard the fastest warships. When no warship was available, as in this case, a fast liner was a good alternative. The *Aurelia* was moderately swift by the standards of her day. Built in 1922, she had a gross registered tonnage of 21,517 tons and could sustain 20 knots. As with all civilian vessels requisitioned for war work, some light guns had been bolted on to the decks here and there, manned by thirteen DEMS (Defensively Equipped Merchant

Ships) gunners against attack by aircraft. To all intents and purposes, though, the *Aurelia* was an unarmed passenger liner with a civilian crew. Still, from an enemy's periscope-view she was fair game in that whatever she was doing was bound to be connected with the Allied war effort, as was indeed the case.

One may as well quote the evidence for the presence of gold on board in Jock Walker's words as they appear in his unpublished memoirs. Substantially, this would have been the story he told Mike Anderson, opening up the whole possibility of salvage:

When we returned to the ship I had completed stowing all of my purchases in the drawers under my bunk when Jack Clarke, the Vancouver chief officer, came to my room. He shut the door and speaking very quietly he said, 'After dinner this evening there is a special job that I want you to take care of, Jock.' Then he went on to tell me that a couple of vehicles would arrive at eight o'clock sharp, under armed escort of South African troops. The vehicles would contain about fifty cases of gold bullion and I was to see them safely stowed in a secure space and locked up. By eight o'clock I was ready and a gang of black longshoremen carried the cases aboard, two men to a case. Shortly after nine o'clock the job was completed and I returned the two heavy keys of the steel room back to Jack Clarke, reported that all was secure and the soldiers and longshoremen had gone ashore. Then I wished 'good luck' to the gold and the Bank of England and promptly put the whole thing out of my mind until much, very much, later.

This is the only known reference to a consignment of gold on the *Aurelia*. Not even her captain, George Goold OBE, mentioned it in the very full official report he wrote nearly a month after his ship went down. We must presume the omission was deliberate and in conformity with orders to maintain the strictest secrecy; he could hardly have been unaware of the consignment if it had been aboard. With the wisdom of hindsight this lends a curious, slightly artificial tone to both his report and a contemporary British Admiralty document which speculated about the sinking as possible evidence of a security leak. It is certainly known there were Axis spies watching the major ports on both sides of the Atlantic. It is perfectly possible that even though the loading of the gold took place after dark, someone with a pair of good binoculars might have taken note of the two trucks making a special delivery under the arc-lights of the wharf. Still, the comings and goings of any Allied vessel would have constituted useful intelligence, with every ship potential prey regardless of what cargo she carried.

In any case the *Aurelia* left Durban with a complement that included 318 crew (mostly Canadian), the 13 gunners and 31 naval ratings, as well as 1,530 passengers. These comprised 500 Italian POWs, 484 British subjects, 313 Poles, 195 Greeks, 29 Free French, 3 Dutch, 2 Norwegians, 1 South African and 1 Yugoslav. There were also two stowaways, both British. She sailed on 3 March. By coincidence this happened to be the very day on which Gazzana received Betasom's radio message redirecting *Michelangelo* to her mid-ocean rendezvous with *Finzi* on the 18th. Gazzana now found himself in the shipping lanes which had lately proved so fruitful to German submariners, and was keeping a sharp lookout for likely prey. Captain Goold adopted a series of zigzag manœuvres in accordance with standard anti-submarine procedure. On 11 March he, too, received a message to alter course. He was to head for Takoradi (a port in Ghana, then the Gold Coast). This new course was all that was needed to ensure that the tracks of the *Aurelia* and the *Michelangelo* would cross. Two days later, they did.

Just before midnight on 13/14 March a torpedo struck no. 4 stokehold on the *Aurelia*'s starboard side. To quote from Captain Goold's official report, there was a 'dull, heavy explosion, but very little effect was felt on deck, no water was thrown up and no flash'. The engines stopped immediately, all lights failed, and without power the steering gear was out of action. The Wireless Officer sent out an SOS 'and although we received no reply, I learned later that it was picked up by everybody in the vicinity'. Goold ordered Abandon Ship. 'The Naval party took charge of the Italian prisoners, helping them down the scrambling nets into the water. We had 499 Italian POWs and an Italian doctor to look after them. They behaved very well, were not at all panicky, but disliked the idea of taking to the water and were very slow in doing so; I promised to pick them up in the boats and rafts as soon as possible. We all had our lifejackets on, including all passengers, but only the crew had the red lifejacket lights.'

About an hour after the first torpedo had struck, a second exploded in an oil tank immediately below the ship's bridge, again on the starboard side.

The ship took a further heavy list to starboard, which increased to about 40° . . . At 0100 I was able to step off the ship into the water, accompanied by the Chief Officer, J. S. Clarke, and Chief Engineer, Mr Cowper, we three being the last to leave. The vessel then slowly righted herself, rose vertically by the bows, and plunged straight down by the stern at 0115, about 5 mins. after we were clear. I swam round for about 2 hours, the Poles and Greeks made no attempt to help me into a boat, so I swam away until a little later I was hailed by a young RNVR Lieut., O'Brien, who had found a waterlogged boat

... He managed to haul me into it, although he was nearly as exhausted as I was, both of us having swallowed a good deal of fuel oil. A short distance away we sighted an upturned boat with two men clinging on to it. We called out to them and they swam over to help us. These two men, Petty Officer Hunter and another officer, Mr Walker, were both young and hefty, and together they bailed out the water from the boat ...

Then Cdr. Begg came along with a Carley float ... Cdr. Begg's party were mostly Italian prisoners of war. Dawn was breaking ... All my Deck Officers, except one who went away in charge of his boat, left the ship at the last moment and were swimming round for some 12 hours before being rescued, and so were most of the Naval party, who had stayed on board as long as possible to look after the Italian prisoners. A lot of people were bitten by sharks; I was not bitten myself during the 2 hours I spent swimming round, but I was smothered with fuel oil which probably kept them away, as they don't like the taste of it. Several people were suffering from barracuda bites; I think the sharks are worse, but the barracuda are more annoying as they bite slowly ...

We had our red sails up, and the yellow square rigged at the masthead of all lifeboats, and during the afternoon of the 14th a Catalina flying-boat flew over, spotted us, and signalled that help was on its way. [This was the first of three Catalinas from a squadron based in Sierra Leone making long-distance rescue patrols in response to the *Aurelia*'s SOS call.] Everyone appeared to expect destroyers to appear immediately, but I warned them it might be some time before help arrived. However, by dusk on the 15th a destroyer, HMSS *Boreas*, and two corvettes, *Petunia* and *Crocus*, appeared ...

These filled up with survivors and on the morning of the 16th the AMC (Armed Merchant Cruiser) *Corinthian* arrived and joined in the search. She left the scene on the 17th and was the last to arrive at Freetown.

Everyone was looked after wonderfully whilst on board, in spite of the overcrowding. I do not know how the two small corvettes, *Petunia* and *Crocus*, managed to feed and equip us so well; it was marvellous, and they did a really fine job ...

Our own Naval losses were heavy, chiefly because the men stayed to the last, helping the Italian prisoners of war to get away, and they also assisted my crew in every way they could. The Italians were not panicky, but acted rather like sheep and were very slow. Unfortunately, the Greeks – about 200 ratings and 20 officers – and the Poles were the worst offenders for being panicky. It is significant that all the Greek Officers were saved, and most of the Polish Officers, whilst our losses amongst Naval Officers were high. I cannot speak too highly of our Naval men, they were wonderful throughout.

I learned later that the submarine surfaced alongside No. 2 boat, whilst I was swimming round. This boat was in charge of Lt. Cdr. Davis who is still in hospital in Freetown. The submarine hailed this boat in English, and asked for an Officer to go aboard. The Italian Army Doctor, whose job had been to look after the prisoners, immediately answered in Italian, the submarine drew alongside the boat, and this man jumped on board; the submarine then pushed off and submerged. A number of Polish women called out *Viva Italia* when the submarine appeared, which made them very unpopular with the British girls in the boat, who refused to have anything more to do with the Poles.

Another, anonymous, report adds a little to the account of the second torpedo. 'The submarine closed to within about 3 cables and examined the vessel by searchlight; then at about 0030 a second torpedo was fired into the sinking vessel. This exploded near the waterline, immediately under the navigating bridge, killing many who were "abandoning ship" ... The second torpedo was a murderous action, for the Officer commanding the enemy submarine had satisfied himself by searchlight that the vessel was not a warship, was now completely immobile, and sinking rapidly.'

The peculiar incident of the *Michelangelo* surfacing and taking a single Italian aboard out of the 500 compatriots she had reduced to shipwrecked survivors in life rafts naturally prompted speculation that somehow the whole thing had been pre-arranged. (Since treasure-hunters are equally conspiracy theorists, Orca was interested in this possibility because it hinted that maybe the gold shipment hadn't after all been such a close secret.) Perhaps the 'doctor' had really been a spy, or else some highly placed and valuable officer whose real identity was a secret? At the time of the *Keldysh*'s expedition, this was all that was known about this mysterious gentleman. Only much later, after Giulio Raiola's book had been tracked down and read in Italy, did Orca learn that not only did the man have an identity, but that he was still alive in the 1970s.

His name was Vittorio Del Vecchio, and he was a young second lieutenant medic who had been captured by the British in North Africa. Because of his personality, as well as his medical qualifications, he was given considerable freedom aboard the *Aurelia* and was able to fraternise at will with the British officers. When Raiola interviewed him in 1972 Del Vecchio was a distinguished man indeed, being a Professor of Medicine as well as Subrector of Rome University. Almost thirty years after the event he gave a vivid account of what had happened. His description of being taken aboard the *Michelangelo* is considerably less sinister than Goold's report made it sound. Indeed, Del Vecchio describes Gazzana as having been most unwilling to take him. Gazzana had surfaced to identify the ship he had mortally wounded, had realised her importance, and had fired the second torpedo to make quite certain she would sink. This was not exactly the gratuitous act it appeared to the writer of the British report. The fact that the liner was not a warship was neither here nor there. It was a large and valuable asset, quite possibly carrying a large and valuable cargo, and as such it had to be sunk rather than merely crippled. In any case, when Del Vecchio shouted to the *Michelangelo* to make his presence known, Gazzana was less than welcoming. No doubt the young submarine commander was shocked to discover he had turned so many of his fellow-countrymen into castaways and was reluctant to single out any one of them for rescue. He would also have heard the *Aurelia*'s distress call and was presumably eager not to linger. Del Vecchio was thrown a grudging rope and hauled aboard even as the *Michelangelo* was starting to submerge.

Gazzana quickly radioed back the coded news of his success to Betasom, complete with a grid reference for the sinking. (Unfortunately for Orca, this turned out to have been 'rationalised' or rounded out to the nearest whole numbers for ease of transmission.) Almost overnight he found himself a national hero, a famous man throughout Axis territory. The *Aurelia* turned out to be the largest ship ever sunk by an Italian submarine, a record that still stands. Newspapers everywhere carried the news of her loss in banner headlines – everywhere, that is, but in the British and Allied-controlled press, where it was not released until over a year later.

Gazzana's last mission had begun sensationally well. The *Michelangelo* headed off for its rendezvous with the *Finzi* on 18 March, a meeting that in the event was delayed because that very afternoon the *Finzi* herself encountered and attacked a British freighter, the 7,600-ton *Lulworth Hill*, damaging but not sinking her. The *Michelangelo* took over, chased the *Lulworth Hill* and finished her off the following day, rescuing a Royal Navy gunner named James Leslie Hull. Gazzana then returned to the *Finzi* in order to take on board 90 tons of diesel fuel and supplies, including enough food for twenty days. He swapped these for his two rescued passengers, Del Vecchio and Hull, who at that time could not have guessed how lucky they were. The *Finzi*, now low on fuel, headed back to Bordeaux with them while the *Michelangelo* turned south and went around the Cape.

There, in the space of a fortnight between the 11th and the 25th of April, Gazzana sank a further five Allied ships, bringing to nearly 59,000 tons his own score in the *Michelangelo*. The submarine itself, under its three commanders, had sunk a record 116,686 tons. Gazzana and his crew became household names in Italy. Betasom radioed the news of the *Michelangelo*'s fame and Gazzana's own promotion, little knowing that the men had less than a month left in which to enjoy their success. By 22 May they were homeward bound off the coast of Spain, approaching the Bay of Biscay, and signalled Betasom that they would berth in Bordeaux on the 29th. And that was the last anybody ever heard from the *Michelangelo*. As with the *I-52*, the silence grew and grew until the inevitable conclusion was drawn. Gazzana and his gallant crew would never receive their heroes' welcome.

Only after the war did the Italians learn the precise fate of their famous submarine. On the morning of 23 May 1943 the British frigate *Ness* was on convoy escort duty about 200 miles west of Vigo. The weather was bad, with rapidly changing visibility. In a sudden bright spell a look-out spotted a submarine running on the surface off to starboard. The *Ness* and HMS *Active* broke away from the convoy to close with the target, which submerged as soon as it saw it had been spotted. With its 'Hedgehog' launcher the *Ness* dropped a pattern of depth charges set to explode very deep, at 600 feet. Her captain, T. C. P. Crick, reported later that among the detonations were two huge explosions which told him he had sunk the submarine. He sent *Active* back to the convoy while he waited for any wreckage to surface in order to make a positive identification. After a long delay (the sub had evidently broken up at considerable depth), some flotsam was seen and retrieved: four tins of Italian coffee, some lifebelts, pieces of wood with unrusted nails in them and a pair of human lungs. Crick duly reported the death of an enemy submarine – probably Italian – although he couldn't put a name to her. But it had to have been the *Michelangelo*. Not only did the position tally exactly with her radioed course but no other Italian or German submarine came under attack that day in that area.

The *Aurelia*, among other vessels, was avenged. A curious footnote was added more than thirty years afterwards when Captain Crick of HMS *Ness* discovered that his own brother had been one of the *Aurelia*'s survivors. Until then, neither man had known of each other's involvement in two stories linked by the *Michelangelo* on her fatal last mission.

The loss of the *Michelangelo* was a terrible blow to Italy as well as to morale at Betasom. Half a century later, with the bathos of material interest, it was also pretty inconvenient for Orca. Had the submarine survived, her log might have given another – perhaps more accurate – position for the sinking of the *Aurelia*. It might also have confirmed Captain Goold's account of precisely where Gazzana's two torpedoes had struck his ship. This was of great concern to Orca since from Jock Walker they had learned exactly where in the liner he claimed the gold was stored. Had that particular room received a direct hit from one of the torpedoes they could hardly expect to find so much as a surviving ingot. Also, the exact point of damage might have determined how the *Aurelia* had sunk on her three mile journey to the bottom, and to some extent her probable attitude on the seabed (assuming an absence of abrupt geological features such as crevasses). This in turn would increase or lessen the chances of cutting a way through her hull into the store room. If she happened to be lying on the wrong side the gold would be unreachable. It was that simple.

Later research revealed a further titbit that greatly intrigued Orca. This was that some years after the war ended one of the youngest British survivors aboard the *Aurelia*, now a ranking RN officer, was posted to Occupied Germany where he encountered an ex-officer of the wartime German Navy. When the German discovered he was talking to a survivor of the *Aurelia* he remarked that the sinking had been quite a triumph. Nettled, the younger man said that it might well have been so for Italy, but it had hardly been any of Germany's doing. 'On the contrary,' the German is said to have replied. 'You'll never know what a hand we had in it, and to what extent it had been arranged for the *Michelangelo* and the *Aurelia* to meet.' By the time Raiola was interviewing retired British Admiralty officers in the 1970s he could get no evidence for this story's validity. He did, however, suspect that not everybody he spoke to was telling all they knew, even thirty years after the event.

So – had the sinking of the *Aurelia* been planned? Or was it merely the fortuitous encounter it appeared? And if a plot, was it because there was gold on board – further confirmation of a valuable cargo? There are still no answers to these questions. Quite probably there never will be, though perhaps one day some document may be declassified that sheds further light on the affair. Back on the *Keldysh* we knew nothing yet of this suggestive story, but we were still free to speculate about whether Dr Del Vecchio might have been an Italian secret service 'sleeper', and if so whether he had courted suicide by somehow aiding the *Michelangelo*. It all began to feel like just another layer of the usual conspiracy stories that seem to surround lost gold bars like greaseproof paper around butter.

Mostly, though, I could not shake off a sense of impropriety. The horror of people left swimming around in a pitch-black ocean, vomiting fuel oil, attacked by shark and barracuda; the cramped community of young men whom fate had labelled as the enemy prowling the sea-lanes in their submarine; the depth charges sinking down towards them from the *Ness*'s launchers: it was difficult to blot all this out, as it was to forget the 392 who died in the *Aurelia*. It was a vision of a far-off war which was nevertheless still poignant in its resonance for someone born during it, who had grown up hearing the stories of men exactly like Goold and Crick and Gazzana, the only difference being that they had survived to become one's school-teachers or the fathers of one's friends. The immediate post-war films were still familiar, too, with their black-and-white starkness, their images of strained, young-old faces in doomed submarines listening to patterns of depth charges exploding ever closer, the awesome melancholy of sonar pings echoing off the vast emptiness of the sea. Add to that the solemn rhetoric of the times, the haunting phrases like 'supreme sacrifice', and it seemed less immoral than downright *incongruous* that fifty years later such things should have shaken down into a simple quest for gold. In order not to see this incongruity one probably needed to be much younger and altogether less beset with memories. And yet there was a latent question of propriety, too. It feels like a covert offence that newcomers should consider picking over the ashes of a war, many of whose millions of combatants and survivors (who lost everything, all the same) are still alive. *Pecunia non olet*, says the

Latin tag: money has no smell. Maybe not. But if not, why should laundering it be among the biggest growth industries of the late twentieth century? We hide our consciences as though in the depths of the sea, and unexpectedly come upon them again three miles down. If they do find *Marlin* on the second leg of this trip I have no doubt they will do the right thing and hold a short, godless service. But what they toss overboard will be less a wreath than a confection of fig leaves to hide conveniently atrophied memories.

TWENTY-THREE

28/2/95

Glary haze, harsh wind yellowing the atmospheric sieves with Saharan dust and heaping up white horses on all sides. We're passing just to the south of the Cape Verde Islands, but they remain invisible. On the starboard lee the wave crests break up in leaning showers and the sun props an intermittent rainbow against the ship's side in a spectral flying buttress.

In the event I have been attending some *Marlin* search zone meetings but must confess my heart isn't really in it. This is partly because I am not myself going to be searching, and partly because the substance of the meetings is predictable. I have the sneaking feeling that Orca ought really to have agreed its target area well before boarding *Keldysh*. This working on it up to the last minute smacks of homework left too late. Tonight at 6.15 p.m. we will have the last such meeting before port. Politics are crackling. Clive is hustling, doing his best to ensure that the people who are staying on for the next leg really do look for the *Aurelia* and don't just conduct the minimum sonar search. He's going around the ship telling them that they need to find the liner just as much as Orca does. Gold on deck means *Keldysh* stays solvent and they keep their jobs. The Orca group will meet in his cabin at 6 p.m. for a pre-meeting meeting so that nobody makes any inadvertent concessions to Anatoly. Even if Sagale-vitch is leaving the ship in Dakar, the great man still wants to be in firm control of what happens on the *Marlin* leg. To be honest, he has never seemed truly collaborative, just as he thinks Orca hasn't been. He plainly wants to leave having fixed the forthcoming search zone so that everyone can be held to it, by signed protocol if necessary. But Clive and Quentin and Mike suspect he'll do his best to fix it too small, committing his henchmen to doing the minimum of work to satisfy the Orca contract. Their plan is to scupper this plot tonight.

Quentin meanwhile informs me of an alleged fact to boggle the mind. Since length × area = volume, try taking a parsec (an astronomical unit equivalent to about $3\frac{1}{4}$ light years, or getting on for the distance to the nearest star) and multiplying it by a Barn (the cross-sectional area of the nucleus of a hydrogen atom). The volume which this prodigious sum yields is 1 cc, or rather less than a teaspoon, which certainly suggests that the nucleus of a hydrogen atom is on the small side. But what is it you've actually got in your teaspoon? Answers, please, on a postcard.

The pre-pre-meeting in Clive's cabin starts out as purely political but degenerates spectacularly. First, the politics. Clive says the point about the *Marlin* search area is that we want the Russians to carry on reading Andrea's files and come up with ideas and suggestions of their own, rather than just adopting ours, i.e., a repeat of the approach which was supposed to make for collaboration in the case of the *Dolphin*. So, he continues, what we shouldn't be doing is flashing around a map of the *Marlin* site which one of the investors himself drew on his computer, because it's very much a preliminary attempt to plot some co-ordinates from the data and might muddy the waters. Far better to let the Russians do their own homework and come up with their own map and *then* see if the two maps have anything in common. Likewise John Wilson (who will be joining the ship at Dakar to replace Quentin as *Orca*'s side-scan sonar expert) will not be told our own interpretations of the data but will be left to form his own opinions. In order to subvert any plans which Anatoly has to ensure the *Marlin* search zone is cut and dried before he gets off the ship, the search area must not be established until after the ship has left Dakar.

To this Quentin says that in any case he wouldn't co-sign any protocol on behalf of a colleague who hasn't yet joined the ship. 'Quite right, too,' says Clive, who goes on to dispute the Russians' interpretation of his carefully-worded Orca contract. (He may be a little miffed that there was enough latitude in it for them to *have* an interpretation other than his own.) So far, he says, their reading is tilted towards considering this as a two month charter which is then possibly extensible, whereas in fact the contract 'clearly suggests' that it's basically a five month charter. If the time on *Marlin* runs out without our having found anything, then under the contract's terms the *Keldysh* ought to be spending extra weeks on site, not high-tailing it for Falmouth, Kaliningrad and penury.

At this point, with a bare minute to go before the main meeting, Ralph explodes. Small damn wonder if the Russians appear disaffected, he says. They've never really been given a chance of proper participation. 'Your investor came up with his computer-generated game plan which you then sat on. You didn't give the Russians or anyone else the complete data to make their own assessment. What kind of a way is this to run a goddam salvage operation?'

Mike, who until now has been sitting slumped with his chin on his chest, perks up and replies acridly that on the contrary, the Russians had all Orca's data nine months ago. I get the impression that this is a conversation they've already had several

273

times together in private. Not only that, but they are probably in broad agreement that there are things about this whole operation far more wrong than the mere question of how and when to fix a search zone. I prick up an inward ear here, but there's no more to hear for the moment because we have to adjourn and hurry off to the boardroom.

In the boardroom we wait. And wait. It's not like the Russians to be late and it's most unlike *none* of them to turn up. Whether Ralph is worried about his alliances or just can't shake his angry mood, it is obvious he is needled by Quentin.

'You can sit there and grin,' he says to Quentin, 'but I can tell you, fella, you came within that much,' (he holds his thumb and forefinger half an inch apart) '*that much*, of being knifed to death by those Russians you insulted the other day. And I'll tell you what, I'm not sure I'd have been inclined to try and stop them.'

The 'insult' Ralph is referring to was a jocular suggestion by Quentin at a meeting that any whores coming aboard at Dakar might pose a security threat. I don't for a moment believe anyone in the room who could understand the remark (made, obviously, in English) was remotely insulted, still less inclined to knife him. They all seem too sophisticated and wry to take umbrage over anything so trivial. Later, Quentin is witty at Ralph's expense (though sensibly not in his presence), referring to 'his fury at my implication that the *Keldysh*'s crew might actually be heterosexual'. This was well observed, but to be fair Quentin had never specified the whores' gender.

When the meeting is belatedly cancelled Ralph invites me down to his cabin where he very decently offers me a gin and tonic (decently, because in default of the Gordon's we lost at Falmouth we've been tucking into his store of bonded Beefeater in scandalous fashion and he can't but know). Then he says, still angry, 'You may quote me on this, James. I have never been on such an ill-planned expedition in my life.' I'm sure he's sincere, but I bet it's not true. People are very fetishistic about planning, but no one ever plans against animosities and mixed motives.

2/3/95

And early this morning we are off Dakar. The first European colony in West Africa, once known (with grisly predictability) as 'The Gateway to Africa'. High blue morning, low white town. On the distant waterfront two brilliant canary-yellow heaps of sulphur dwarfing cranes and silos. We have plenty of time to admire these twin pyramids since, despite all the radio messages to an agent here over the last three days, no one seems to be expecting us and there's no available berth. The Russians gather on the bridge deck. 'Africans,' they say. 'What do you expect? Bunch of monkeys.'

In fact, the whole ship is permeated with unease. The crew are jittery and have already been assigned a rigorous roster of guard duties so that no gangway will ever be left unattended and there will always be someone hanging over the rail on the harbour side to watch for agile intruders swarming aboard *Keldysh* as if on lianas. The hours pass, the sun climbs. The crew fish over the side, hauling in easy bucketloads of glittering catch. From the galley ventilators drifts the scent of fresh frying. Viktor Brovko leans on the rail next to me to explain that five or so years ago the *Keldysh* was impounded in Sierra Leone for alleged spying. The exact charges were vague and seemed to have something to do with the ship's electronic and underwater capacities to 'subvert' that country's defences. For nearly ten days the vessel was in the grip of the local military and the event was clearly traumatic in that it has left an indelible Africaphobia in all who were aboard. 'Everywhere – in every passage below, up on the bridge, down in the holds – these black savages with automatic weapons, primitives. We were terrified.' It had been a diplomatic impasse. Moscow had to send their Foreign Secretary, Eduard Shevardnadze, in person to sort it out. He had met Sierra Leone's top brass on the *Keldysh*. 'The boardroom was full of these Africans with medals and ribbons. Great warriors, no doubt. After that we were allowed to leave. But now you will understand why we don't like West African ports. Later we heard the Sierra Leoneans had been acting on a request from Washington via the CIA because the US Navy wanted us out of the way for a week while they did something to their SOSUS network somewhere not far off the coast. I believe that,' Viktor adds ingenuously.

If this sounds like paranoia we should take into account Viktor's utterly different experience of life compared to that of the average gentle Western reader. This quiet, middle-aged engineer comes from a background where even consummate skill and dedication were no protection against arbitrary terror. His father was an aeronautical engineer at the time of Stalin's great post-war purges. In those days, before a Soviet test pilot took off the engineers had to sign a statement certifying that the plane was airworthy. One day the USSR's most famous test pilot took off and was killed. Next morning Viktor's father went to the office carrying the suitcase he always kept packed and ready, knowing he was headed for Siberia. In fact, he was wrong. All his colleagues were arrested but he was spared because owing to an administrative muddle he alone had not signed the document . . . All of which puts the *Keldysh* Russians' seeming naivety over contracts in a very different light. It was all in our minds. They know everything there is to know about putting a signature to a document. Small wonder they have been so insistent on drawing up protocols for Orca to sign. At times they must have longed for the boot to be on the other foot enough for them to be escorting the lot of us to a waiting Siberian express.

Eventually we're assigned a bunkering berth, after which we shall be able to tie up on the town side of Dakar harbour. No sooner are we moored and taking on fuel than the quayside is swarming with tall, thin Senegalese merchants in beautiful robes who arrive at a run. On strips of cloth they set out equally tall, thin wood carvings. Had Giacometti ever had a West African phase, his sculptures might have resembled these. There are also sacks of glum parrots. Warily, the first Russian scientists descend the gangway and start buying souvenirs. Dakar may be potentially dangerous but it's exotic, and nothing brightens up a drab apartment in Moscow or Kaliningrad like a touch of Africa, chosen with your own hands beneath a tropic sun... That's Dakar to them. To Quentin, Dakar is little more than the Gateway to Europe; an airport from which he can shortly leave and be reunited with his family. To Clive, Dakar is where he hands over not unregretfully to Simon: a rendezvous fraught with fresh opportunities for things to go wrong, for stores and equipment not to have arrived or to be inextricably impounded by Customs. For Andrea and Mike, Dakar is a halfway house with the Project's possibilities for success already reduced by 50 per cent. Mike has often been heard threatening to leave the ship here, so disheartened has he become. Not even the parrots look as gloomy as he.

And for me, Dakar is the base used by the Piccards, father and son, in the autumn of 1948 for testing FNRS 2. This was the prototype bathyscaphe, the submersible which would soon decisively take the world's depth record away from Beebe and Barton who had so bravely dangled over the abyss in their cramped sphere ($4\frac{1}{2}$ feet internal diameter!), half a mile down. In those days, of course, Dakar was a French naval base with all the engineering and fuelling facilities the Piccards might need. Though Swiss nationals, the Piccards were considerably wooed by the French, who had their own fish to fry. Indeed, the next bathyscaphe, FNRS 3, was taken over by the French Navy who slightly modified the float but used Piccard's FNRS 2 capsule design down to the last rivet. Somewhat miffed but full of Swiss dignity, the Piccards at once shifted their scene of bathyscaphe building and testing from the Toulon/Dakar axis to the Italian eastern seaboard, where they built the *Trieste*. It is interesting that nearly half a century later, when syntactic foam has made obsolete the cumbersome and risky metal floats holding thousands of gallons of petrol, the size of the capsule Auguste Piccard originally designed remains unchanged. A sphere of two metres' internal diameter is now common to all deep ocean submersibles of whatever nationality. The reason for this apparently lies in some quite complicated physics. Piccard had done his sums right and put his own life where his calculations were. He lived to descend to the deep ocean bed nearly two miles down, and later to see his son reach the deepest known place on earth in 1960. He died in 1962, aged 78.

3/3/95
Simon arrives from London looking dapper but burdened, like a slightly tarnished corvette captain. John (Quentin's replacement) arrives looking like a Scottish elder. Clive, who with Quentin and myself is leaving tomorrow, grabs Simon and disappears into Orca's stateroom for an emergency debriefing before a meeting with Anatoly, who it appears is also leaving on the same flight as ours. He and Natalya are probably in the midst of packing and composing sealed orders for Bogdanov.

Eventually Quentin and I tear Simon and Clive away for lunch ashore in a restaurant overlooking a stony stretch of beach from which the *Keldysh* is welcomely invisible. A froth of bougainvillaea encloses us. A small jetty below stands up to its ankles in low tide while children and grey birds on stilts (which I think of, no doubt erroneously, as egrets) investigate the crusted pools gurgling in its shadow. It is a memorable luncheon. The food tastes like the long-withheld promise it is and combines with relief at being off the ship for the first time in six weeks. There is also the lightening knowledge that one will shortly be flying far, far away from search zone meetings and the bickering, politics and clashes of will which are inseparable from enterprises where 'the stakes are high' (as their participants tend to put it).

Simon asks sensible, well-informed questions about how people and equipment have borne up under the strain. He himself evinces no more than a slight irritation that we didn't find the *I-52* – certainly nothing as self-indulgent or counterproductive as reproach. 'On to *Marlin*,' seems to be his attitude, outwardly brisk and purposeful whatever his inner misgivings. With all those millions of dollars and their investors' expectations now weighing entirely on him and the outcome of this second leg, these must be considerable. I admire this, even as I assume these steely types with Wall Street experience must be quite used to risking other people's money as well as their own necks. This is, after all, the man who was prepared to leap off Clifton Suspension Bridge before being arrested in the nick of time, even as one of his companions was haplessly bouncing and twanging two hundred feet below him.

4/3/95
Farewells are always awful, especially when one is leaving as a parolee and bidding adieu to cell-mates who have still to complete the other half of their sentence. One feels such a rat,

albeit a rat with an internal broad grin. On the quay at dawn amid the lumpy sacks of parrots and the heart-of-darkness Giacomettis there are a good few misty eyes, while Mike is frankly in tears. I give Andrea a sisterly hug. I love her solidity, both physical and mental. It is very hard to imagine the circumstances in which she would go to pieces. Balanced and tenacious, she lets go neither of the facts she so ruthlessly unearths nor of her own self-possession. It is very agreeable to have had such a cell-mate, someone who was herself once imprisoned on a trumped-up charge in a stinking eastern gaol just as I was nearly thirty years ago in South America. Gaolbirds and adventurers, we are, and not very regular guys at all in most other respects. It's a real bond.

One good thing is we're all far enough away from England not to feel diffident about weeping (for rats, like crocodiles, do shed the occasional tear). The trip has indeed been an emotional experience. The Russians, who are experts at leave-taking and tearfulness, watch and wave sympathetically from the rail. I'd guess some of them will be well pleased to see us go. At the last moment I sprint back up the gangway to embrace my fellow aquanauts of 'the writers' MIR'. Sergei is wearing the full Anarchist's rig in which I first noticed him: hooped T-shirt, mega-beret and beard. If I say I shall never forget him, I really believe it to be true. He surrounds himself in my mind's eye, as he does in the flesh, with the autonomous zone of the complete and confident human being. In a word, he is what the Jews call 'Mensch', virtually a definition of the estimable. His beard is soft and warm on my cheek.

From the moment we leave the quay the journey itself is long, hallucinatory, wonderful. Buoyed up by departure and the grey oxidising wings of an Aeroflot Ilyushin 62, we fly to London by first going directly south to Conakry in Guinea. Where else?

This is my favourite airline by far; the only one which takes the trouble to turn even the shortest flight into an adventure. From Conakry we embark on the long hop across the Sahara's heart to Malta, flying the length of Mali and crossing the Hoggar mountains. As we do so we pass unseen those mythical ne-plus-ultras, Timbuktu and Tamanrasset. From his window seat Quentin becomes simultaneously excited schoolboy and geology teacher. The air is as clear as glass and for 2,000 miles reveals a landscape nearly indistinguishable from the seabed we have just been mapping. Had we been able to see the bottom of the Atlantic with equal clarity in the full glare of noon we should have observed nearly identical dune formations and sediment movement, the different colours produced by old sand coming to the surface and new sand disappearing beneath it as currents slowly mimic the effects of wind. Watching the desert's patterns of drift, the river-like deltas and windings formed by centuries of sand on the move, one could hardly imagine a better demonstration of the earth's surface being constantly in flux, whether on land or under the sea. It shows I was wrong in the MIR: the seabed down there and this African terrain are clearly contiguous.

Anatoly and Natalya sit together further up on the other side of the cabin. A long way back in disgrace sit a grey-haired Russian and his wife who had often helped us retrieve bottles of Ralph's gin or cans of McEwan's from the *Keldysh*'s bonded store. He had always struck me as a kindly fellow with a charming smile. It now seems he has been summarily sacked by Anatoly and ordered back to Moscow, having been unmasked as a member of the Russian Mafia. There is, of course, no law that says *Mafiosi* have to look like villains any more than vicars have to look like child molesters. A hugely drunk Anatoly lurches towards us somewhere over uttermost Algeria and confides tearfully that once back in Moscow his own life will be worth less than a row of beans. The degree of anarchy in Russia is now such that he confidently expects to die shortly after landing. Somehow this news ought to be more sobering than it is. Later, he perks up to the extent of performing a feat which in retrospect is still fairly incredible. Now even drunker, from two rows up and across the entire width of the cabin he shies a single orange segment straight into Quentin's open mouth. They must be at least 16 feet apart, yet it doesn't look like luck. Somewhere under all that vodka a vastly competent engineer who knows all about motor skills and the dynamics of trajectories is paying his last flirtatious respects to 'Inspector Huggett'.

5/3/95
No point in dwelling on a night spent on airport benches in Moscow, or on the Heathrow greetings which eventually followed. It was a marvellous journey.

One final oddity, or coincidence, is that on the evening of our arrival the chance vagaries of British TV programming arranged a counterpart to the preview of the *Keldysh* we'd had while waiting to sail a couple of months ago. The first thing I see on getting back to London is a film about the *Titanic* showing Ifremer's submersible, *Nautile*, going down to retrieve objects from the wreck for an exhibition. These include, bizarrely, a 3-ton bollard which is laboriously winched up into daylight, a most unremarkable lump of iron. The rapaciousness of the whole enterprise is glossed over by various poisonous twits on board the mother ship. They all wear logo-emblazoned T-shirts and effortlessly use PR phrases like 'The most famous ship since Noah's Ark.' The *Titanic*, as exploited by RMS *Titanic*, Inc., is being carefully marketed as far more interesting than it actually is. Or rather, since I now know some of the scientific reasons why it is in fact interesting, they are promoting its least significant aspects as being of terrific historical value. Not a single mention of rivers of rust or rustsicles throughout the programme. Nothing about iron-eating bacteria. Just objects, objects, *objects*. It's all very American; as if a wretched liner dating from 1912 were old enough to qualify as an archaeological site. It would surely have provoked Thomas Hardy to withering verse.

Nautile's pictures are excellent and I view them with proper respect since I now know how hard-won they are. On the other hand the 'storyline' or narrative imposed on the exploits of the idiots up on deck is a flimsy farrago of pretend suspense. I make a mental note that if ever there's a question of scripting a filmed account of Project Orca we must scrupulously avoid all those predictable shots of faces lined with tension staring at sonar screens; the out-of-sequence clips of all-purpose technological bustle (cranes lifting precious toys over the rail, transponders being dropped, hydraulic pumps being dismantled on deck); the re-enacted whooping of people clustered around an intercom loudspeaker pretending to learn for the first time that whatever was being looked for had at last been found. I don't suppose we'll succeed. That's the genre, complete with the now-obligatory soundtrack of the sort of electronic noise Hollywood deems appropriate for the ocean deeps. There is too slim a chance of doing anything of real interest for such a dim medium as television since everything has to look and sound the same. By the time a real adventure has been scrunched up and packaged to fit that tiny little screen and a producer's tiny little imagination, it looks like a dozen such things one has seen before.

Why is this? I suppose because underwater films, like salvage work, are made possible by glamorous and ingenious technology, and technology is all too easy to film. But those of us who have been on a deep ocean treasure-hunt know that much of the real fascination lies elsewhere, in the people and not in the machines, which by themselves are merely inert tools. This should be obvious but somehow isn't. Most fascinating of all is that it isn't obvious to the very people engaged on the hunt.

TWENTY-FOUR

Back in Italy once more, I remained in touch with Quentin, Clive and Andrea via the same old telephone screwed to the wall of the same old bar. News arrived from Simon aboard the *Keldysh* as they repeated the sonar lawn-mowing exercises over a new patch of sea.

> We are on site in the *Marlin* search zone and this bulletin is being written fifty-two years to the day, indeed to the hour, after *Marlin* was torpedoed. The conditions are almost identical; it's a dark night with a sliver of moonlight, there is a very gentle wind from the SE and the sea shimmers with a black, inky stillness. In these conditions of immense tranquillity it's difficult to grasp that within a few miles of where we are, maybe less, 1,800 people took to the boats and in the resulting chaos and confusion 392 lost their lives. Tomorrow morning in a short ceremony we will be laying a wreath on the site.

Then came heartening news: one of the MIRs had found and retrieved six shoes, including a pair. If the bottle brought up during the search for the *I-52* had been made the subject of several imaginative scenarios, these shoes were even more suggestive. What article of clothing was a suddenly-ditched passenger most likely to shuck off? Precisely. Moreover, several showed signs of crude mending, one even with a nut and bolt – the sort of repairs one might expect POWs to have carried out with whatever materials were to hand. In general, the styles looked old. The only problem was that nobody aboard *Keldysh* was enough of a shoe historian to know when such things as plastic insoles began to be used. Still, Simon's report to Clive in London showed his conviction:

> [The shoes] were all recovered in a small area (maybe 150 metres by 100 metres) and I have no doubt there were more because we were unable to search thoroughly. To my mind the range in quality and size would [otherwise] be difficult to explain, except of course it is probably representative of the range of people on the *Marlin*; the coincidence would be too extraordinary if they were not in fact from the ship. Needless to say there are doubters on board – MA [Mike Anderson] in that ever-discerning way of his announced almost immediately that the shoes were from the fifties (!) and therefore couldn't be from *Marlin*.

Eventually the shoes were examined by an expert. Some of them might indeed have been of the right period, but at least one turned out to be a 'winkle-picker' of the late fifties/early sixties style, with a one-piece sole and heel unit (an innovation which apparently dated from the mid-fifties at the earliest). Still, Orca's novelistic ingenuity could easily account for its unwelcome presence by assuming it had been tossed overboard from a passing cruise liner by a disgruntled member of a skiffle group returning from a gig in South Africa, sheer chance having made him choose the exact moment when his ship happened to be over the *Aurelia*'s grave. Failing that, it may be that Mike was right after all. I did eventually see the shoes for myself as they lay soaking in Simon's guest bathroom in London. They had about them an awesome poignancy, and I remembered Robert Ballard finding a pair of boots lying on the seabed at the *Titanic* site and seeing in them an emblematic pathos, not least because he assumed they had settled there while yet encasing their long-vanished owner's feet. I also recalled the skip on the quay at Falmouth into which the Russians had thrown the old shoes they were replacing with brand-new pairs, as well as a black and white picture of a mountain of Jewish shoes taken at one of the concentration camps by an Allied photographer in 1945. It is a strange thing about shoes. They are not inert, like cast-off clothing, but manage to retain a terrible vulnerability.

That episode turned out to be the high spot of the *Keldysh*'s search for the drowned liner. The sea hid its secret well and gloom inevitably settled over the expedition. Alone of the Orca group, Andrea did not fly home from Africa or the Canaries but stuck it out with the *Keldysh* all the way back to Falmouth. By the time they arrived, the expedition's failure to find either of its two targets had been somewhat assimilated. The conviction remained (as presumably it always will on treasure-hunts) that 'we had come incredibly close' – not an easily provable assertion – and there was already talk of a new expedition to return to both targets.

I was not at Falmouth to see the *Keldysh* dock but I can well imagine Andrea being right when she later recounted her sadness at taking leave of her hosts – something distinct from the despondency of their joint failure. The only one left of the original crew of British buccaneers, she would surely have earned the Russians' respect and affection for her professionalism as well as for her tenacious loyalty to the project she had worked on for so long. She did report there had been 'an unholy scramble' to get all the data off the ship in Falmouth, especially the rolls of sonar print-outs.

Because of the way Orca was constituted – and it is pointless to deny that by April 1995 cracks were obvious along factional lines – the most comprehensive post mortems presumably took place between Simon, Clive and the investors. As for the rest of us, we had the sad air of confederates who had been briefly but vividly yoked together and were now going our own ways again. Mike was incommunicado in Cornwall; Quentin was in Japan on Geotek business; Ralph was in Hollywood; Andrea was in Walthamstow; I was up a mountain in Italy. So there never was a meeting in which everyone reassembled to lick their wounds constructively. It is easy to see why; but it was, I believe, a mistake. Even had we not made some resolutions for the future – if indeed there was to be a future for Orca – we might have aired some resentments which, in the pressure of the ensuing months, showed every evidence of festering.

I shall come to the nature of that pressure in a moment; it was in any case so dramatic it could scarcely be ignored. In the mean time I was able to look back a little more objectively on an experience that for me had been one of the most memorable of the last ten years. On balance, I was full of admiration for an enterprise which in many respects was very far from a failure, no matter that success had up to now eluded it. Certainly I knew better than before the sheer complexity involved in organising a salvage operation. That Simon and Clive – respectively a banker and a solicitor – should have raised more than $3 million, collected a team, hired a foreign ship and technical expertise and completed two legs of the deepest-water search ever undertaken struck me as a triumph of will, logistics and sheer self-confidence. It still does. Indeed, I would willingly join any future expedition of theirs, if asked, in the knowledge that they would have learned from their experiences on that first *Keldysh* trip.

It was always going to be a gamble, of course. That had been clear from the outset and was part of the attraction. That aside, there is no doubt errors were made. I still think that in the final analysis Orca's financial management constituted a cabal that was perceived as separate from – and overriding – its own small element of salvage professionals. This fatal split existed despite Clive and Simon's most earnest attempts to democratise decision-taking and concern themselves with the most technical aspects of salvage work. Both worked hard to assimilate and master details of maritime law, complex facts of underwater physics, the propagation of acoustic signals, the computerisation of time-lines (the juggling of all the log-book and other data on the sinkings) and several other daunting techniques. Both knew the *Dolphin* and *Marlin* research files backwards. Nor could anybody ever have accused them of being unwilling to involve themselves in practicalities, whether risky or downright boring. Both went down in a MIR, and they each spent long hours in the sonar lab as well as closeted in Anatoly Sagalevitch's office.

Yet by the time Simon had begun his search for the *Aurelia* after Clive, Quentin and I had left the *Keldysh* at Dakar, the notion of a team had degenerated somewhat, as accounts sent from the ship by Simon in mid-March made clear.

I think this really is what all those Hollywood films were about. Whether they concerned a hunt for treasure or a spectacular and meticulously-planned robbery, the enterprise usually hinged on issues of character which, unless held in check, jeopardised everything. It is curious to reflect that none of this need ever have been acknowledged had Orca found its targets, and would never have been spoken of had it retrieved the gold. Success blots out such issues as being no longer relevant. This is why most accounts of famous salvage enterprises that yield the longed-for millions tend to an odd flatness and a technological triumphalism. The doubts and dislikes and splits that underlie these adventures are instantly swallowed up in the brainless grins of people pictured holding double handfuls of gold sovereigns. In that sense there is nothing to be learned from success.

And from failure, whether temporary or not; is there anything to be learned from that? It will never be possible to assert that Orca's team problems materially altered its luck, but from time to time I still look up from whatever I am doing and turn the idea over in my mind. Maybe after all we infringed too many maritime taboos in our blithe, landlubberly fashion. Perhaps we whistled too much. Perhaps Clive and Quentin never should have taken that torn half of the dollar bill down to the seabed with them. 'Very bad luck, taking money to that place.' I can still see Anatoly's face saying this as he snatched it from my hand and tore it to shreds. Neither belligerent nor shocked, his tone of voice was simply emphatic. He might have been quoting Young's modulus to prove to a first-year engineering student why his submersibles couldn't fail to withstand a loading of 500 atmospheres. It was something anyone with half a brain would know.

Meanwhile, Andrea and I did meet in London at the end of April when she had wound down a little after her three months at sea. By then she was able to draw some rueful and pertinent conclusions about the trip. Most of these did not differ greatly from my own; they were simply better informed and more evidentially reasoned. The fact of the matter was, Orca had not given itself anything like enough time for such a huge undertaking. It had spent twelve and a half sonar days looking for *Dolphin* and seventeen looking for *Marlin*. This was absurd when stacked up against all those *Central America*s and *Titanic*s. At the beginning of this book I said that Mike's plan to find and salvage not just a single deep-water wreck but *two* on the same expedition suggested a gamble amounting to 'a case of greed overcoming prudence'. Apart from the phrase's governessy flavour, I think I was wrong in that what finally overcame prudence was not greed at all but inexperience.

In any case, our empty-handedness so far was no reason for total despondency. As Orca thought, what was needed was to go back to the investors and convince them that the gold was still down there for the taking. A second expedition surely couldn't fail to find one or other vessel since so much of the basic bathymetry and sonar work had been done. Indeed, a return trip was already being planned when in the middle of July a bombshell exploded in the form of headlines in the world's press. Somebody else had found the *I-52*.

Orca was stunned. The news brought its scattered team together as nothing else could, messages flashing between them which ranged from the sour to the incredulous. It seemed that an American, Paul Tidwell, had used another Russian research vessel, the R/V *Yuzhmorgeologiya*, to re-survey the *Dolphin* site a scant two months after the *Keldysh* had left it. The *Yuzhmorgeologiya* lacked the advantage of submersibles aboard, but it did have first-rate sonar and ROV imaging equipment and apparently took some good pictures of the Japanese craft. Evidently the submarine hadn't imploded as Ralph had asserted it would. It was practically intact but for a gaping hole where the Mk. 24 mine had struck, sitting upright on the bottom in an area of smooth sediment next to a small escarpment. The position was seven miles outside the area covered by Orca's survey, which suggested a discrepancy in interpreting the data.

According to *Time* magazine Paul Tidwell, a Vietnam veteran, and his team had found the submarine on their last sonar line, five weeks into the expedition and $250,000 over-budget. That was on 2 May, but the news did not break until 19 July. One would have thought it left Orca with nothing much to say or do other than make philosophical noises and turn all its attention to the *Aurelia*. One would have been wrong. All manner of conspiracy theories were privately aired, each carrying its potential for legal action. One such scenario required there to have been collusion between 'our' Russians and Tidwell's. 'Our' Russians had actually found the submarine on one of the MIR dives without an Orca member aboard and had decided to keep quiet about it in order to sell the co-ordinates for a better price. (Suddenly everyone remembered how elusive Target 1 – the most promising of all – had been, with the Russians claiming there was nothing there and Orca not convinced they had ever found it. Another scenario held that it was a plot hatched by our Mysterious American, or else it was a scam enabling outsiders to 'buy into' Orca's original and still-secret target, the *Aurelia* . . . The *Guardian* report (19 July 1995) moved Orca's paranoia along nicely. Orca was described as 'a rival British salvage group in the race to find the wreck':

> The British group, also using a Russian vessel, the *Akademik Keldysh*, reportedly refused an offer from Mr Tidwell to collaborate on the hunt and set sail for the area before the US team . . .

This certainly amazed me. I had never knowingly heard Paul Tidwell's name before the news broke, much less suspected that he and Orca might have been in contact even before we had set sail from Falmouth back in January. Who was in cahoots with whom? Perhaps this was none of a fly-on-the-wall's business. However, some of the Orca team seemed as taken aback as I was. Once again there was a pervasive sense of there being wheels within wheels, of things to which one had not been made privy, of rationed or privileged information. The Orca management must have noticed this too since it felt it necessary to issue a confidential statement to the shareholders firmly denying Tidwell's allegation. They said they had first heard Tidwell's name mentioned by the Mysterious American with the US Navy contact who had sold us the wreck's allegedly classified co-ordinates. Only after the *Keldysh* had left the site did this gentleman fax Orca saying that a Paul Tidwell might be willing to work with them. That was the extent of any 'offer of collaboration'. There had never been any direct communication with him ...

Who knew what to believe? Who now cared, anyway? It was the new situation that was interesting. As suggested at the beginning of this book, wrecks in international waters are mostly fair game for whoever can get their hooks into them, making possession pretty much ten-tenths of the law. The I-52 was now the perfect example of a bird in a bush. Tidwell might have found it but he was still a long way – three miles, to be precise – from laying a finger on a single gold bar. The newspapers spoke of some scheme he had for pumping foam into the submarine in order to raise it, prompting irreverent memories of the man who had proposed raising the *Titanic* by pouring millions of ping-pong balls down a tube into her interior. In the case of Tidwell's proposal, at least the theory and the physics made sense even though the practice would undoubtedly prove difficult and vastly expensive (as a preliminary, the hole in the submarine's hull would have to be sealed somehow).

At this point Orca began congratulating itself on having had the prescience to write into its contract with the *Keldysh* a five-year embargo on anyone other than Orca using the MIRs to dive on either of the two targets. Since there were so few other submersibles with a 5,000-metre capacity it would seem that Tidwell's group was stymied. One obvious way out of the impasse was surely to do a deal: a joint expedition to salvage the

Japanese gold using the MIRs and splitting the proceeds, on the principle that half a bird in the hand is better than nothing, especially when the divided corpse is still worth millions. To date, though, no such agreement has been reached.

Orca did have an entirely justified grievance over the way the press had unquestioningly swallowed Tidwell's account. In interviews he managed to imply that not only had he found the *I-52*, but alone had unearthed its history by pioneering archival work. In fact as we know, the sinking of the *I-52* and the presence of 2 tons of gold aboard her was common knowledge in the salvage business and had been since the late 1940s. As for the archival discoveries, it seems certain that he had at his disposal exactly the same background information and log books that Andrea had dug out, no more and no less, with the possible exception of the Mysterious American's allegedly still-classified data. It is conceivable, of course, that it was this last that made the crucial difference. In that case Paul Tidwell is to be congratulated: it wasn't dumb luck but access to superior information.

It might appear that a real divergence between these two very different *I-52* expeditions lay in the way the respective sets of data were treated. Orca used its signed-up members as a think tank, giving them the files and urging them to work out their own ideas as to where the search zone should lie. Then it pooled these conclusions at a series of meetings, some of which were still taking place even as the *Keldysh* neared the spot. One of the investors himself produced plots for both targets on his computer that were added to the pool. For all the implied democracy of consultation, though, the data were still treated as something of a state secret, heavily restricted. Tidwell, by contrast, appears to have instructed his project manager to give the same data to a commercial search company, Meridian

Sciences Inc. of Maryland, who re-plotted everything from scratch using software that, in *Time*'s words, '"re-navigated" the *I*-52's course and adjusted by about 32 kilometres the Navy's official estimate of the sinking site'. Yet both boats were doing analyses right up to the last moment. It turns out that the analysis that led Tidwell to the wreck was still going on two days before they were due to leave the site, and clearly he struck lucky by sheer good fortune.

I was not, of course, on Tidwell's trip, so have no more idea of his outfit's internal organisation than is to be gleaned from an account in Meridian's house magazine. This implies his greater reliance on buying-in outside professional expertise, having one company (Sound Ocean Systems) provide a project manager and with Meridian itself supplying an operations director and a sonar expert. The trade-off of such an approach must be the advantage of dedicated salvage expertise weighed against the increased possibility of security leaks.

It looks as though Orca took the hint. Probably it assumed the *Aurelia*'s secrecy was by now compromised. In any event, before launching a return expedition to the site in early 1996 it showed its *Marlin* data to three different professional groups for evaluation, without telling any of them it had been to the site the previous year. The result was 'a strong consensus' as to where the search zone should be, an area which largely overlapped the one already searched. For this return trip Simon Fraser was once again aboard a Russian vessel – the irony is absurd, since it was the very ship Paul Tidwell had chartered with such success, the *Yuzhmorgeologiya*. When once more Simon returned empty-handed I felt a real disappointment. A year had gone by since the *Keldysh* trip and some of the associated memories had dulled a little, but I found I still keenly wanted sheer good fortune to smile on Andrea and Mike Anderson, in particular. More, I knew that had Simon's excursion found the *Aurelia*, a full salvage operation would immediately have been planned and it seemed likely that many, if not all, of the original team would once again assemble on the *Keldysh*.

It could still happen. That ought indeed to be a light-hearted reunion, full of madeira and ping-pong. I think people would be willing briefly to drop their assorted depressions and business commitments for the fresh chance of seeing millions brought up, dripping and freezing cold from their deep entombment, to lie warming on deck in the African sun.